DATE DUE

Hesketh Pearson
by Himself

Biographies by Hesketh Pearson

Hesketh Pearson
by Himself

HARPER & ROW, PUBLISHERS
New York

To my friend
MICHAEL HOLROYD

Contents

Illustrations

'The web of our life is of a
mingled yarn, good and ill together:
our virtues would be proud if our
faults whipped them not; and our
crimes would despair if they were
not cherished by our own virtues.'

Shakespeare

Publisher's Note

These memoirs in the American edition start with Hesketh Pearson's school days, beginning at the age of nine. For the reader's information we summarize two brief chapters from the British edition of this book (omitted from our edition) which deal with the author's early years and with his forebears.

* * *

Hesketh Pearson was born in 1887 at Hawford, near Worcester, the descendant, he says, of "energetic and earnest ancestors," an inheritance that he feels may partly account for what he calls "my own laziness and levity"— though as to his laziness if not his levity, the reader of his memoirs may wish to take exception.

Pearson's father, a well-to-do landowner, who though "not rich" kept three carriages, a brougham, a dogcart and a wagonette, two horses and a pony and "the usual indoors staff" (about twelve) of a small country house, was an imposing figure, invariably friendly but rather awe-inspiring. A heavily built man, six feet tall and immensely strong, he was good at every game or sport he took up, putting more vigour into them than most men put into earning a living. As a young man he was sent to Australia where, deprived of funds from home, he had been shrewd and self-confident enough to live by his wits for six months. He had another accomplishment outside sport, being gifted with a singing voice of such range that he could sing in tenor, baritone and bass with equal ease and potency.

From the seventeenth to the nineteenth century, the Pearsons were wealthy landowners. The author's father belonged to the "squarson" class of society: squires whose younger sons became parsons; both his grandfather and great-grandfather took Holy Orders. His paternal grandfather was rector of Suckley in Worcestershire, a rural dean and Justice of the Peace.

Through his mother, Hesketh Pearson was a great-great-nephew of Francis Galton, as well as a direct descendant of Robert Barclay, the eminent Quaker apologist, and of Erasmus Darwin, the noted sceptic, poet and philosopher.

Pearson's maternal grandmother was a Moilliet from the Genevan banking family. His mother's interests, which were wholly artistic, were fostered by her education in France and Germany. She is described as being devoted to her children, energetic in her domestic duties and social activities and so susceptible to other people's sensations that she never knew what it was to be bored. Hesketh Pearson considered that he had inherited, along with his father's stubbornness, some of his mother's hasty temperament. Her father, a wealthy vicar, was a strange clergyman who "never wore a round collar." An expert rider and driver of horses, he had been Master of the Worcestershire Foxhounds before entering the church. He lived at Ettington, near Stratford-on-Avon, and it was here the young Pearsons regularly spent their Christmas holidays.

Pearson was one of five children, who "within certain limitations" were allowed to run wild in the woods and fields and along the streams of Hawford, and were, he recalls, "as happy as children can be." He was nine years old when this existence came to an end and his father, in the interests of the children's education, moved the family to Bedford.

At this point in his life, Pearson's narrative begins.

PART

I

1

'The Happiest Years'

Some time during my schooldays my father's cousin, whom we called Uncle Ted, spoke grave words to me: 'Remember that you are now enjoying the happiest years of your life.' I knew in my bones that this was a lie, but inexperience prevented me from questioning it.

It would be difficult for any boy who does not conform to type to be happy at school, and in my case it was impossible because I could not or would not learn whatever did not engage my interest. I therefore absolve the masters who struggled with me, though I am inclined to think that one's education has been in vain if one fails to learn that most schoolmasters are idiots. Sir Walter Scott agrees with me: 'No schoolmaster whatsoever existed without his having some private reserve of extreme absurdity.' Once Scott believed he had met a sensible specimen, but soon regretted his error: 'God forgive me for having thought it possible that a schoolmaster could be out and out a rational being.' The excuse for the poor pedagogues is that they have to deal with far too many boys, and as most normal healthy boys are pests the wonder is that masters remain sane. In any case the boredom of teaching the same old thing over and over again, to say nothing of the enforced company of embryons, would drive any intelligent man crazy, which perhaps explains why so few intelligent

3

men take the risk. But I was luckier than Scott. Out of the thirty-odd masters who tried to instruct me, I did happen to run across two whose humanity called forth my liking and gratitude.

Learning is as much a faculty as teaching, and I dare say I would have found more sympathetic masters if I had shown less resistance to being taught. But I must have been subconsciously aware that when a fellow is a fool compulsory education is wasted on him and when he's intelligent it's useless, because in the first case he is incapable of absorption, in the second he follows his natural line of development and teaches himself only what he wants to know. I am aware that school and college education, the cramming into boys of facts and information and so-called erudition, is necessary for those, the great majority, who wish to spend their lives in routine jobs; but nothing of this nourishes the intelligence, which is a wilful individualistic quality. Thus we often find that the fellows who strained their faculties at school in order to pass examinations are useless at anything but the work for which they have been trained, while those who slacked at school are more adaptable and intelligent in after-life. I have no panacea for the problem, but speaking solely for myself, after being taught how to read and write, add, multiply and subtract, all of which I learnt from my governess at Hawford, I should have been left to follow my own bent, which, as time went on, would have led me to history, literature and French, the only subjects that ultimately interested me at school, where most of my time was wasted on Latin, mathematics and algebra.

Dr Johnson says that in his day boys were flogged into learning. Perhaps that partly explains his curiously warped nature. In my case I was flogged out of learning, assuming I had the least disposition to learn. The first school to which Jack and I went was a private institu-

tion kept by a man called Blake. Known as Orkney
House School, it was in Clapham Road, Bedford. The
headmaster, Blake, was a flagello-maniac. Nothing gave
him greater pleasure than thrashing boys, though pike-
fishing was another of his hobbies. He was a tall clean-
shaven man with lumbering gait, grey eyes, high forehead, thin lips and inflexible jaw. He wore steel-rimmed
glasses, through which his cold eyes glinted ominously.
I am the last person to draw an objective portrait of
him, since he was the only individual who ever aroused
my hate. He seized every possible excuse to thrash me,
and I know he enjoyed the exercise because I occasionally heard him smack his lips. Something obstinate in
me prevented me from howling over the pain, and this
made him pile it on. I can recall two occasions when he
flogged me so hard that the cane went limp in his hand
and he had to throw it away. Innocent of such matters
in those early days, I could not perceive that he was
simply a sadist who released his lust on my behind. I
think that I was his 'star' victim, though the majority
of boys received his ministrations at one time or another.
Hardly a day passed without some wretched lad being
told to 'Go into my study'. I derived a single advantage
from Blake's school: the worst things that have happened to me since leaving it have seemed relatively
mild in comparison with those five years of helpless
misery, and I would far rather have died at any period
of my existence than go through them again. So much
for 'the happiest years' of my life.

But it would be false to leave the impression that I
was perpetually unhappy between the ages of nine and
fourteen. My nature is resilient. No sooner had I passed
out of that hateful gate at the end of the gravel path
leading up to the school than my spirits began to soar;
and holidays were always a joy. In those days Bedford
was a small county town of less than thirty thousand

inhabitants. There were practically no big industries; the chief business was agriculture; and as the town existed mainly for its schools, the resident families were mostly of the retired army and navy officer or independent gentry class. We lived at No. 31 Shakespeare Road (since, for some inscrutable reason, changed to No. 53) and the front of our house looked onto fields with no intervening buildings, while at the top of our road the town finished and the country began. When freed from school, we ranged far afield, trespassing in woods, bird-nesting, and making ourselves unpopular with land-proprietors. I soon formed close friendships with other boys of my age. The two brothers who suited my milder moods were Gerald and Sidney Hemsley, the two who joined my more vigorous escapades were Leslie and Rex Tetley.

I can only remember a single evil deed perpetrated with one of the former. Sidney and I kept pigeons, and after experimenting with various breeds we got about a dozen white fantails. The woodwork along the top of our next-door house was being painted a sort of reddish brown, and the birds rather liked it, spending much of their time transferring the paint to their feathers. When they were completely discoloured and resembled no flying creatures ever seen on land or sea, we sold them to a schoolfellow as red fantails, a rarity only to be found on the upper reaches of the Amazon. We made a handsome profit on the original outlay and advised the purchaser to let the birds out fairly soon as they were liable to die of despondency if denied freedom. He followed our advice, and the birds promptly returned to us. We kept them encaged until their feathers were white again, and when he complained that his red fantails had disappeared we said that he had neglected to keep them warm enough and they were probably on their way back to South America, perched on the mast of a cargo boat.

We then assured him that in this country white fantails were far more adaptable and home-loving, showed him ours when they were back to normal, and he bought them again. I fancy I was the financial genius behind this *coup*, which suggests that I might have been a successful stockbroker.

With the Tetleys, however, my most piratical instincts were unleashed. We modelled ourselves on Captain Kidd, and nothing was safe from our maraudings. The antics of European dictators in the thirties of this century reminded me irresistibly of our behaviour at about the age of twelve. We raided fruit-gardens, insulted tradesmen, laid traps for harmless pedestrians, threw stones at mobile objects, punctured bicycle tyres, stole money, lit bonfires, climbed trees, crawled over roofs, swarmed up haystacks, and lied like Trojans when caught red-handed. Two incidents will illustrate our Hitlerian conduct, which in those days was called original sin. There was a gentleman who lived at the top of Waldeck Avenue, which was renamed Warwick Avenue in the delirium of anti-German fever during the 1914 war. For some capricious reason he objected to a habit Rex and I had formed of ringing his front-door bell and leaving hurriedly. Like England when Hitler was flinging bombs as we threw stones, the gentleman took a lot of rousing, but suddenly one evening he popped up from behind a privet hedge and cut off our retreat. He asked why we had rung his bell. Our explanation that we had done it for fun seemed to him inadequate. He boxed our ears, knocked our heads together, and threatened retaliation on a larger scale if we continued to be funny. Naturally we could not allow things to remain as they were, and late one night a week or two later we hurled a couple of bricks at his ground-floor window. He must have been waiting for us because he was in full cry at our heels before we had sprinted a hundred yards up the road. To save ourselves from immediate chastisement, Rex and I took refuge in my home garden. As a consequence, my father had to pay for a plate-glass window, my payment being made across his knee.

The second incident was of a more serious nature. A certain milkman evoked my hostility for some reason that has escaped my memory. He had a morally vindictive expression, was earnest in his occupation, and never made that cheerful note on the top register which denoted the presence of his fellow-milkmen. So I determined to teach him a lesson to make him if possible more sprightly. Loading my airgun with slugs in my bedroom at the front of the house, I awaited his appearance. When he came into view the sight of his red walrus-moustache hardened my heart. I leant out of the window, aimed carefully, and scored a bull's eye in the centre of his overcoat, the impact making him jump and sending me into fits of laughter. The upshot of the downshot was an interview between the milkman and my father, and a further interview between my father and myself.

As I recall this period of my life, it seems to have been passed with a tender bottom and sturdy lungs. It was difficult for me either to sit down or to sober down. Rex Tetley and I had an odd effect on each other; we could hardly meet without laughing; the world had clearly been created for our amusement, our own rascalities and other people's respectabilities being equally funny. We had not acquired a moral sense, a personal standard of behaviour, and all the precepts in the world were for us like water on a duck's back. I dare say we were much like other boys except that we were more daring in our outlawry, more careless of the consequences, and more abandoned in our hilarity. Even the solemn ceremony of Confirmation failed to subdue us, and the

bishop who laid his hands on our heads as we knelt together before him no doubt ascribed our convulsions of
mirth to religious emotion. More extraordinary still was
the occasion when Blake placed us at his own table within three feet of his ruthless eye. With the full knowledge
that our backsides would be flayed if he perceived our
condition, we could not help shaking with laughter
throughout the ordeal. Blake, totally unable to conceive
such a possibility, doubtless attributed the trembling
table to an attack of nerves on our part.

How I managed to get into the top class of his school
I do not know; but the master of the second form was
an extremely sympathetic fellow named Blow, and it is
possible that under his tuition I made some progress.
From the look on Blow's face when at the end of my
last term Blake made some extremely displeasing remarks about me in the course of his breaking-up speech,
I felt sure that the second-master's view of the headmaster coincided with mine; and sure enough Blow
shortly left the school to take private pupils. He was a
rattling good chap. Finishing with a distasteful topic,
I met Blake once again after leaving his place of torment.
At about the age of twenty-one I was standing with my
mother at the church door following the Sunday morning service when Blake emerged and stopped to speak
with her. As I showed no sign of recognition, my mother
turned to me and said: 'Surely you remember Mr
Blake?' Though I now regret having made her feel uncomfortable, I am not sorry that I replied: 'I remember him so well that if I saw him drowning in the river
I would throw stones at him from the bank', on which I
turned my back and walked away. Explaining my behaviour to my mother afterwards, I had to give a
synopsis of my life at Orkney House School. She could
scarcely believe it and asked why I had not told her at
the time. I could only say that, though I had often cried

in privacy, my pride must have been greater than my pain.

It may have been partly due to Blake, who was always full of biblical sentiments, that I did not warm towards religion. At least he opened my eyes to the type of person who professed Christianity, the retributive type which enjoyed the act of punishing others for not being like itself. Fortunately one somehow develops a moral sense in spite of a Christian upbringing, because one soon perceives that people create a God to suit their dispositions. As my friend Colin Hurry put it:

> A God in man's own image,
> Head, heart, and trunk and limbs,
> With man's own petty passions,
> And a horrid taste in hymns.

I must have been vaguely aware of this by my early 'teens, as it never occurred to me that the religious tenets of the church expressed universal truth. In fact I used to think they were the private opinions of the clergyman who gave them forth. It happened that I liked the Reverend A. Haig, vicar of St Martin's, where we occupied the front pew. He prepared me for Confirmation in a rather sad manner, but he was a good fellow whose health had been undermined in the East, and his black beard, white face and tired look gave the impression that he would have been happier in a hermit's cell. His condition was not improved by rigorous fasting throughout Lent, and by the time Easter arrived one wondered whether he would survive the services. He was not popular because his preaching was as doleful as his appearance, and the congregation which had been large when he arrived became slenderer with the years of his ministration. He believed in what were then called High Church doctrines, and he soon brightened up the proceedings with colours and vestments, which made him less popular than ever, Bedford being one of the last strongholds in the Midlands of nonconformity and Low Church principles.

My parents did not care for his innovations, but their innate conservatism kept them loyal to St Martin's. Father certainly objected to Haig's twenty-minute sermons. He considered that a man could say all that was necessary on any subject in ten minutes; and the moment a sermon began he ostentatiously pulled out his gold hunter, flipped it open to consult the time, closed it with a click, and gave his attention to the discourse. If the ten minutes he allowed were exceeded, he would produce his watch, look at the time, sigh, close it with a snap that was quite audible in the pulpit, and become restless. I remember a Cowley father named Hollings who came to preach on the Sundays of one Advent. He droned along for over half an hour, dead to the sighs and snorts and watch-snappings from our pew, and after the second Sunday father simply stopped going to church, becoming a Christian again at Easter when Hollings had withdrawn to Cowley. Father had a strange habit of always arriving for the morning service from three to five minutes late. Whether this was done because he enjoyed a solitary march up the aisle or because he did not wish to admit he was a 'lost sheep' in the general confession, we never made out. In any case he had to breakfast early in order to get there in time for the *Venite*. His usual breakfast-time was twelve noon and lasted an hour, but on Sundays he had to be down by 10.45 and eat a hasty meal in about ten minutes. He never went to bed before two or three in the morning, sitting up with his pipe and monthly magazines and sometimes falling asleep in his armchair. Once or twice I heard him snoring peacefully at 6 a.m. when I was on my way to the river for a swim. Another of his peculiarities was that he liked to sip from the chalice at Holy Communion before the rest of the communicants, possibly feeling that his fellow-Christians were unclean, the result being that though our front pew gave us a good start the family did a slightly undignified sprint to arrive first at the altar rails. Since we only attended Holy Communion once in two months, those who had won the race in our absence regarded us with unchristian eyes when we beat them to the winning-post, especially when it was almost a dead heat.

What interested me more than anything else was the demeanour of the communicants as they returned from the ceremony down the chancel steps. Some tried to look as if they had passed through a great experience, others were a little sheepish, others put on a nonchalant expression as though the occurrence were normal, a few were tight-lipped as if they had done their best and would do it again. Very few appeared natural, perhaps because they could not feel the emotions which they thought they ought to have experienced. My mother was always quite natural, but then she never pretended anything she did not feel and criticized what she disliked in the official religion. For example, she disagreed with Athanasius that those who had done evil would go into everlasting fire, and when that creed was being intoned she closed her mouth firmly when the rest of the congregation were repeating the passage. She also disbelieved in the resurrection of the body and remained silent when the Apostle's creed affirmed it. From her I would have learnt to question dogma, had I not been a natural sceptic where official faiths were concerned.

While mother was soon involved in all sorts of social and artistic activities, father devoted his life to sport, though as time went on he became vicar's churchwarden, chairman of the Town and County Club, of the Discharged Prisoners' Aid, and several other things I have forgotten. I fancy he was also on the committee of the Bedfordshire County Cricket Club and the local Croquet Club; and I know he was captain of the Golf Club because by his personal influence the movement in favour of Sunday play was temporarily held in check. This was rough on those who worked hard during the week, but it was a typical example of the calm, unimaginative way in which he imposed his personality. We learnt long afterwards that he was generally known as 'Pompous Pearson', and we witnessed many instances of his suppressive power. For instance, he disliked the sort of stories told in male clubrooms, and the moment he walked into a room where the occupants were amusing themselves with risky or smutty yarns a hush fell upon the assembly, like a schoolmaster's entrance into a noisy classroom. Golfers are notoriously explosive when they foozle shots, and one of them uttered a 'Blast!' within our hearing when I was caddying for father, who jerked his thumb over his shoulder in my direction with an admonitory 'Now, now!', and the player passed on with chastened mien, his feelings unrelieved by a further selection of expletives. In the winter months father's marksmanship got him innumerable invitations to shooting-parties, and he made something of a reputation at curling when the conditions were favourable. At about the age of sixty he attended the opening of a shooting-gallery at Bedford School, scoring eleven bulls and an inner out of twelve shots, and so beating the next best, a master named Columbine who had won fame at Bisley.

All through our schooldays father remained an awe-inspiring figure. We did not dislike him, but we kept out of his way. He was just but not generous, and whenever we wanted anything we applied to mother, who was a permanent shield between him and us, sparing him worry and us punishment. I was her chief cause of vexation because I simply could not keep out of mischief. I was a thief when it suited my purpose, incurably adventurous, unteachable, and utterly irresponsible. Twice I ran away from school, but returned as soon as I felt hungry. Lectures and beatings had no effect on me, because so happy was my nature out of school that I always forgave myself for whatever I did, and I was willing to make a physical self-sacrifice in the interest of my personal pleasure.

As I so frequently did things to which my elders objected, it followed that I was occasionally caught doing them, and on one such occasion my father's spiritual stature was lessened in my eyes. I had been forbidden to climb up the side of our house, at the corner of which there were sections of projecting brick giving precarious hand-and-foothold. To be forbidden to do a thing, as Adam and Eve knew, was an incitement to do it, and I was more than half-way up the building one fine afternoon when father, quite unexpectedly, arrived on the scene. 'Come down at once, Posh!' I heard from below. He always called me 'Posh' because I reminded him of someone he had known with that name. But I was in a strategically sound position for bargaining, and I gave as my condition for an immediate descent that I should not be caned. He was too nervous to withhold the promise, and I came to earth. Having naturally assumed that corporal punishment was all I had to fear, further clauses in this gentleman's agreement did not occur to me, and my faith in his honesty was gravely shaken when I was consigned to a dark room for several hours, with bread and butter for sustenance. Of course I did not accept the situation. My bedroom was darkened by a Venetian blind, which by some device on this occasion could not be raised. The first thing I did was to pull out the slips of wood which made the blind. I then stepped on to the outer ledge of the window and performed a first-class bit of acrobatics by seizing the gutter that ran along the bottom of the roof, swinging myself up to a crawling position above it, and scrambling at great danger to the very top of the roof, from which I announced my safe arrival in stentorian tones. On seeing me in that parlous position, father was so horrified that, without any haggling on my part, he capitulated, promised complete exoneration, and begged me to await the arrival of a ladder. I shouted that he need not bother as I knew an easy way down, and while he held his breath I clambered across the roof from front to back and got into the house through the window of my sister's bedroom.

What he would have said and done if he had known about a favourite game of my sisters and myself, I cannot surmise. By my early 'teens I had dragged my two sisters into multifarious malefactions, Elsie the elder willingly, Baby (as we called Evelyne) hesitantly. Elsie was soon crawling after me along roofs at the imminent risk of death, the two of us creeping stealthily downstairs in our night attire when we were supposed to be fast asleep. We invented the queerest games, one of which we called 'Post Office', when we wrote cheques, exchanged stamps and issued postal orders, spelt at first by Baby 'Post Lauder', which caused much merriment. But our chief game was 'Church', and we only indulged in this on Sunday evenings when father was safely immured in his club. We draped ourselves with all sorts of vestments, such as antimacassars, cut stoles out of curtains, made bath towels serve for hoods, and bought mortar boards to complete the outfit. Whenever money was required to obtain such necessaries, I would apply to my godmother, Aunt Adèle: 'Please send £1 at once, or £2, as I must buy some books.' She usually obliged, though when she satisfied a demand for £5 she thought it advisable to tell mother, who naturally laid a veto on further applications.

Fully arrayed as doctors of divinity, we issued forth from a bedroom-vestry humming a tune which ran up and down the scale, with a specially gloomy one for Lent, and entered the schoolroom, wherein a desk had been placed on top of the table for the preacher, and chairs for the two priests who formed the congregation. Each of us preached to the other two, and there was a good deal of scarcely suppressed mirth from the auditors and much frowning from the pulpit when occupied by Baby. I can remember one high spot when Baby, having taken as a text 'It is more blessed to give than to receive', reasoned the matter out and decided that if the precept were universally followed everyone would be giving and no one receiving. A shout of laughter greeted this conclusion and the preacher sensed a conspiracy on the part of her dearly beloved brethren to mock her most deeply conceived thesis. She revenged herself on us by taking exception to my High Church practices. At that time certain Anglican clergy were introducing incense during their services, and I decided that we should follow their example with our limited means. I therefore produced an aspidistra in a pot, and as we circled the schoolroom humming our melody I ceremonially sprinkled the plant with brilliantine hair-oil from a bottle. Baby thought the whole business too ritualistic, savouring of Popish idolatry, and after a sort of Lambeth Conference between us I agreed for the future to reserve the oil for my hair, especially as the aspidistra did not seem to be flourishing under the treatment.

Feeling that we should carry our message beyond the schoolroom, we sometimes paraded along the corridor, down the front stairs, and into the drawing-room, where mother sat with her book or embroidery. To her amazement, and perhaps amusement, we gravely circled round her in full vestments and gave her the benefit of our musical and sartorial composition. Had father suddenly entered through the front gate, there would have been a most unholy stampede.

2

Happier Years

At the age of fourteen I left Blake's hell-house and went to Bedford Grammar School, now called Bedford School. I had won a prize at my preparatory school, heaven knows for what but probably for spelling, which came naturally to me. The prize was a book which I may or may not have read, though I remember the title: *Tad: or Getting Even with Him.* I was a singularly backward boy, too much taken-up with fun and games to look at books, and totally uninterested in the fairy tales that were read to me as a youngster. Kipling's Jungle Books failed to impress me, together with all the other yarns by Henty, Manville Fenn, Ballantyne, etc., which were devoured by contemporary youth. The first stories I ever read with pleasure were those about Sherlock Holmes, who for me was a real figure, not a figment of the fancy. I began with *The Hound of the Baskervilles*, which was being serialized in *The Strand* during my first year at B.G.S. Then I went back to *A Study in Scarlet, The Sign of Four,* the *Adventures* and *Memoirs*, after which *The Return of Sherlock Holmes* appeared monthly while I was still at school. Soon after my first acquaintance with Holmes I came across Doyle's *Brigadier Gerard*, and revelled in his adventures. Perhaps the only other stories which

18

gave me almost as much pleasure during my schooldays were half a dozen of Stanley Weyman's novels.[1] I did not share in the juvenile admiration for Rider Haggard and Cutcliffe Hyne, while all the famous figures in mythology and fairy lore bored me with their miraculous doings. I needed actuality, which I found in that believable and likeable superman Holmes, and humour, which made Gerard so fascinating.

My brother Jack had far outdistanced me in learning and was several forms ahead of me when I entered B.G.S. Throughout our scholastic period we were not on good terms and had no friends in common. I had a quickly-aroused and violent temper, and as he used to tease me frequently our fights were sometimes ferocious. I recall an occasion when I chased him round the garden with a sword, father's intervention saving bloodshed. In a stand-up fight he could beat me easily, but when mad with rage I was a fearsome antagonist. I cannot explain the cause of my tempers, which were liable to break out under provocation for very many years; indeed it is only within the last decade or so that I have got the better of them. They were always over in five minutes, and I used to wonder why other people remembered what I had said to them in a fury when I had not the faintest recollection of it half an hour afterwards. The symptoms were curious. I seemed to see red shutters going up and down before my eyes and I felt as if something inside me were about to burst. In that condition I exploded, saying outrageous things in a virulent manner, quite unconscious of what I was saying and how I was saying it. One inherits these temperamental things as one does a physical weakness, my particular malady

[1] *Francis Cludde, A Gentleman of France, Under the Red Robe, Count Hannibal, The Long Night, The Abbess of Vlaye.*

coming perhaps from a batch of maternal ancestors, since my mother had a hasty temper which she usually managed to hold in check.

My temper may have been exacerbated by my hatred of compulsion, and school life is one long compulsion. I was a born rebel, like some of my forebears, and I rebelled against a discipline which seemed to me futile. But in those days my sense of injustice must have been instinctive, not rational. Besides, I objected to instruction that did not stimulate my curiosity, and no master could make me interested in mathematics or the classics. This may have been the fault of the masters or of my own lack of co-operation, probably six of one and half a dozen of the other.

With the vague idea that army discipline would be good for me, my parents decided that I should study for Sandhurst, and I joined the C & M (Civil and Military) side of Bedford Grammar School. My first form-master was Rice, who played cricket for Gloucestershire. An agreeable fellow, he always gave me the impression of being preoccupied with something outside the class-room, perhaps dreaming of hitting six boundaries in an over. I think he did his best with me, but it was not enough. The silly notion then obtained that, in the weekly hour given to English, boys should gain their introduction to literature by learning poetry. We sweated through Scott's *The Lay of the Last Minstrel, The Lady of the Lake* and *Marmion*, reciting stretches of them which we were given to learn as part of our homework. It was all gibble-gabble to me, and trying to remember it a penance. Rice could not understand my inability to memorize the stuff and gave me up as hopeless. I can still remember looking through the window at the playing-field on a fine sunny day, and thinking of making a century at cricket or bowling a hat-trick while reciting automatically:

The way was long, the wind was cold,
The minstrel was infirm and old;
His withered cheek and tresses gray
Seemed to have known a better day.
The bat, his sole remaining joy,
Was carried by another boy.

'Bat!' roared Rice: 'Another boy!' He glared at me. 'This is *The Lay of the Last Minstrel*, not the Cry of the Last Cricketer. Start again; and if you don't put a little more meaning into what you are saying, you'll get a wicket where you least expect it.' Such was the crude magisterial humour of my youth, and it went with a bang. But it was not the way to make me love Scott, and in fact I detested him. Even the novels we were given as holiday-tasks failed to excite me. I was bored by *Ivanhoe* and *The Talisman*. Had the masters been gifted with some critical sense and picked on *Rob Roy* or *Quentin Durward* I might have warmed to the author. As it was, I did not get to know the real Sir Walter till I was twenty-three, and his greatness as a man was unknown to me until at the age of forty I read his *Journal* for the first time.

Rice's disgust over my failure to make sense of Scott was trivial compared with his rage when, at the end of my first term, I was awarded nought in an algebra paper. He could not contain himself. It seemed to him a comment on his failure as a teacher, which was partly true because he had not explained the object and meaning of algebra, and to this day I do not know why the nonsense was invented. He lost his hair and shouted at me, which did not help me to consider algebra a rational science. Many years later I met him on a golf course, shook hands, and asked if he remembered me. 'Remember you!' he exclaimed: 'You are the only boy in my experience who scored a duck in an algebra exam.' I

remarked that it was a distinction to be so freshly remembered. But he was furious at the time, and insisted
on my being sent down to a lower form. In retrospect
I regard this algebraical 0 as my outstanding scholastic
achievement. It signified my instinctive knowledge that
for me algebra was a waste of time and would have no
place in my life.

The following term I found myself under a master
named Rolfe, a strict person whom I never much liked
but who stimulated my interest in French, in historical
novels, and in Napoleon Bonaparte. His whole life was
in his work, which he took with deadly seriousness.
There was no laughter in his class-room, and all of us
were rather frightened of him. He had dark red hair
and a longish pointed red moustache, and sometimes
looked extremely severe. Rigid discipline reigned during lessons, and inattention invariably resulted in a
caning. He was a good teacher, if too austere, but he
could not explain algebra to me, and I soon reached
the lowest place in his form for arithmetic. He caned
me twice, but they were rather formal operations and
I did not feel animosity on his part or mine. One of
these punishments was earned by a remark I made about
Charles II, my interest in whom had been aroused some
years earlier. I have already referred to an admirable
person named Turner who took horses across the Severn
not far from our old home. Once he put Jack and me
aboard a dredger in midstream where we heard that
many relics of the battle of Worcester were constantly
being brought up from the bed of the river. The master
of the dredger informed us that King Charles II had
swum the river at that identical spot and was about to
land on the opposite bank when in the nick of time he
caught sight of Oliver Cromwell waiting for him and
swam back again. I dreamt of this achievement on
several occasions, but later study has convinced me that

the story was apocryphal. Anyhow it aroused my interest in the fugitive King and at school I enjoyed reading about him in the history-books. The whig histor-
ians, in trying to whitewash that strangely unattractive
figure William III, did their best to blackwash Charles
II, but the worse they made him appear the more I
liked him; and when we had to write an essay on the
theme, mine erred on the side of hero-worship. One
sentence, a justification of myself, would have been
approved by my hero: 'His only fault was laziness, and
this is a virtue.' But it was not approved by Rolfe, who
greatly admired Oliver Cromwell and said that a boy
who could hold such a man up as a model of regal
rectitude would come to a bad end. I replied that
Charles himself had come to a good end and I asked
for nothing better. He called me impertinent, and I
suffered three stripes for the Merry Monarch, which
made me wonder whether I ought to have an oak-apple
leaf tattooed on my bottom since Charles was not alive
to decorate me with the Garter.

I took far more interest in my masters than in the
lessons they tried to impart, and quite unconsciously
the bent of my mind was already in the direction of
what in time became my chief concern in life. Our
headmaster, J. Surtees Phillpotts, fascinated me. He had
practically created the institution, which in his time
rose from a local grammar school of about 200 boys to
a notable public school of 1,000 boys. As he strode on
to the platform for prayers in the hall, with his long
grey beard, flowing gown and mortar board, he looked
like Zeus or Jupiter or an Old Testament prophet.
Occasionally he treated us to what we called a pi-jaw,
which I chiefly liked because it went on for half an hour
and practically eliminated the first morning lesson.
Once he took his text from Genesis, 'Unstable as water,
thou shalt not excel', and I felt that this applied to me.

Not only was my nature unstable as water, but I could not conceive myself excelling at anything. But I accepted the situation manfully, being more anxious to enjoy myself than to get into the sixth form or become a monitor. My general inadequacy was brought home to me one day when the whole school were drilling. Something must have amused me because my laughter was heard by our instructor, Serjeant-Major Sim, who called 'Halt!' and advanced purposefully in my direction. ' 'Oo laughed?' he demanded, looking at me and the three others who formed the delinquent four. I admitted the crime. He commented ruthlessly on the weakness of my face and what seemed to him its idiotic expression, concluding with the words: 'You'll never come to no good.' He might have revoked this prophecy if, some ten years later when I was training in an officers' cadet corps, he had heard a more formidable serjeant-major hold me up to the rest as a model marcher in this phrase: 'Keep yer eyes on that lanky bastard at the 'ed of the squad if yer want to know 'ow to drill.'

Phillpotts was equal to any situation, and when one morning the citizens of Bedford formed a procession to the school, accompanied by a band, to demand that the boys should be given a holiday because Mafeking had been relieved in the Boer War, the big central door was opened, the hall was quickly packed with patriots, the boys were sent up to the galleries, and the Old Chief delivered an impromptu harangue, received with yells of delight. He then stooped down from the platform, shook hands vigorously with a thousand or more townsmen, freed us for the day, and probably spent the rest of it having his arm massaged.

Passing over the other masters who instructed us in German, drawing, geometry, geography, chemistry, physics, and so on, I shall dwell briefly on two who would have been better employed managing coconut shies. One was a clergyman named Massey, called 'Pot' on account of his belly. He lost his temper easily, his small reddish beard bristled with wrath, and like all fat little men in that condition he looked funny. An answer I gave to one of his questions annoyed him, and he trembled with rage, which made me laugh. Insensate with fury, he picked up an ink bottle and threw it at my head. I caught it neatly and threw it back, catching him on the belly, where it broke and deluged him with ink. He was so utterly confounded that he remained for several seconds with his mouth open, staring at me as if he could not believe his senses. Gradually he became conscious of what had happened, said nothing at the time, but at the end of the lesson took me down to report my behaviour to the headmaster. The Old Chief had retired, and our new one was J. E. King, who had been headmaster of Manchester Grammar School before coming to us. He listened to Pot's account and then asked what I had to say. I simply explained that I had made a good catch, returned it, and could not be blamed for Mr Massey's failure in the field. King sent me out of the room, had a heart-to-heart talk with Pot, and I heard no more about it. From that moment I had complete confidence in the new 'head', who was conspicuously fair.

The other master who gained my strong disapproval was named Yule, which appropriately rhymed with Fool. He had a high opinion of himself and put on a good deal of 'side', being good-looking in a conventional sort of way. For some reason or other he took our form in English for a term, and started to plague us with Shakespeare's *Macbeth*, a wholly unintelligible play to anyone who has not experienced some contact with the outside world and the struggle for power. We were given a speech to learn by heart, a difficult involved

speech which has fogged many Macbeths I have since
seen on the stage:

> If it were done when 'tis done, then 'twere well
> If it were done quickly. . . .

This I was called upon to recite. I gabbled off the words
dutifully and sat down exhausted by the effort. 'Stand
up, Pearson.' I did so. 'I should be interested to know
whether you understood a line of what you have just
uttered?' 'Not a word, sir.' This was a truthful reply,
but being a fool he thought me impertinent and his
vanity was touched: 'Then your understanding is about
to be quickened. You will write out that speech fifty
times, and at the conclusion of the exercise you may
have a dim idea of what it is about.' The sycophants in
the form considered this a rare joke and laughed
heartily. But I did not think it funny because his imbecility prevented me from playing cricket for several
afternoons while I wrote out that wretched speech until
I loathed the name of Shakespeare as much as I detested
Macbeth. Yule had committed the sin against the Holy
Ghost, but no doubt he thought himself clever. True,
I enjoyed several performances of the plays given by
F. R. Benson's company at Bedford, and a master named
Dasent made me laugh when he took the part of
Fluellen in *Henry V* after several of us had failed to
grapple with it; but I refused to read the man whose
ridiculous rigmarole had made me suffer, and but for
an accident at a later date one of my greatest pleasures
in life would have been denied me by the folly of an
idiot.

Dickens by the way was lucky: he escaped the con-
tagion of school: and so he started from scratch. Possibly the masters thought him too realistic; in which
case they were wrong as usual, for a boy can appreciate Dickens while it takes an intelligent man to under-

stand Shakespeare or Scott. I remember being given
Lorna Doone to read when I was recovering from an
attack of jaundice. Naturally I took a jaundiced view
of the book and have never looked at it since. For illness
as well as holidays one's reading must be in tune with
one's mood.

Not that I ever opened a book on holiday if I could
help it; there were far more exciting things to do. We
used to spend some weeks at the seaside every summer.
My first sight of the sea was from Bexhill, which was
then (1900) in the process of being built. Here I stayed
with the two Hemsleys and their mother, bathing most
of the time and occasionally making trips to the hinterland. It became a joke in my family that whenever I
related anything remarkable in my experience it had
always occurred at Bexhill, no one being in a position
to contradict it. Another holiday I spent with a B.G.S.
friend named Mears and his mother at Torquay. But
as a rule the family went together, Jack and I to
Lowestoft with mother, all of us to Hunstanton twice,
Jack and I with several other fellows to Aberdovey,
where incidentally I swam across the mouth of the
Dovey at low tide, did not feel like swimming back,
borrowed a pair of trousers at Ynyslas, and returned by
train. That was in 1902 because I remember the old-
fashioned cannon near the quay being fired to celebrate
the coronation of Edward VII.

The year before I went alone to stay with a French
family at Le Havre. My father took me to Southampton
and put me on board what a porter called 'the Avver
boat', much to father's amusement. I can still remember
the name of the family, Cornille de L'Avergne, and
their address, 8 Rue Auguste Dolphus. Several other
English fellows were staying there, and we were supposed to converse with one another in French. We
bicycled all over the neighbourhood, received a French

lesson daily from one of the ladies who owned the place, and were encouraged to air our knowledge of the language at every meal. As a result I could speak almost like a native by the end of the holiday and had started to dream in French. It is one of my regrets that I was too lazy to keep it up, though I read the Musketeer series of Dumas, Hugo's *Les Misérables*, and two or three of Balzac's novels in the original before my innate indolence mastered me. Apart from being nearly drowned in the Seine during a boisterous day when we were warned not to bathe, a feat of mine caused consternation. One of the boys locked me in my bedroom for fun. With some experience of climbing walls, I got out of the window and with no handhold slowly worked my way along a very narrow ledge directly above the road, at the end of which I lowered myself to the top of the garden wall and jumped down. It was considered an impossible achievement and only the fact that I appeared in the garden while my bedroom door remained locked convinced the others that I had done the deed. Several French pedestrians who had watched the performance from the road called to express their alarm and present their felicitations, after which my annoyance at having been locked in passed off.

Up that road very early every morning came the fisherwomen from the harbour, and I still remember their cry, which sounded like 'Rat-om-ard-cherrum-chee-chee.' I have always been very sensitive to street-cries, which I usually manage to interpret after a while, but apart from the obvious 'homard' in this one I remain in ignorance of the other fish in the huge baskets the women carried.

Several times in the last years of the century Jack and I stayed with our maternal great-uncle, Lewis Moilliet, at Abberley Rectory. His father had owned the Hall, and his twin-brother Keir, who lived at Malvern, had continued the family banking business at Birmingham. Uncle Lewis was rector of Abberley for some forty years, and had been in love with my father's cousin Fanny, whose hunting accident had left her supine at The Elms till the end of her life. He remained a bachelor. With him we drove all over that beautiful countryside, and visited relations, such as the Cameron Galtons at Shelsley Grange. To our great delight he also took us to Ombersley where we spent a day with Albert and his family. It was the last time we saw our youthful hero. We were soon on friendly terms with our uncle's coachman, Bishop, and his housekeeper, Mrs Elliot, the first of whom did not relish all our heinous escapades. Uncle Lewis, though a genial fellow, was a serious churchman, and once boxed my ears because I asked whether one would get tired of eating unleavened bread, which was specially made for his Holy Communion services. After that I kept clear of religious themes, though I was innocent of offence.

During the spring, summer and autumn weeks which we spent at home during the holidays, I and my friends lived either in or on the Ouse, the best of all bathing and boating rivers. There were few reaches or inlets within ten miles of Bedford that we did not explore in Rob Roys or Canadian canoes, and when we could not afford them we spent the days in and out of the water at some spot with sloping banks on which to lie, chief among them being 'the pops' (poplars) in a field between Bedford and Clapham, now profaned by the gardens of new houses. The Ouse, a tranquil river, sometimes flooded the surrounding meadows, and the weirs became dangerous. One fatality lingers in my memory for a special reason. Two girls and a young man were in a boat that toppled over Bromham weir. The man saved himself, but the girls were drowned. The accident caused a sensation, and half Bedford walked or bicycled

out to Bromham for the funeral. My sisters' nurse was
still with us, and she took me to the village, where we
joined the throng to look at the masses of flowers and
the two coffins in their grave. The whole business had a
most unfortunate effect on me, and I developed a morbid
view of death and its external trappings. I still have
an exaggerated loathing of all the paraphernalia of
mortality.

But in spite of the risks of cramp, weirs, weeds, water
lilies, and other things I was warned against, I could
not keep away from the river, and once I was bathing
when I should have been in bed with a temperature,
the result being that I was laid up with some complaint
for the rest of the holidays, to my disgust, and for the
first two weeks of a new term, to my joy. All of us suffered the usual juvenile illnesses, measles, mumps,
whooping-cough, chicken-pox, etc., and the moment we
were down with one of them mother sent for Cousin
Nell. In those days many families had some spinster
aunt or cousin who rushed to the rescue on occasions
like these, and my father's cousin, Ellen Ellison, nursed
us through all our ailments with angelic patience and
professional competence. She was a sweet and good
woman, a sort of efficient saint, but engrossment in
religion eventually turned her brain.

Our illnesses, which we managed to enjoy with our
toy soldiers and magazines (*The Boys' Own Paper* for
Jack, *Chums* for me), had one drawback: they kept us
away from active games. Both of us were keen on cricket,
and I loved acting episodes with my sisters and friends.
It seems that in the improvised dramas we performed
I always insisted on playing the villain, because when
Gerald Hemsley saw me as a professional actor at Liverpool in the part of a murderer in 1928, he was vividly
reminded of the days when I had throttled or stabbed
the other members of our youthful casts, never permit-

ting any form of judicial retribution for my murky deeds. Another outlet for my superfluous energy was carpentry, and my sister Elsie surprised me recently by saying that I used to make serviceable shelves, tables and chairs. All I can remember is that I badgered my mother for a carpenter's bench, a plane, a brace, a bradawl, saws, screwdrivers, chisels, and so on, and that I spent a lot of time making a lot of noise.

The only school game I enjoyed was cricket. I hated 'rugger' for which B.G.S. was famous, because I suffer from claustrophobia, and I usually found myself beneath a heap of other boys when the 'scrum' caved in. I preferred long-distance running to anything else, and I quite liked coxing the Paulo-Pontine boat in the house races, my light weight more than my ability being the main qualification. Though fond of playing certain games, I have never been at all interested in watching others play them, or in the results of their prowess, and so I have failed to share the absorption of my fellow-countrymen in cup ties, test matches, Wimbledon tennis, golf finals, horse races, and so on. Once, on entering a famous restaurant, the manager greeted me with: 'Well, sir, how about the great race?' 'What race?' I asked in complete ignorance. 'Sir!!!' he exclaimed, reeling backwards. I then learnt that the Oxford and Cambridge boat-race had taken place that day. I am not proud of this isolation. I think it a pity that I am incapable of feeling the competitive thrills of the mass of mankind. But so it is.

My real interests were foreshadowed in 1903, when I had reached the age of sixteen. Elsie and I decided, or more likely I decided and Elsie agreed, to produce magazines. Hers was called *The Thunderer*, mine *The Lightning*, and we kept them up for three bi-annual numbers, starting with the second half-year of 1903 and finishing with the second half-year of 1904. Hers have disappeared, but two of mine, the first and third numbers, have survived. I have just gone through them, and am amazed by their immaturity and naïveté. I have since read essays by boys of fourteen that put these to shame. Mine was certainly a very slow growth, and my education did not begin until I had left school.

The magazine was of course written by hand and sent the round of uncles, aunts and cousins, each of whom was requested to return it and pay one shilling for the privilege of reading it. 'I think that it is worth 1/-', I wrote in the preface to the first number, 'as I have spent many precious minutes or hours in writing it, whereas I might have been doing other things.' My native laziness is apparent throughout, many pages being filled with pictures and press cuttings: six pages taken from some daily paper about the death of Pope Leo XIII, with his photo on a seventh; three pages about a murderer named Samuel Dougal; twelve pages describing the death of Napoleon; a lot about Joseph Chamberlain. 'As you know already', I interrupted the sequence of events, 'this magazine is chiefly devoted to summarys (*sic*) of famous mens lives and their photos. I am now going to give a few of these in succession and am then going on to do something else.' There followed a great deal about the reigning monarch, Edward VII, containing this self-indulgent phrase: 'When Prince of Wales, the King was not at the early part of his life what he should have been, but many of us are the same, so do not comment on his sins till you are sure that you have none yourself. (Note: Chapter 6, St Luke, verses 41 & 42.)' The reference is to the mote in our brother's eye and the beam in our own eye, and it is clear that I wanted readers to consider their own vices before jumping to any conclusion about their editor. Charles I next had an innings, with severe comments on that 'ill-bred cur' Oliver Cromwell. Then came a comparison between

Lords Roberts and Kitchener, with illustrations, followed by a pen-portrait of Sir Arthur Conan Doyle, described as 'my favourite of all bookwriters'. The magazine included school stories of an almost incredible artlessness, comic stories that were only funny because they were supposed to be so, verses that received the courtesy-title of poetry because they rhymed, and a write-up of its rival: 'The Editress (or rather author) of: *The Thunderer* is my sister, so of course I would say nothing against it except that mine is the best.' The Prince and Princess of Wales and the Duke of Connaught also received favourable notice.

My third and last number contained a bloodthirsty serial story of myself as a bandit, but was almost wholly devoted to pictures and sketches of eminent men. Charles I kept cropping up, as well as Napoleon and Joseph Chamberlain. The editor stigmatized so harshly the treatment of Napoleon by the English that he must have anticipated a flood of protests, to prevent which he wrote: 'I don't want any letters from any of my readers saying that my language is a bit too eloquent on this most painful subject, because if I receive them, they shall be torn up and put in the fire without ceremony.' The severance of the French Republic from the Vatican was a topic of the time, and I admire the fine reticence of the editor on this subject. Assuming that many priests would take refuge in England, this is how he dealt with the question:

'Why should we English take French people within our country because they are expelled from France?' The answer is easy:—Because we are a free country. Therefore we cannot, even if we would, turn them out. Instead then of taking all the outcasts of foreign powers, why do we not give up becoming a free country? Because the greater number of our population don't wish it.

'Why not?'

'I can't tell you.'

Along with my literary efforts I began to invent all sorts of curious words, like a character then in the womb of time, H. G. Wells's Mr Polly. These indicated ideas and moods beyond the confines of the English language. They amused my mother, who repeated them to her friends. Clearly these strange new cacophonies hinted at a subconscious desire to express myself; and as clearly the preoccupation with famous men's lives pointed to a future biographer. But who could have guessed this at the time? Not I.

My complete failure to learn anything that bored me kept me in Rolfe's form for several terms, until he got tired of seeing me in the same place. My father heard from the school authorities that perhaps I had better be transferred to the Mercantile Class. After a vain effort to persuade me to study the classics and become a clergyman, since there were a few fat livings in the gift of the family, he agreed to the transfer, and my last two years of schooling were spent in the M.C. under H. W. Barnes, known affectionately and familiarly as 'Podgy'. All the failures of the school eventually came to roost in his form, owing to the general view that fellows who were no good for anything else were good enough for business. Podgy was the nicest and most sensible master I ever met, and I became really fond of him; indeed I actually began to take some pains with my work, and ended up top of his form. Not that I found this achievement very difficult, most of the others being less inclined to labour than I, and very little intelligence is needed for scholastic work if one takes it seriously. Memory is the chief asset, and though I could not be bothered to remember all the stuff I ploughed through I soon got into the way of learning what I thought would be useful in examination. Two subjects I really got to like: history and French, the consequence being that I walked ahead of everybody in both, and even beat a Parisian lad named Pourée in the final French exam, earning a tribute from the French master, Le Jeune, who called me 'a good bye, a very good bye' and expressed a hope that he would find as good a 'bye' as I the following term. It was fortunate that I left at the end of that term, for such is the nature of schoolboys that I would have been nicknamed 'Good-bye' thereafter.

In the belief that life away from home would be good for me, my parents made me a boarder in Barnes's house for the last four terms of my pupillage. Podgy had called it Merton House after his Oxford college, and it was situated in Kimbolton Road, at the other end of Bedford, being the last house but one before the fields and hedgerows started. I was fairly happy there, as happy as I could ever be in a state of restricted liberty. I liked most of the other fellows, about thirty of them, and there was very little bullying. In most other boarding-schools, if the memories of their one-time inmates are to be trusted, there was a good deal of love-making between the older and younger boys. So far as I know, and one gets to know most things in these small communities, B.G.S. was fairly free of it. About a third of the school consisted of boarders, and I never heard that any of the houses festered with lust. This may have been due to the immense emphasis laid on games and athletics. So far as our house was concerned, the main amorous interest centred on girls seen in St Peter's Church, where we attended morning service. In those days there was no school chapel, and the official school service was held first at St. Paul's and afterwards at Trinity Church in the afternoons, each house attending its neighbouring church service in the mornings. Long conversations took place in our dormitory at night about the relative attractiveness of the girls to be seen at matins. Of course we all had chums, mine being a fellow called Newman, who was sometimes ragged for his habit of kneeling down and saying his prayers at night, there being occasions when one could not see him for pillows. But such relationships were entirely innocent of sex, and my sole experience of carnality was when a boy of my own age aroused my curiosity in onanism and made a practical demonstration on me to prove its delights. He failed to convert me. I got bored and suggested some other form of recreation.

We had tremendous bolster-battles in our dormitory. We got into trouble with the matron if our pillows were dirty, so we used bolsters instead. A boy was always posted outside the door to keep watch and give warning of hostile approach. Many years after leaving school a contemporary told me that I had once been detailed for the duty, but that my excitement over the fight had diverted my attention as a guard. Suddenly I dashed into the room crying 'Cave, you fellows, here's Podgy!' At the same moment Podgy loomed behind me. He must have heard my warning, but he took no notice of it, merely advised one fellow who had dived for his bed leaving his feet dangling over the side that he would sleep better if covered up, and retired. During a half-term holiday a chap named Innocent and I spent a day at a farm not far from Kimbolton. We bicycled back in the dark, and as we returned long after the regulation hour we expected trouble. But I had prepared for this. On being told to report ourselves, we entered Podgy's sanctum and presented him with a brace of rabbits before he could speak a word of disapproval. He grinned, thanked us, and frankly admitted that we had stymied him. Such was Podgy, a delightful and lovable person with a keen sense of humour, and whenever I revisited Bedford I called for a talk with him. Shortly after I left school he took Holy Orders and with the erection of the chapel he became the school's chaplain. He died during the 1914 war.

While in his house I joined the School Corps, of which he was an officer, and we were inspected by two generals who had been famous in the Boer War: Methuen and Gatacre. This thrilled me because I had taken considerable interest in that campaign, and my first hero was Sir George White, the defender of Ladysmith. There are early snapshots of me posing, left arm akimbo, as I had seen him in a picture. I thought for a while that soldiering would be great fun, especially pig-sticking on the North-West Frontier, but on leaving school all I wanted to do was nothing except enjoy my freedom. I left after the summer term of 1905, with small Latin, less Greek, no mathematics, an almost pathological hatred of punishment and cruelty, a violent objection to routine, and a firm disbelief in compulsory education, which I shared with Sir Walter Scott, in whose letters many years later I came across this: 'The knowledge which we acquire of free will and by spontaneous exertion is like food eaten with an appetite; it digests well and benefits the system ten times more than the double cramming of an Alderman.'

Though a scholastic education had taught me nothing of value, I first became conscious of beauty during my state of pupillage. On a tranquil Sunday evening in summer I was paddling a canoe on the Ouse. At a spot I can still see in the mind's eye I let the boat drift across the stream and sat for a while entranced by the deep shadows of the woods on my left, the rich green fields on my right with the line of pollards beyond, the violet sky, the clouds red and pink in the sunset, and the distant sound of bells from Kempston church across the meadows. I was sixteen years old at the time, and when the bells ceased ringing I felt a little ashamed of an emotion that filled me with happiness and yet made me want to cry. I paddled back viciously to Bedford in an effort to overcome the feeling and get back to the normal world of exercise and muscle.

3

Revelations

Our next-door neighbour in Shakespeare Road was
Alfred Strover Williams, managing-director of The
Royal Mail Steam Packet Company. At the request of
my father, Williams gave me a job in his company, my
school record having proved conclusively that the respectable professions were beyond my competence. I do
not know what else my father could have done. I had
shown no aptitude for anything and no preference for
any kind of employment, whereas my brothers were
both keen on engineering and went through an appren-
ticeship at Crewe. Father was not a far-seeing man,
and it would have called for divine prescience to fore-
see my future.[1] All professions were the same to me:
they meant work, and I disliked work. I wanted to enjoy
myself, and earning a living was not my idea of enjoyment. So I went into the city as I would have gone into
any other place, to make as little effort as possible and
get as much amusement as I could. To say that I had a
modicum of curiosity in the sort of work I was to do

[1] Yet I must have been vaguely conscious of my destiny because
at the age of eighteen I subscribed to *The Bookman Illustrated
History of English Literature* by Thomas Seccombe and W.
Robertson Nicoll, in twelve monthly parts, which was the best
investment I ever made in my life and which I still possess,
though the original covers of the different parts are somewhat
ragged from over half a century's wear and tear.

would be a wild overstatement of the fact. To this day
I have but the vaguest impression of my labours. But
I was interested in many of my fellow-employees and I
can see them in my mind's eye today as clearly as I
noted their mental and physical peculiarities during the
two and a half years I spent in their company, from
September 1905 until March 1908. The city of those
days was good ground for the study of human oddities;
though unfortunately the staff of the R.M.S.P.Co. had
not been engaged for the purpose of providing me with
raw material for my future studies of life, and far too
much of my time was passed in meaningless drudgery.

Having returned from a holiday with Cousin Nell
at her Overton home near Ellesmere, I accompanied
Williams to the firm's chief office at 18 Moorgate Street
in the city. The day was cloudless and beautiful, and
he said to me as we walked along that it augured well
for my future in business. Had he left out the last two
words, he would have been right. What I discovered
for myself while I was in the city was of more value to
me than all the Company's shares. My salary was ten
shillings a week, out of which I had to buy my lunches
for six days. My first job was in the Transfer Department, which consisted of two others and myself, our
chief being a most lovable character named D. W.
Allport, who was so absent-minded that he used to look
for his hat when it was on his head and his spectacles
when they were on his nose. Deeply involved as a radical in politics and a nonconformist in religion, he was
an eloquent public speaker. He recognized at once that
I was wholly unfitted for my work, but he was remarkably sweet-natured and sympathetic, and I never heard
him speak an unkind word. Once I put his gentle spirit
to a severe test. His desk was excessively untidy, papers
all over it in no kind of order and mixed up with ink
bottles, india-rubber, rulers, pens, pencils and other

utensils. I inherit a sense of tidiness from my mother and cannot bear to see things left lying about, pictures crooked, carpets rucked, and all that sort of thing; so I took advantage of his absence one day to put everything in order. Expecting to hear a cry of delight when he caught sight of his desk next morning, I heard a groan, followed by dead silence, then a tremendous rustling of papers as if the south-west wind had got in amongst them. He did not complain; he suffered in silence; but I heard from his second-in-command that as a consequence of my passion for neatness he could not lay his hands on anything he needed for the next week or two, after which disorder reigned again and by plunging his hand here and there into chaotic masses of stuff he found what he wanted and sighed with relief. I learnt from this incident that one should leave ill alone.

His second-in-command was a Scot named R. R. M. MacKintosh, who eventually succeeded him as head of the department. MacKintosh was a rather secretive fellow who told me little about himself, though I did my best to pump him. He too had a very nice nature, never lost his temper, never got rattled, was always kind, courteous and humorous. As time went on I became very fond of him, and on finding that he often went to the theatre I badgered him with questions about the players he had seen. It happened that Sir Henry Irving died during my early weeks at the office; and as the one thing I had intended to do on coming to London was to see him act, his sudden death on tour deprived me of my sole ambition. MacKintosh had seen him in many parts and sometimes imitated his mannerisms. I could have listened for hours to such talk, and I am sure that Mac-Kintosh interrupted his labours as often as possible to satisfy my curiosity, but in the middle of some reminiscence his conscience would smite him and he would break off with: 'Well, we must get on with our work.'

At one period our work consisted of transforming £100 shares into £60 ordinary and £40 preference stock (my terminology may be as shaky as my memory on such a tedious theme) and we spent weeks filling in new certificates. But when not engaged in talking of books, politics, or the theatre, I spent much of my time looking out of a window that commanded an alley, and the rest of it making official journeys in the city: to Robarts Lubbock the bankers, where I suppose I handed in cheques, and to the Custom House, passing which many years later with a friend I happened to mention that 'I used to go in there with specifications and things like that.' 'Things like what?' 'Specifications.' Which about sums up my complete ignorance of what I was doing and my total lack of interest in it; though, oddly enough, I can vividly remember the face of the man to whom I used to hand the specifications, just as I can still see a pedlar outside Robarts Lubbock and hear his croak: 'Pretty collar studs.'

At the beginning of my city career I lived at home, leaving Bedford every morning by the 8.40 train, and St Pancras every evening by the 5.45; but in November 1905 I started to live in London, at first with the family of a dear old lady named Sara Goodwin, at 93 Fitzjohn's Avenue, Hampstead, where I had a wonderful view over western London from my bedroom window at the top and back of the house. After her death I shared digs with my future brother-in-law, Bernard McCallum, at No. 23 Gayton Road, the most depressing thoroughfare in Hampstead. Every morning before breakfast in the warmer months I used to bathe in the Highgate ponds, in the colder months to practise golf shots on the Heath. For some years I was keen on golf and had managed to reduce my handicap to twelve, playing a fairly steady game, when I made the appalling error of taking lessons from a professional, who corrected all my mistakes of stance, swing, grip, etc. and wrecked my play; from which I learnt that we should teach ourselves everything, in sport as in art, forming the styles that are natural to us.

London was, and is, a wonderful place to me, forever fresh and fascinating. Before 1905 I had only visited it once, when Jack and I put in a few summer weeks of 1900 with our cousin, Laura Johnstone, at Chiswick, and were shown the sights; St Paul's Cathedral, Westminster Abbey, the Tower of London, Madame Tussaud's, and taken to the Egyptian Hall in Piccadilly for Maskelyne and Cook's mysterious performance, to the Zoo where the snakes made me shudder, and to Earl's Court Exhibition, where we witnessed a battle between Britons and Matabeles, rifles *v* assegais, called 'Savage South Africa,' and went round in the Great Wheel. Motor buses and cars were just beginning to vie with hansom cabs and other horse-drawn vehicles in the early months of 1906, and among the minor amusements in the streets were the caustic comments of horse-bus drivers as they passed the stationary Vanguard motor-buses that had broken down: 'D'yer want a lift or a 'orse?' 'Try goin' backwards!' 'Walking's quicker!' 'Spit on yer 'ands and pull it!' The street-cries always intrigued me, and one of them kept me guessing a very long time. Just outside Moorgate Street station a fish-monger stood by his shop and yelled at the passers-by: 'Ory-et-stibbet, keb and lob-ster, keb and lob-ster.' 'Keb' was obviously 'crab', but I was bothered by the first part of the cry until many years later I happened to note the contents of another fishmonger's shop and received enlightenment: 'Ory-et-stibbet' meant 'oysters and turbot.'

My father paid for my lodgings, clothes and fares. This included breakfast and dinner, but I still had to make ten shillings a week cover the cost of my midday meals; and as I wished to visit the theatre at least once a week, I had to lunch frugally in order to save the necessary half-crown. There were quite a few suburban theatres which the West-End 'stars' used to visit on their tours, and one of them was the Camden, about two miles from Hampstead. Here I saw popular players like Forbes-Robertson, Martin Harvey, Fred Terry and Seymour Hicks. My Aunt Eva was then living in London, and she asked me what I would like to see in the West-End. In spite of the fact that I had already seen a fit-up company do the play at Towyn when Jack and I were staying at Aberdovey, I did not hesitate over the choice, and she took me to the Duke of York's where William Gillette had revived *Sherlock Holmes*. He did not realize my idea of the great detective, but of course I was thrilled by my first visit to a West-End theatre.

At the age of nineteen I experienced the four major revelations of my life, as a result of which I grew up. Much nonsense is often talked about the people and things that are supposed to influence a man's character. But our natures are irrevocably settled at birth. What happens is that in the early stages of growth our minds are clogged with a lot of useless knowledge and warped by hearing so many fatuous opinions that we do not know ourselves until something occurs to clarify our true natures, the influence we acknowledge being merely a disclosure. No one's nature can be changed: it can only be revealed by another's stimulation. The light shines from without but the illumination occurs within; and ultimately the only person by whom the intelligent man is profoundly influenced is himself.

The revelations that enabled me to see and be myself came in this order: Oscar Wilde, Shakespeare, Beerbohm Tree, Bernard Shaw. To two of those four I am permanently indebted for liberating my mind, to the other two for releasing my sensibility.

Soon after I began to live in London I came across a book called *Sebastian Melmoth*, which contained a number of passages from someone's writings and a complete essay called *The Soul of Man Under Socialism*. Reading it was like waking up after a long sleep. I suddenly saw things, not as I had accepted them in a comatose condition, but as I instinctively perceived them to be. It was not a conversion: it was a recognition. And this, I believe, is the reality behind all so-called conversions, which, with mentally conscious people, are simply fulfilments of their own personalities. I immediately became intensely interested in Mr Melmoth and asked everyone I met if they knew anything about him. No one had ever heard of him. Then a fellow in the office named Standage lent me an anonymous book called *De Profundis*, and when I asked for the author's name he behaved in a very mysterious way, telling me that the fellow's name was Oscar Wilde, but that as he had been imprisoned for an unmentionable crime I had better forget it. That of course was quite enough to make me remember it, and when I discovered that he had also written what by then had become my Bible, *The Soul of Man Under Socialism*, I determined to go on mentioning the man until I had discovered his unmentionable crime. I must have been strangely innocent because the fellow with whom I shared digs, McCallum, though ignorant of literary matters, told me the dread secret, and I thought it comical that a man could have love-affairs with members of his own sex. But I was not in the least shocked, and all my life I have been surprised by the moral indignation aroused by that particular malady. Hatred being the child of fear, I can only assume that the resentment aroused by homosexuality must be due to some internal disquietude in those who express it. Anyhow, I was so much attracted by what I had read that I spent hours searching for Wilde's works, in those days a perilous occupation because his name was still never breathed in public and one was liable to be insulted by the sellers of books and such bystanders as overheard a request for, say, 'Oscar Wilde's *Intentions*'. At length I managed to collect odd copies of his works in second-hand bookshops at bargain prices, all of which I sold later at a considerable profit, when I bought the Collected Edition.

While still in the early stages of the Wilde fever I was granted another revelation. Staying with one of my school friends at his Shropshire home, a rambling old country-house not far from Shrewsbury, where conversation was restricted to hunting, golf and shooting, I looked for a book with which to pass a day of cataclysmic rain. The house was bookless except for a copy of the Bible and a volume of Shakespeare's plays in execrable print, an austere choice between the boredom of church and the anguish of school. I decided to be a martyr and began to read *Hamlet*. The opening scene held me and I galloped through the play with increasing excitement. I re-read it immediately after lunch the same day. That did the trick. I entered a new world, which expanded with every play I read, and to such a degree was I carried away that I sometimes wept with joy. Looking back on those days, I seem to have walked on air. My imagination was released, my sense of beauty set free. The City was no longer a prison where I did purposeless jobs but a place of magic where, sitting at my desk or wandering through the streets, I could dream of Shakespeare's poetry and characters. My fellow-clerks must have thought me, if not mad, at least 'not all there'. Indeed I was not all there or even partly there: I dwelt in an ideal world beyond the City's horizon. I quoted from *Hamlet* and *Macbeth* in replying to questions, and what was supposed to be a shipping business became for me a Shakespeare business.

At about this time I was taken out of the Transfer and put into the Outward Freight Department. The Secretary of the company was a boisterous bully named Forbes, who strongly objected to my going over his head and appealing to the managing-director to compensate a fellow who had been unjustifiably sacked. The victim received a decent sum and I incurred the displeasure of Forbes, who shoved me into a much busier branch of the business, where I would have no time to interfere in matters that did not concern me. The only matter that concerned me then was the poetic drama, and I soon became friendly with two other fellows of my own age, C. H. Burt and H. C. Kemp, injecting them with some of my enthusiasm for Shakespeare and his high priest, Beerbohm Tree.

It would be impossible to over-estimate the effect on me of Tree's Shakespearean productions, which made visual the imaginative drama within me. He opened my eyes to the beauty of music and painting, and his own personality kindled my instinctive propensity to hero-worship. The hours I spent in his theatre were the happiest I had known, even though my stomach was audibly demanding the food I had sacrificed in order to pay the price of entrance, and I nearly always had to face the walk back to Hampstead after the play was over, having had nothing to eat since breakfast. The all-round acting at His Majesty's was far better than it had been under Irving at the Lyceum, and even though Tree frequently miscast himself, especially in leading tragic parts, the fascination of his curious character more than made up for his inability to sustain heroic rôles. I have seen several actors who could give technically better performances than he did of Richard II and Malvolio, but none who could give me half as much pleasure. The only part he played which left me dissatisfied was Hamlet; but this did not matter, since the finest conceivable representation of Hamlet was given by his contemporary Johnston Forbes-Robertson, who was so perfect in the part that every other actor who has played it in the last half-century seems in retrospect to have been either affected or commonplace. Incidentally I first saw Robertson's Hamlet at the Coronet Theatre, Notting Hill, in 1906, and another dozen times at various theatres before his retirement.[1] But one remembers his own performance and nothing else, his scenery being shoddy, the playing of the other characters second-rate; whereas Tree's productions were memorable and wholly enjoyable, the acting excellent, the stage-management thrilling, the scenery exquisite, the music delightful, the whole atmosphere enchanting. He was a great artist.

The fourth and final momentous revelation of my City days took place at the Court and Savoy Theatres, where I saw the early productions of several plays by Bernard Shaw. After the so-called well-made plays of the popular playwrights, Pinero, Jones, Sutro, *John Bull's Other Island, Man and Superman* and *The Doctor's Dilemma* came like the fresh air of an oasis in the desert. Such a revolution had never before taken place in the history of the British drama, for even Shakespeare had followed Marlowe. The unique achievement of Shaw was that he gave his generation a good shaking, made them question everything and think for themselves. He with his speeches, prefaces and plays, and Wilde with his conversation, essays and witty dialogue, destroyed the complacency, pretentiousness and conventional morality of the Victorian Age, and

---

[1] In the year following his death I drew Bernard Shaw's attention to Ellen Terry's statement that she preferred Henry Irving's Hamlet to any other she had seen. 'Her love of Henry blinded her judgment,' said G.B.S. 'Irving's Hamlet was simply another aspect of Henry Irving, Forbes-Robertson's was the Hamlet of William Shakespeare.'

everyone who hates humbug and cares for freedom of thought must be eternally grateful to them. I remember foolishly declining to see *Major Barbara* because I had heard that it dealt with the Salvation Army, which with its 'Come to Jesus' hysteria grated on me. If people could only be made religious by an onslaught on their emotions, I felt that the sooner the nation denied God the better. Though *Barbara* can hardly be described as propaganda for the Salvation Army, I like it less than any of Shaw's longer plays.

The acting of the entire cast at the Court was first-rate, but my most vivid memory is Ellen Terry in *Captain Brassbound's Conversion*, the part written for her. The play that made the greatest impression on me was *Caesar and Cleopatra*, done by Forbes-Robertson at the Savoy for four weeks only. The character of Caesar had been created by Shaw for Robertson, whose performance was flawless. Somehow I raked up the money to go three times, and the play remains one of my favourite works in all literature, enriched for me by the unforgettable tones of Forbes-Robertson's voice and the dramatic diction of Shaw, who read it to me at my request when he was past eighty and brought every character to life. No one could have foreseen that *Caesar and Cleopatra* would have a wider influence on literature than any other work produced in that age. Shaw's naturalistic treatment of a historical theme was the spring from which flowed a stream of novels, plays, films, histories and biographies, in which both subjects and periods have been dealt with in a humorous, satirical, naturalistic modern manner. At its worst this method has the effect of mere iconoclasm; at its best it produces a living picture, like Shaw's.

So much for the revelations that had an immediate and permanent effect on me. Other pleasures that I enjoyed in those two and a half years, but which did not

help to create self-realization, were the novels of
Dickens, Thackeray and Balzac, the music of Wagner,
several works by Fielding and Smollett, some stories by
Kipling and Stevenson, and the easily digestible
romances of a few popular contemporary authors, particularly W. J. Locke.

In short my head was full of literary fancies, my
spiritual nature responding to the apocalypse of my
natural masters, as I sauntered through the streets and
alleys of the City during the lunch hour, stemming the
craving for food as best I could by thinking of the book
I could buy or the play I could see with the money I
should have spent on a beefsteak. As one who has always
enjoyed his meals, I thought it strange even at the time
that I should sacrifice so much for my urgent needs;
but in those days spiritual nourishment meant far more
to me than physical well-being. Sometimes I went to
a lunch-hour service at St Peter's or St Michael's Church
in Cornhill, sometimes to an organ-recital by Reginald
Goss-Custard at St Mary Le Bow, now to meditate for
a while in St Paul's Cathedral or St Lawrence Jewry,
now to cross London Bridge and stroll round Southwark
Cathedral, where the stones had been trodden by the
feet of Shakespeare. But I was young, and hunger
gnawed, and passing an A.B.C. or a Mecca café I could
not always resist the temptation of a roll and butter
with a cup of coffee at a total outlay of fivepence. Then
I would return and probably spend the afternoon filling
in bills of lading, which I find, on reference to a diction-
ary, were 'papers signed by the master of a ship, by
which he makes himself responsible for the safe delivery
of the goods specified therein'. Of this I have remained
ignorant until the present moment, but I filled them in
all the same, and how I managed to keep Shakespeare
out of them, if I did, is a mystery. I remember answering a telephone enquiry about freightage in such an odd

way that the instrument was seized by a fellow-clerk, who apologized to the man at the other end, dealt with the subject in a more practical manner, and then asked what the devil I had meant by talking about rats. I must have answered the enquiry in Shylock's words: 'Ships are but boards, sailors but men; there be land-rats and water-rats, land-thieves and water-thieves—I mean pirates.' The prospective customer probably thought he had rung up a lunatic asylum by mistake.

For some unearthly reason I fancied a job in a bank. If I know my nature at all, the idea may have crossed my mind that a bank was a cosy sort of institution where one sat behind a counter in much the same way as my sisters and I had played at 'Post Office' and chatted to any clients who wanted to talk about the theatre. But beyond doubt it also occurred to me that a visit to China would be rather pleasant, and I applied for work either to the Chartered Bank of India, Australia and China or to the Hong-Kong and Shanghai Bank. I can never be certain which it was, but I know that China came into it. The manager of the concern I chose received me courteously and asked whether I had any banking experience. I dealt with that question easily. Then he asked why I wanted to join his staff. The answer to that was easy too: I did not care for my present job. 'But are you interested in banking?' he enquired. 'Not in the least,' I assured him. 'Then, Mr Pearson, I do not think I shall require your services.' That concluded the interview.

My head was in the clouds not only during office hours but at periods of complete freedom while I roamed about Hampstead Heath. Even during my holidays the main subjects that occupied my mind were never absent for an hour. One holiday I spent with my brother Harry at Cannock Chase, where in those days there was an extremely attractive golf course laid out in a piece of scenery as pretty and wild as anything in Scotland. My preoccupation with other matters so often took my eye off the ball that my game steadily deteriorated. Another fortnight's holiday, as well as two extended Easter week-ends, were passed with my Uncle Walter's family at Emery Down Vicarage in the New Forest. I loved my uncle, and our talks when walking or bicycling or playing golf or sitting up late at night were always pleasurable. He told me that during his chaplaincy at Ajmer he had spent the whole of one hot season going through the plays of Shakespeare. He had a theory that all nightmares were due to fear of particular things, not a general fear of life as many people supposed. This was certainly true in my own case, because my two recurring nightmares were (1) that I was back at my preparatory school, and (2) that I was caught up in some terrible piece of machinery which was slowly crushing me to death. Both were claustrophobic in effect, and the latter was directly due to my dislike of machines. I used to read the lessons for Uncle Walter on Sundays, and once, when he suffered a sudden return of malaria and could not get a locum-tenens at short notice, I had the temerity to take as much of the service as a layman can and even, such is the audacious self-confidence of youth, to intone the Litany. The church is still standing.

I saw a good deal of two other relations on Sundays in London: my great-great uncle Francis Galton, then about eighty-five, and Aunt Eva who kept house for him after the death of her father. At lunch or tea at 42 Rutland Gate I met, among other notabilities, Mary Coleridge the poet, Ralph Inge, the vicar of All Saints, Ennismore Gardens, afterwards Dean of St Paul's, Karl Pearson, who later became the first professor of Eugenics at University College and wrote a monumental biography of Galton. I paid little attention to the talk on science, and what attracted me to Uncle Frank, as we called him, was that he could discuss the things I liked. I even managed to persuade him to take tickets for Tree's production of *Nero* at His Majesty's Theatre, and though his hearing was defective he admired the magnificence of the show. He also gave Aunt Eva and myself seats for the Court Theatre, but did not accompany us on account of his deafness.

One of his achievements interested me: he was the first to make a science of finger-prints as a means of identification. After seven years' hard labour he had produced a Finger Print Directory, which resulted in seven years' hard labour for a good many other people and displaced all the other systems then in use, including that of Alphonse Bertillon, whose method of bodily measurements had previously held the field. One day Conan Doyle, who wanted to question my uncle about the various finger-print systems, came to lunch, and I had a first and last view of my boyhood's hero, who disrelished my enthusiasm for Sherlock Holmes at the expense of his historical novels. My curiosity about finger-prints was perhaps due to an early absorption in the pre-digital methods of Holmes, because Galton's other accomplishments left me cold, and I received a severe lecture from one of his female disciples for talking throughout lunch about Shakespeare and Shaw when I ought to have been concerned with the epoch-making works of my uncle. She took me into a corner to deliver her reproof, which concluded with the words: 'You should be proud, *proud*, of being his nephew.'

Another female who reproved me was our landlady, whose language reminded me so much of Shakespeare's Mistress Quickly that I made notes of it and many years later revived her character in a short story which was published in the *Cornhill Magazine* for September, 1932, not because the editor Leonard Huxley cared for the story, but because he loved the character. When my future brother-in-law and I engaged our 'digs' at 23 Gayton Road we asked her name, and thinking she said 'Tellard' we always called her so, though we later discovered it to be Taylor. She had married again, but in conversation she was always recalling the maxims of her first husband, which must have been a little vexing for her second. My first attempt to reproduce her eloquence occurred after she had delivered herself on the subject of food. Influenced by Bernard Shaw, and hoping to become as witty as he if I followed his regimen, I suggested a vegetarian diet for a week or so. Her reaction was prompt and decisive:

'Lettuces and tomatoes never agreed with no one. What my husband always said was "Steak for the stomach" he said "and vegetables for the collywobbles" he said. There's nothing like a good raw Porterhouse for a pick-me-up and nothing like prunes and potatoes for a lay-me-down. Except spirits, of course, which picks you up in moderation and lays you down on Bank Holidays. Not that I don't know that one person's butter ain't another person's parsnips, as my husband used to say. No, nor I won't argue about it, Mr P.,' she continued breathlessly, as I opened my mouth to enquire what her husband had meant by 'collywobbles'; 'I never will argue about anything. I just like to say what I think, and leave it to other folks' better natures to come round to my way of thinking. But I never will talk politics— that I do debar. Whenever my husband started politics, I used to lock up the valuables and leave the house. He wasn't happy unless he could have at least one good row a week, and then he used to sulk up to dinner-time the next day. But *de mortuary mensa mensam*, as he used to say, and all's well that ends respectable. So what's it to be: a nice steak and chips or shepherd's pie?'

At a moment of excessive penury, when I was dying

to take a pal to one of Tree's Shakespearean revivals, I asked her to lend me a pound, and the following conversation ensued:

'Now don't tell me you've been getting into trouble, Mr P. I couldn't believe it, not with a face like yours.'

'Fact is I want to take a friend out and I'm stoney at the moment.'

'A friend? Oh, I see! Well, well; some calls 'em one thing, some another. So what you're wanting is, as my husband called it, the *quid pro Joe*—he always would call them quids, though who Joe was I never could make out, though I had my suspicions. All right, Mr. P., you can have it and welcome.'

'Very kind of you indeed. But it really is a friend, a chap in the office.'

'You go and tell that to the submarines,' was her sole comment as she left the room in search of her purse.

I had my hat and coat on when she returned, in order to spare myself the pain of listening to a further selection of moral reflections. She handed me the money, saw me safely to the door, and when I was half-way down the steps outside gave me the benefit of a life-time's observation:

'Them that go out with a pound usually come in with the milk.'

In this particular case her suspicions were unfounded, but she was a shrewd woman and no one, as she once informed me, could pull her leg 'with impudity'.

Though not exactly a cheerful soul, she sometimes hummed, and was clearly in a humming mood when she brought my cup of tea one fine summer morning. After saying that 'the late bird gathers no moss', she stood by the window humming two notes like an asthmatic cuckoo. Suddenly she broke into speech:

'I do like a morning that *is* a morning, so to speak. You can see St Paul's Cathedral today, which my husband used to call "a great globe of itself" and he's seen a thing or two, take it from me. "I've been all around the gerkin", he used to say, "and what I haven't seen isn't worth worrying about." And nor it wasn't, neither, I give you *my* word. Them was the days to see things, before these motors came along. Alykon[1] days—that's what I call them. What's the use of tearing about the place so fast that you can't stare at things?'

I agreed that there was much in what she said, and then dropped off to sleep, which must have ruffled her because she treated me with some aloofness for several days.

Just as Mrs Taylor could not help bringing her husband's mixed maxims into her everyday speech, so was I incapable of keeping Shakespeare or Wilde or Shaw or Tree out of my conversation, and I perceive now that I probably bored people with my pet themes; but in my favour it may be said that I was always greatly interested in the opinions of others and did my best to make them talk of what interested them. I have a sad memory of an old school chum, Gerald Hemsley, who stayed with me in Hampstead for a week-end. On Sunday I took him for a long walk over the Heath, in the course of which I discovered that we had nothing whatever in common. He remained interested in the things that had pleased us at school, all of which I had outgrown. I tried hard to make him discuss literature, politics, music, the theatre, even religion, but he answered all my questions monosyllabically and apathetically. We came to the western edge of the Heath, a path leading from the rear of the Bull and Bush inn to the Spaniards, on the left of which in those days were palings which cut off the Heath from the meadows that ran down to Golders Green, then four cross-roads without a house in sight. Along this path

[1] Halcyon.

we went, myself struggling to maintain a conversation about anything but our past doings. At length I tired, and while we were climbing the bit leading up to the Spaniards Road, where the roots of trees almost form steps, I made a final effort: 'Do you ever read anything?' 'Yes.' 'What?' 'Marie Corelli.' Ever since then I have named that steep path 'Corelli Climb'. Gerald, known to all of us as Jum, was a dear fellow, and I am not at all sure that the incident I have just described does not reflect on me.

Beyond doubt I became something of a nuisance in the office, where I spread the views of Shaw and advocated the formation of a clerks' trade union. All young men with sensitive natures rebel against existing institutions. The youth of twenty who does not think the world can be improved is a cad; the man of forty who still thinks it can is a fool. Forbes, who had kept a sharp eye on me, got to hear of my subversive opinions and in the absence of Williams on holiday sacked me. But Williams, while reinstating me, advised me to resign as soon as I could get another job. Well, I have never been keen on jobs of any kind; but if there was one kind of employment the prospect of which did not make me sick, Tree alone could provide it. So I wrote him a letter begging to be allowed to walk-on or do anything else at His Majesty's Theatre. I had no particular urge to act, but the thought of being connected with Shakespeare and Tree thrilled me, and if my sole occupation were to be the splashing of water on the deck of the vessel in *The Tempest* I should feel contented. Besides, I fancied that life in the theatre would be pleasantly lazy and intelligently sociable. I got as far as the pillar-box with that letter, but I never posted it.

4

Pleasantly Lazy

Something much better than a job turned up: at the age of twenty-one I inherited money from Aunt Alice. She and Uncle Ted, both of them father's first cousins, had recently died, leaving their money to my brother, my sisters and myself. Jack came in for a pretty large sum from Uncle Ted, my sisters got most of Aunt Alice's money, and I, the least promising of the family, received £1,000. It was a happy day for me, and perhaps not unhappy for the firm, when I resigned, Williams giving me a free passage to Mexico in one of the Company's boats. I said, and possibly believed, that I would get a job there, but what I really wanted to do was to see the country that Prescott had described so vividly in *The Conquest of Mexico*. Also my friend Standage had already gone there, and I felt sure that he would help me to find work if I felt disposed to do any.

Before sailing I passed some weeks of glorious freedom. I took my mother to see her friends in the neighbourhood of Worcester, Stratford and Abberley, and went to several West-End theatres with my sisters. Two friends in the office managed to get holidays which they spent with me. Burt and I put in a fortnight at Paris, staying at the Regina Hotel in what was then the Place Jeanne d'Arc, and seeing *Samson and Delilah* at the opera (not yet allowed at Covent Garden), *King Lear* at the Odeon, *The Barber of Seville* somewhere else, and Sarah Bernhardt in a play with an Egyptian setting. I had already seen her as Phèdre at the Royalty Theatre, London, obtaining a certificate of illness from a friendly doctor who lived beneath us in Gayton Road, standing for six hours in the pit queue, and wondering what would happen if a member of the firm chanced to pass by and recognize me. She howled and cooed very effectively, and played the gamut with her voice, but I never felt for a moment that she forgot herself in the part. Burt and I were both addicted to Napoleon, which meant visits to Versailles, St Cloud, Fontainebleau, the Louvre, etc., and of course a pilgrimage to the Invalides. I dragged him unwillingly to see the house where Oscar Wilde had died and the Hôtel Voltaire where he had once lived. There were moments when my interest in Wilde clashed with our dual interest in Napoleon; but as his host I always gave way, especially as I had not yet quite outgrown the Napoleonic hallucination. A trifling incident remains in my memory. I was excessively fond of cream, and sitting outside the Café de la Paix I saw on the menu 'Pot de crême'. Thinking I would at last be able to have a large pot of cream all to myself, I was disgusted beyond words when something that looked like custard was placed before me. I am still searching for a restaurant sensible enough to serve as an undiluted course a pot of cream.

After that Kemp and I went for a few days to Edinburgh, where we put up at an old-fashioned hotel in Princes Street called McGregors. We drove about in a hansom cab, the driver of which gave us a remarkable amount of misinformation, including the statement that the statue of Charles II (Carolus Secundus) was that of an eminent Franco-Scottish monarch named 'Cairols Singles'. We took a car to drive along Tweedside and saw Abbotsford on the opposite bank; but I believe my main reason for choosing Edinburgh was to see Forbes-Robertson as Hamlet at the Lyceum, which we did on the night of our arrival, entering our box after the opening scene because the wheel of the hansom had come off on our way to the theatre.

I also cut short a holiday spent with my Aunt Adèle and her husband Archdeacon Bree at Allesley Rectory, near Coventry, the instant I discovered that Forbes-Robertson was playing Hamlet at Birmingham. The Archdeacon was a cousin, two or three times removed, as well as an uncle by marriage. He was close on ninety, twice the age of his wife, when I went to stay with them, but still walked seven miles every morning about his estate. No smoking was allowed in his house, and even my father, when there for the shooting, had to smoke his pipe out-of-doors or in the servants' hall at night after they had gone to bed. As in grandfather's house, punctuality was inexorable, and I am not surprised that father limited his visits to two or three days. The living of Allesley had been in the Bree family since the time of Charles II, and when Uncle William died childless at the age of ninety-seven the line of succession which had continued for 250 years was broken.

Having witnessed every play in Tree's annual Shakespeare festival, I went home to bid my parents farewell. As I was about to visit the New World, it seemed appropriate that I should receive a lesson in the brotherhood of man, and my father, of all people, gave it by practical demonstration. While we were waiting for a train on the platform of Bedford station, a porter struggled to get a large heavy basket onto his luggage-truck. Seeing his difficulty, my father quickly went to his assistance, stooped to clutch the bottom of the thing, and with a single mighty heave lifted it into place. I profited from the lesson. Through the carriage window he said 'God bless you!' and reminded me never to forget my prayers.

I had already stopped saying them with any regularity, but I nodded my head to comfort him.

It was a pleasant trip to Mexico on an old 3,000-ton cargo boat, which stopped at various Spanish ports, Vigo, the Canary Islands and Havana. I learnt enough Spanish during the voyage to find my way about Mexico, though not enough to read *Don Quixote* in the original. At Havana we reached the town by a street of one-storey buildings, the fronts consisting of large folding doors, through most of which we saw women of all colours and nationalities, some of them swinging in hammocks. An open door meant an invitation to enter. Not from prudery but disinclination, I maintained my virginity. At Vera Cruz I experienced great difficulty in getting my large gramophone through the customs house. The officials were under the impression that it was lethal. After some delay I paid enough to make me abandon such a costly travelling companion, and as far as I know it is still in Mexico City. The early part of the train journey from Vera Cruz to the capital was slow, the scenery superb. We climbed about 7,000 feet in a few hours, and I appreciated the obstacles that Cortes had encountered.

After an agreeable fortnight in Mexico City, with an exciting earthquake thrown in, I spent a few days with Standage, whose primitive surroundings, coupled with a murderous neighbour, did not encourage me to seek a job in his concern; and then stayed for a while at Orizaba, where I stupidly attempted to climb the volcanic mountain of that name, over 18,000 feet high; but about half-way up it I started to vomit blood. While recovering from this adventure I went for a walk and suffered one of the most unpleasant experiences of my life, caused by the fact that I am a victim of claustrophobia, hating small rooms, closed windows, and anything tending to suffocate, especially crowds. Nothing could induce me to go down a mine or in a submarine, and I even disliked underground railways.

Four or five days after my mountaineering expedition I set forth on foot to explore the district north of Orizaba and came to a thick bit of jungle country, which I tried to penetrate. The going was heavy until I had gone about a mile, when the undergrowth thinned and at last gave way to clearings and trees. As it was no longer necessary to keep my attention fixed on my progress, my mind began to wander, and for a long time I must have drifted heedlessly. I was conscious only of the pleasant shadows of the trees and of that weird humming and buzzing sound—the whirring, all-pervading insect life of the tropics which affects one's hearing like a chronic aural catarrh.

On and on I wandered, letting my feet take me where they would. And then, quite suddenly, I became fully conscious of my surroundings. I cannot describe the sensation except by saying that it was like waking up, as one sometimes does, in a condition of absolute awareness. I stood still and looked about me to get my bearings. I seemed to be in a dark tunnel of greenery. A pathway stretched behind and ahead of me, losing itself in a gloom of green. On either side of it was thick bush. The foliage met above my head, but looking down the tunnel I could see occasional shafts of light where the covering growth parted and let in the sun.

I began to retrace my steps. I walked and walked, but the tunnel seemed endless. Eventually I arrived at a spot where the path forked. Which should I take? I had utterly lost my sense of direction. I took the right prong and went forward at a pace that made me perspire. Again the pathway forked, and again I kept to the right. I had lost my watch a week or so before and had no idea of the time, but it seemed to be getting darker. Or was it only that the foliage was getting thicker? Yes, that was it, for I now became conscious of the dank, sickly reek of sunless vegetation.

I could feel my heart thumping with the exertion. Would this tunnel never end? It was like a maze. Perhaps I was going round in circles. At the thought I came to a standstill. Suppose I was just going round and round. Surely there must be some way out. How did I get into it? Where was the sun? I looked up at the green roof above me, but no ray came through it. Where I stood was twilight; but it was brighter farther on. I pressed on towards the light, but it seemed to recede. Always it was twilight where I stood and brighter farther on. I stopped again. And this time I strained my ears for the sound of anything human that might direct me. I listened and listened, but no sound penetrated the everlasting hum, the shrill song of the insect world.

With an appalling suddenness I was seized with a feeling of utter isolation. It came upon me while I was listening breathlessly for a human voice, for the bark of a dog, for the sound of anything that could break through the all-enveloping tic-tic-zz-zz of insect life that wrapped me about and drummed and buzzed in my ears. It was not merely a feeling of solitude, of which I am fond. It was as if I were cut off from all human relationship, from the life of my kin and my kind; as if I were surrounded by a blank wall of impenetrable darkness and invisible horror.

For a while I fought against this feeling with all my might. I started off again down the path, but I could not shake it off. I hurried, I ran, but it grew upon me. Again I stood still, telling myself aloud that the feeling was idiotic and meaningless and that if I wanted to escape from this maze I must use my intelligence, not give rein to my imagination. And while I stood there, fighting down my fear, I became aware of a sound, scarcely audible at first, unmistakable at last. It was the sound of something or someone moving in the bush to my right. I faced round and held my breath, staring into the thick growth a few feet from where I stood. The sound was intermittent. It ceased—continued—ceased again—went on again. Was it a man or an animal? A footstep—possibly—but a dragging uncertain footstep. A rustle of leaves, a snapping of branches, a dull thud as of someone or something falling—then silence—and for me suspense.

My heart was beating unevenly, now loudly, now imperceptibly; there was a kind of prickling about the top of my head; and I noticed that my throat was dry. I tried to call out something in Spanish, but no sound came. I held myself in and tried again. A hollow croak issued from my lungs, which frightened me as much as the silence it broke. Up to now I had been controlling my breath, either stifling it altogether or letting it go in sharp staccato bursts. Now I could control it no longer and I realized the terrible strain that had been put upon it by the hoarse, long-drawn, half-sobbing sighs with which it came and went.

How long I stood there choking and gasping I cannot say. The dread of the unknown was upon me and the limit of my endurance was almost reached. A crash in the undergrowth not twenty yards away shook me through and through and left me quivering. Sheer panic gripped me. I turned and ran, ran, ran, not knowing why, not knowing where, conscious only of some immense and elemental horror at my heels.

I was found the next morning by a *peon*, bruised, bloody, insensible, crumpled up at the foot of a tree that must have cut short my wild escape from my own imagination. . . .

Incidentally the half-caste fellow who found me, having obtained assistance, conveyed me to the French hotel at Orizaba where I was staying, and did not steal a cent of my money. He even appeared surprised when I recompensed him. Yet a few drinks of *pulque* might have made him quarrel with and murder a friend. There were several slaughterous cases of the kind while I was in Orizaba.

I wrote an account of this experience, which appeared in *The English Review* some twenty years later; and when Hugh Kingsmill commented on it I felt as surprised as an actor in whose playing of a part a critic discovers strange meanings of which the performer is wholly unconscious. This was how Kingsmill saw the episode:

'This adventure is one of those rare occurrences which, without any wresting of what actually happened, form a perfect reflection in the physical world of a spiritual experience, in this instance the sudden uprush of the terror inspired in the soul by its imprisonment in matter. The episode can be enjoyed for its own sake, as a very fine example of direct unadorned narrative. But its chief fascination for me is in its allegorical significance—young Mr Love-Life straying from the path into a pleasant wood, having lost the watch given him at the outset of his journey that he might regulate his time aright, not squandering precious moments in idle divagations from the way. Even in *The Pilgrim's Progress* I do not know any moment more dramatic than when the narrator suddenly, in a tunnel of dark greenery, recovers his awareness of his surroundings, or any trace of spiritual despair and isolation more poignant than—"Where was the sun? I looked up at the green roof above me, but no ray came through. Where I stood was twilight; it was brighter farther on. I pressed on towards the light, but it seemed to recede. Always it was twilight where I stood and brighter farther on." '

Returning to Mexico City, I obtained an interview with the President, Porfirio Diaz, at Chapultepec.

Three years later he fled for his life; but he had given, relatively speaking, peace, order and prosperity to his country for a generation, a record unparalleled in the history of the South American republics.

One of my fellow-passengers on the cargo boat knew a lot of people in Mexico and had given me a letter of introduction to a man who owned an estancia some ten miles from the capital and who had literary leanings. I sent my letter of introduction and received an invitation to stay with his family. A delightful visit was marred by the attentions I paid to his very pretty daughter, because a young Spanish neighbour was extremely jealous, and when he caught us embracing he threatened to shoot me. It soon became evident that he intended to do so, and after we had enjoyed each other's company for one more day she begged me to leave before he turned up for dinner. In the hope that she would be able to meet me in the City, I left. But she wrote that she dared not take the risk, and I never saw her again. My senses had been so much excited that the only thing I remember doing in Mexico City after receiving her letter was to walk into a brothel, where I was shown into a room in which a naked girl was washing herself. I turned round immediately and walked out. There were limits to the means of gratifying my senses.

The sight of the jealous lover lurking in the street where I lodged expedited my departure; and as my brother Harry had told some Canadian friends that I might be visiting them, I took a boat from Vera Cruz to New York, where I arrived in a heatwave. After a bit of sight-seeing, and toying with the notion of applying to E. H. Sothern for a job in his Shakespearean company, I proceeded by train to Montreal, where I stayed at the Windsor Hotel, had a look round, and was relieved of some cash by the hard-up story of a stranded Englishman. Thence to Toronto, putting up at King

Edward's Hotel, and spending a yachting week-end on the Lake with Harry's friends. A visit to Niagara Falls made me homesick, and I went on to Quebec for a few days at the Château Frontenac, where I read Gilbert Parker's *The Seats of the Mighty* and succumbed to another hard-up story from a man who lived at Levis on the opposite shore and had invented something that would make a fortune if he could exploit it in England. Like an idiot I parted with a portion of my rapidly diminishing capital, and soon lost sight of him. I have a dim idea that his invention had something to do with harness for horses; but as I can never take the smallest interest in any sort of invention, my enquiries into his were perfunctory.

My interests were always of a literary kind. Strange how much of one's nature never changes. All of us are partly mad: that is, we have our little personal fads that remain with us through life, the more sensible among us being conscious of our peculiarities, secretly rather ashamed of them, and knowing quite well that they illustrate a streak of craziness which has got to find some sort of expression, whether mischievous or innocuous. My own form of abberation is quite harmless, and known to no one up to now except my wife. It started with me at the age of fifteen, when I pestered my mother to give me a blackboard and a large number of differently coloured chalks. On that blackboard I wrote a list of my most valued belongings, heading it in capital letters BEST THINGS. It happened that one of Jack's friends came into our schoolroom, read those words, and started to call me 'Bes-tings' whenever we met, which riled me so much that one day I threw a book at his head and caught him clean on the nose, which bled. It was a matter of pride with him to say 'Bes-tings' when next we met, but he spoke half-heartedly and soon gave it up. I wish I could remember what those best things were, though I am fairly certain that they included a copy of Milton's poems, from which I would quote at length when I preached to my sisters, a Life of Napoleon by (if I am not mistaken) a hero-worshipper named Morris, and some pictures of Edward VII for which I had got my mother to make a velvet case (still in my possession) with the letter N surmounted by a crown embroidered on the front, the point being, I suppose, that even the King was subservient to Napoleon.

Throughout my life I have had this mania of hoarding a few select books, my bibles, which are the only possessions I cherish, just as other men treasure their pictures or coins or ancient silver or period furniture or stamp collections, or their old bats, guns, clubs and rackets. While I was travelling in Mexico and Canada my 'best things' went with me in a handbag which I can still visualize, and consisted of Shakespeare's tragedies in a limited and rather luxurious edition, Shaw's *Plays for Puritans*, Boswell's *Life of Johnson, Intentions* and *The Soul of Man* by Oscar Wilde, *A Tale of Two Cities* by Dickens and *Vanity Fair* by Thackeray. Since then the bibles have undergone permutations and have now reached a final selection, the titles of which I propose to keep to myself.

From Quebec I took a boat to Liverpool, and I shall never forget the joy of being in London again. I might have been away fifty years instead of five months. It even charmed me that there was a fog, and I swallowed great draughts of it as I strolled down the Strand. Taking a room at the Grand Hotel, Trafalgar Square, I suddenly discovered that less than £100 was left of the £1,000 I had started off with, and another letter to Tree might have been written if brother Jack had not come to the rescue. With some of his money he had bought a motor business in Hove and was about to open

a showroom in King's Road, Brighton. He thought it
would not be a bad idea if I were to manage the showroom. I found myself in complete agreement with him,
though I knew nothing whatever of motor-cars or their
accessories, and in September 1908 I went to Brighton,
where at first I stayed with Jack in Clarendon Man-
sions. After his marriage in the spring of 1909 I lived
in various digs and for a while occupied a house in
Hove.

My two years at Brighton were among the happiest
of my life. I loved the country all round, which was
then (1908-10) practically unspoilt. One could walk
along the cliffs to Newhaven without a building beyond
Roedean School to mar the views, the pretty little village
of Rottingdean being completely hidden in its valley
until one came upon it. Going west, one found amid
leafy lanes the small townships of Worthing, Littlehampton and Bognor; while inland the lovely weald
was dotted with tiny picturesque villages. I walked,
bicycled and motored all over the countryside, in those
days motor-cars being rarities on roads that would now
be called tracks.

My friend Burt, still going to the City every day, lived
with his two sisters in Clifton Road, not far from the
old parish church at the top of the hill, and I frequently
visited them at week-ends. He and I talked endlessly
of everything under the sun, and often when I left their
house at night he would accompany me half-way to
wherever I lived, and then I would see him home again,
and then he would retrace his steps with me, and so on
until we had temporarily talked ourselves out. He was
becoming very religious, that is churchy, and I was
moving in the opposite direction. He asked me to go to
St Bartholomew's one Sunday evening to hear Father
Cox, the vicar, hold forth. It was to me an unpleasant
occasion because the sermon was about hell, and the

preacher tied himself into knots in his efforts to reproduce the physical torments of the wretched victims cast
into it. Cox came to supper with the Burts after the
service, and I felt that I was there under false pretences,
as I had not believed a word of his horrible discourse.
Eventually Burt followed Cox into the Roman Church,
and I heard with dismay that he had destroyed all the
works of his favourite author, Maeterlinck, because they
had been placed on the Catholic *index expurgatorius*.
But in the Brighton days he had not crossed the border-
line.

Indeed, if one of us might have been certified as mad,
it was I. Soon after my managerial appointment I
decided to take the Burt family for a motor trip. Never
having handled a car before, I asked a driver to show
me what to do and was initiated into the mysteries of
clutch, footbrake, handbrake, starting-handle, throttle,
and so forth, the lesson lasting about ten minutes. I then
set off in our 14 h.p. Star car and called for the Burts
without misadventure. They got in, and the journey
started with a terrific jolt which they no doubt thought
an inevitable part of the mechanical process. How I
got down the hill, through North Street and along
Marine Parade, I do not know, but a benign fate
guarded me, as it does drunken men, and by the time
we reached Beachy Head I felt myself an expert driver.
The return inland through Eastbourne must have been
tricky in spots, but my mood was one of self-gratu-
lation and I remained serene. Approaching Preston,
however, fate side-slipped and the car skidded across
the road into a ditch. I said something about cars being
as vulnerable to banana-skins as human beings and
helped everyone out. With herculean efforts Burt and I
pushed, pulled and lifted the thing back on the road,
and to my surprise the engine responded to the starting-
handle as if nothing had happened. When I deposited

the family safely at their home, I broke the news that
I had never before been at the wheel. Their exclama-
tions embraced admonition and admiration, the former
predominating. This ditching episode should have
taught me a lesson, but at the age of twenty-one the
memory of such warnings is brief, and with even less
preliminary instruction I mounted a motor-bicycle,
dashed off, mistook the throttle for the brake, collided
with a wall, and stayed in bed well bandaged for a
couple of weeks

When I felt fit again I asked Burt to spend a few days
with me in Brussels. He gladly agreed and we put up at
a hotel in the Boulevard Anspach. I cannot recall its
name, but I vividly remember my meeting with a girl
who was staying there with relations. She was of
medium height, not pretty but attractive, with hair that
sometimes looked brown, sometimes bronze, lively hazel
eyes and quizzical expression. I was alone in the sitting-
room one evening reading a paper when she came in,
gave me a challenging look, and asked for the news.
I could still speak French fairly well, and we were soon
talking thirteen to the dozen. Suddenly she enquired if
I ever went to Paris. I replied that if she lived there I
would make a point of going. Without a word she produced a card, wrote down her name and address, and
told me to let her know when next I went. The rest of
our stay in Brussels made Burt rather irritable, because
I disappeared for no apparent reason at odd moments,
if I saw a remote chance of a few words with Julie. I
felt so excited that I wanted to go straight to Paris, and
would have done so if she had not said that her holiday
would last another three weeks.

Burt was still in the grip of my early enthusiasm for
Napoleon, with which I had infected him, and we spent
a day going over the field of Waterloo. Owing to my
amorous condition an impish mood overtook me; and

while he was looking reverently at the spot where Napoleon had stationed himself for the greater part of the battle, I quoted Oscar Wilde: 'As long as war is regarded as wicked, it will always have its fascination. When it is looked upon as vulgar, it will cease to be popular.' Burt thought me inharmonious, and when that same evening I said that I wanted to buy a book I had seen in a shop near St Gudule Cathedral, and we had to run up a hill to get there before closing-time, he was excessively vexed to find that I had bought a Tauchnitz edition of Wilde's fairy tales, *The Happy Prince.* His temper was not improved the next day, which we spent at Antwerp. As our boat left the quay for England and sailed down the river Scheldt, we had our last view of the cathedral spire, which, said Burt, had been compared by Napoleon to Mechlin lace. I murmured that it reminded me of *The Happy Prince.* Silence descended upon us until we disembarked.

A month later I was off to Paris, preceded by a letter. I still had a little money left from my legacy, and brother Jack raised no objection to the trip on hearing of its laudable motive. He was easy-going, kind-hearted, extremely generous by nature, equable in temperament, such good company that his mere presence kept everyone in high spirits; and my unbroken fondness for him dated from those days.

A fortnight in Paris at the age of twenty-one in the company of a vivacious girl, much of it spent in learning how to make love, is 'paradise enough'. She told me that no Englishman understood the sexual side of love unless taught by a Frenchwoman, and I think she was right. Vague memories of dining somewhere in the Bois, a noisy evening on Montmartre in the company of French youths and girls who may or may not have been artists, a comedy or a tragedy at some theatre, a motor trip to St Germain or St Something: no doubt it was all very pleasant, but what made it rapturous was Julie's company. We parted with protestations of undying devotion and an oath on my part that I would be back in Paris as soon as I could beg, borrow, steal, or even earn some money. And so I would have been if, a few weeks later, I had not been captivated by another girl.

At that time there was a theatre called the Grand in a turning off the road running up to Brighton station. It had once been known as the Eden, and in my time was the home of melodrama, commonly known as 'the blood-tub'. Every week we used to go to plays like *Women and Wine, The Worst Woman in London, The Ugliest Woman on Earth, The Sign of the Cross, The Silver King*, and enjoy ourselves hugely, but not in the way the authors of those works had intended we should. Sometimes our laughter jarred on the other playgoers, who loudly demanded our withdrawal, but as a rule we managed to keep our mirth within bounds with the aid of our pocket-handkerchiefs. The heroes were applauded, the villains were hissed, and the characters were often warned by the audience of the pitfalls prepared for them.

Every Christmas the Grand put on a pantomime, and Robinson Crusoe was the theme of the one produced on Boxing Day, 1908. I went with a business acquaintance to a performance in the first week of 1909, and saw a chorus-girl who made my heart miss a few beats. She was a brunette with large dark eyes, a Grecian profile, and a perfectly proportioned figure. I learnt her name from an attendant, and in the interval sent her a note with the largest box of chocolates I could buy in the theatre. The note said that I would be at the stage-door after the show. That began an affair that lasted for two years. For all I know she may still be alive, so I had better change her name to Bella. She lived in

Brighton with her family and had a sister almost as pretty as herself. I cannot honestly say that she had much intelligence, and as far as I could make out the only book she had ever read was *Alice in Wonderland*, but her sense of fun made her good company and her sudden rages made her look extraordinarily beautiful, so that I sometimes provoked them for the pleasure of beholding a tempestuous Venus and the satisfaction of mollifying her.

In due course I heard from Julie, broke the news to her, and heard no more. Bella and I explored the country all round Brighton, mostly by car, and lived in the moment without a care for the future. I managed to hire one of those arches under the King's Road, level with the beach, and many of our evenings were passed in it, though we made a weekly visit to the music-hall shows at the Hippodrome or the Alhambra. Of course I thought myself in love with her, but later experience has taught me that my feeling was ninety per cent lust. I doubt if one can tell the difference before the age of forty. But however my emotions were apportioned, Bella made Brighton glow for me in the radiance of youth, giving it a permanent place in my affections, and to this day it remains my favourite town after London.

Naturally there were ups and downs in our relationship. She sometimes got a job as 'an extra' at the Theatre Royal, and once I saw her walking in St James's Street with an actor in that week's play. For the first time I knew the meaning of jealousy, wrote her a stinging letter, and left it at her home. She arrived after the night's performance at a house I shared with two other fellows between Hove and Portslade. She was in a flaming temper, and looked so magnificent that I begged her to stay like that. She promptly went berserk, and I had an uncomfortable quarter-of-an-hour, as she got in several telling swipes before I was ready for them. But soon we were on excellent terms, and she made amends for the onslaught.

I left Brighton in September, 1910, and she sometimes came up to see me in a Westminster flat I occupied with a friend. But by that time our association was cooling; and when, early in 1911, I heard that she was going to marry, I experienced a curiously irrational sensation, something between irritation and relief. I saw her once again, during the nineteen-twenties, in the tube lift at Leicester Square station. She was smartly dressed, very erect in figure, thinner than she had been, and with a determined expression on her face. I did not recognize her for a few moments, and she gave no sign of recognizing me. The past came back with such intensity that I went home and wrote a short story about our association. But it was overcharged with sentiment, and I did not try to get it published. I was in love again and had begun to realize the profound truth of Oscar Wilde's remark: 'Each time one loves is the only time that one has ever loved. Difference of object does not alter singleness of passion. It merely intensifies it.'

Whether with or without Bella, I enjoyed every day of my two years at Brighton. I often went to see plays in London by train, and several times by car, though the latter mode of transit in those days might mean a night on the road with tyre punctures or defective carburettors or a seized engine. My ignorance of elementary mechanics may be judged by an episode. A very pleasant fellow named Rawlinson was put in charge of the showroom when I became manager of the business at the garage headquarters in Hove, and one day he and I set out for Margate. All went well until we reached Canterbury, when the car appeared to be, in his words, 'conking out'. We left it at a garage and had lunch, after which he went to see what had happened. Returning, he said 'The big end has gone.' 'Who's taken it?' I asked. Recovering from a fit of laughter, he explained with care the function of big ends. Rawlinson and I used to play billiards when business was quiet, as it usually was, at a place called the Seahouse Hotel, where an admirable marker with a withered arm taught me all I ever knew. I inherited my father's excellent eye, steady hand and sensitive fingers, for I showed signs of becoming a good player, but I dropped the game on leaving Brighton.

The three West-End plays of 1908-10 that remain most clearly in my memory were Tree's production of *The School for Scandal*, George Alexander's famous revival of *The Importance of Being Earnest*, and Lewis Waller's *Henry V*, each of which I saw at least half-a-dozen times. Waller's was the most perfect performance of a Shakespearean hero I have ever seen except Forbes-Robertson's Hamlet. Shakespeare still filled my mind, and I sometimes persuaded the Burt family to join me in reading his plays aloud. I shocked a clergyman, the Reverend Felix Asher, vicar of Holy Trinity, by saying that the plays of Shakespeare meant far more to me than the Bible. 'Do you realize that you are putting Shakespeare above God?' he asked. 'If God wrote the Bible, yes,' I replied. 'That is rank blasphemy!' he exclaimed. 'From your point of view,' I agreed. In spite of which he continued to see me.

Asher was a master at Lancing School as well as a Brighton vicar, and I enjoyed the talks we had together. The religious belief in which I had been brought up was rapidly giving way to scepticism, though I still experienced discomfort about the future of the soul and the apparent meaninglessness of mortality. One afternoon I had a revelation. Wandering along on the top of the Downs behind Brighton I was attracted by the appearance of the little village of Poynings at the foot of the Devil's Dyke and descended to explore it. Having seen

the church I strolled through the graveyard reading
the inscriptions on the tombstones. Depressed as usual
by such lapidary texts as 'Thy Will be Done', my
melancholy deepened at the thought of doleful church
tunes like that used for 'On the Resurrection Morning',
and I was about to leave God's Acre in a mood of pessi-
mistic repugnance when, turning a corner of the church,
I saw a tombstone with a poem on it. It marked the
grave of a man who, I heard on enquiry, had been
struck by lightning on the Downs, and the poem was
part of the dirge in Shakespeare's *Cymbeline*, all of
which I knew by heart:

> Fear no more the heat o' the sun,
> Nor the furious winter's rages;
> Thou thy worldly task hast done,
> Home art gone, and ta'en thy wages;
> Golden lads and girls all must
> As chimney-sweepers, come to dust.
>
> Fear no more the frown o' the great,
> Thou art past the tyrant's stroke;
> Care no more to clothe and eat,
> To thee the reed is as the oak :
> The sceptre, learning, physic, must
> All follow this, and come to dust.
>
> Fear no more the lightning-flash,
> Nor the all-dreaded thunder-stone;
> Fear not slander, censure rash,
> Thou hast finished joy and moan :
> All lovers young, all lovers must
> Consign to thee, and come to dust.

In a moment my apprehensions seemed to vanish.
What I had previously regarded as merely a perfect
lyric now appeared as a spiritual illumination, and I
clearly perceived, what I must always have felt
obscurely in my bones, that one's life could be a blessing

or a curse without the least reference to what might or might not happen beyond the grave; that it was all-sufficient, an end in itself; that it would close either in the peace of cessation or in the peace beyond human understanding; and that it did not matter which, since both meant the annihilation of the human mind with its cares, the human body with its tribulations. A mood of extraordinary serenity followed my phase of difficulty and doubt, and I have never since worried about the mystery of the universe, the ultimate truth, the nature of God, or any other insoluble problem.

A very different sort of adventure occurred during my Brighton days, a pure bit of bravado resulting from a bet. In the bar of the Royal York Hotel I happened to run across a few fellows who had just taken part in the London-to-Brighton walk. They were remarkably pleased with themselves, and in order to deflate them I said that anybody could do the walk with a bit of practice. My bluff was instantly called, one of them betting me £5 that I could not do it at a stretch in twelve hours. I took the bet on condition that I would be allowed two hours for refreshment on the road. He agreed and said that he would accompany me, starting from the Old Steine at midnight. I was a good walker, but I had never done more than thirty miles in a day and did not realize that there is a big difference between thirty miles mostly on grass and fifty-two entirely by road. I did not even bother to change my light shoes for heavy boots, and was idiotic enough to wolf two pounds of strawberries and a pint of cream shortly before starting. There is no need to enumerate my many agonies, which began with a terrifying stitch before we got to Crawley, where we knocked up someone at the George Inn and had a breakfast of eggs and bacon soon after 5 a.m. By the time we reached Reigate the soles of my feet felt raw all over, and I could scarcely rise from my chair after a nasty lunch at Sutton. The last part of the journey would have been sheer torture if I had not been so exhausted that my movements were automatic and the pain in my feet was almost numbed. We reached Charing Cross just before two o'clock, and I received £5, with which I took my companion to the Adelphi Theatre, where we saw Martin Harvey in some Spanish play. By that time I felt that the only alternative to entering a hospital was to keep moving, and after the matinée I suggested a stroll on Hampstead Heath. He favoured it, and we walked from Jack Straw's Castle to the Flask at Highgate. Except for the effort of getting up after sitting down, I was beyond pain, my feet being quite torpid. Having absorbed a few sandwiches and washed them down with plenty of beer, we were able to face another play, and saw Lewis Waller in Conan Doyle's *The Fires of Fate* at the Lyric. I left London by the midnight train for Brighton, and passed the next two or three weeks supinely, with enough blisters on my feet to arouse the doctor's admiration.

One more experience of my Brighton period is worth recording. I met an eminent man of letters and kept pretty full notes of the occurrence. The first play in which I had seen Tree perform was *Nero* by Stephen Phillips, a poet who is now as absurdly underrated as in the first decade of the twentieth century he was grotesquely overpraised. He held the same sort of position in public estimation as, say, Eliot and Fry held some forty years later, but his success as a dramatist was far greater than theirs. When George Alexander produced Phillips's *Paolo and Francesca* in 1899 the literary and dramatic critics compared him with Sophocles, Dante, Racine and Tennyson, while his poems were ranked with those of Milton, Rossetti and Swinburne. What had actually happened was clear enough. Ever since Shakespeare the poets had been trying to write blank-verse plays.

Keats, Shelley, Byron, Wordsworth, Coleridge, Swinburne, Browning, Tennyson: all of them had done their
best, but owing to their lack of stage-sense they had
failed. Shakespeare as an actor knew his job, and
Phillips, also an actor, had mastered stagecraft. The
joy of seeing well-constructed poetic plays with thrilling
incidents and effective 'curtains' made the critics think
that here at last was a worthy successor to Shakespeare,
and as the verse was on a par with Marlowe's they felt
justified of their dithyrambs. Tree's production of *Herod*
repeated the success of *Paolo*, and *Nero*, helped by an
amazing stage-picture of the burning of Rome, crowned
the author's reputation, making even more money than
the others. But Phillips could not withstand success. It
went to his head and drove him to drink, which increased his innate morbidity and melancholia. The
quality of his work deteriorated, and his version of
Faust was only saved from failure by Tree's scenery,
music and effects. When I first set eyes on the author, a
year after that production, his success had vanished,
his reputation was in process of eclipse, and the man
himself was sinking under the influence of drink and
depression.

I did not know him by sight, but when I heard a
stoutish thickset man addressed as Phillips in an East
Street café, and when in the ensuing conversation it
became clear that he was a poet, I turned my chair
and had a good look at him. He was largely-built, with
a square jaw, light eyes, and a set satirical expression.
His companions were ragging him, but he gave tit-for-
tat and his opinions were so forceful, his enunciation
was so clear, that soon he had the attention of all the
diners. When asked by the manager to tone down his
voice or his opinions he became excessively rude and
remarked among other things that the wine was un-
drinkable. I next ran across him in the pub, within a

few yards of King's Road, where I used to play billiards. He sat in the corner of the bar with a large
glass of whisky by his side. His hat was drawn over his
eyes, and he glowered in a semi-fuddled condition at
the other occupants. Being then a rather nervous, hesi-
tant youth, it took me a little time to summon the
courage to address him, and if I had known what was
to follow I would never have risked it.

'May I introduce myself, sir?' I asked.

'No, you mayn't,' he snarled back.

I turned away after that, and was just leaving the
pub when he shouted after me:

'Who the devil are you, anyway?'

I returned and told him my name.

'Don't know you,' said he, adding after a pause,
'Don't want to either!'

'You are very polite.'

'Go to hell!'

We seemed to be hitting it off pretty well, so I continued the conversation:

'I know *you*, though. You are the author of some of
the finest verse of the time, and I want to tell you how
much I admire your work.'

'Rubbish!' he answered: 'that's what they all say,
but they don't encourage me to go on with it. A poet
in England is a fool. He is also an anachronism. England doesn't want poets. She wants Kiplings. In fact
she doesn't know what she wants—and I hope she
suffers for her blasted absent-mindedness!'

'If you'll excuse me for saying it—' I began.

'I won't excuse you for anything, damn you!'

'Then,' said I, adopting his lingo, 'I think you should
consider yourself damned lucky! There are a dozen
poets of equal genius to yourself practically starving, or
doing hackwork to keep themselves out of the gutter;
while you have had success after success, greater success

than any dramatic poet has had since Shakespeare. I really don't know what you've got to grumble about.'

'When I allowed you to introduce yourself to me—' he started. 'You didn't.'

'Be silent! When, I repeat, I allowed you to address me without giving myself the pleasure of kicking your backside, I imagined—God forgive me!—that you might have something to say that hasn't already been said by every Grub Street growler in the kingdom. You are talking poisonous rot, man! But I will smother my present inclination to throw a glass of execrable whisky over you because I want you to name the dozen poets of equal genius to myself (as you so abominably phrase it) and also because you do not appear to be yet out of your 'teens.'

'I mentioned a dozen at random,' I replied; 'but you have doubtless heard of Davidson, Watson, Noyes, Newbolt and Bridges—to say nothing of those three obscure little scribblers, Hardy, Meredith and Swinburne.'

'Don't try to be funny!' he sneered. 'Humour is not a virtue of the cradle. You'd better be toddling home, or your nurse will be getting nervous. Wait a moment, though! Now you *are* here, you can make yourself useful. Get me another whisky.'

'Delighted,' I said: 'I had no idea poets could be such charming companions.' I went to the bar, got his drink and took it back to his table. He seemed to be half-asleep and I had to poke him in the ribs before he was aware of my return.

'You still here!' he cried. 'Whatever will Mammy say?'

'Drink that, you fat-gutted old beast,' I angrily rejoined, 'and then say your prayers.' I did not wait for his comments.

I had no intention of speaking to him again, but fate

intended otherwise. Whenever we met at the pub I frequented he addressed me with a mixture of politeness and rudeness. Two or three of his remarks have lingered in my memory:

'Hullo! Still studying the poets? Why not try to climb Parnassus yourself? If you look in your atlas, you'll find Parnassus in the heart of Germany. The railway porters of that country read Shakespeare. Have a drink!'

'The only truly generous people in the world are drunkards.'

'The romantic attitude towards life leads to the Thames or to Hanwell.[1] Christ was crucified because Jerusalem had neither. I prefer a public house to both.'

'A love of stomach is the beginning of wisdom.'

One day I asked him for the meaning of a line in *Paolo*: 'O! and that bluer blue—that greener green!'

'I haven't the least idea,' he said. 'I am a poet, not a statistician.'

At last I understood what had happened to the man. It was a rainy boisterous day at the end of the year, and I caught sight of him turning into a side-street off the Brighton front, his loose cape, with mackintosh underneath, ballooning from the massive shoulders as he struggled round the corner. Having nothing better to do at that moment I followed him into his den. He was reasonably polite, if a trifle morose. We drank each other's health and sat by the fire. We were alone except for a mouldy-looking old bloke muttering to himself in a corner. I started the ball rolling:

'Why did you suddenly break away from lyrical poetry and begin writing rhetorical verse?'

'Why did Shakespeare?' he parried.

'He didn't—not in the sense I mean. There is even a strong lyrical current beneath the stilted style of his

[1] Hanwell: a well-known lunatic asylum in this period.

last plays. He remained a poet to the end—even in prose.'

'And is there no poetry in my *Nero*, my *Sin of David*?'

'Yes, of a high-falutin, pretentious kind. But it's the work of a poet who's running away from poetry, not of a poet whose poetry is running away with him.'

'Ah, but I had to take time by the forelock, and a poet should never woo the success I sought.' He was silent for a few moments before continuing: 'Every man has a turning-point in his career. It's merely a question of whether he keeps to the path he set out on or sidetracks his ideals. My turning-point came immediately I had written the last line in *Paolo*. Every rhythm in that play I felt, every touch of true poetry in it was a part of myself. I, too, loved as Paolo loved. This was my very *cri de cœur*—' and he recited the lines commencing:

O God, Thou seest us Thy creatures bound
Together by that law which holds the stars. . . .

He recited musically, in a high-pitched monotone, with a keener feeling for sound than sense. Having finished it, he spoke in a weightier manner than was usual with him:

'But I couldn't keep to that level in poetry or in life. I wasn't strong enough. Things happened. Stupid, vexing things. And I was ambitious. I wanted renown. . . . I love life too well—the good comfortable things of life. I sacrificed my poetry for pounds and pence. Though (who knows?) perhaps I had no more of the real stuff in me. A poet must live his poems; and when he ceases to live them, he ceases to write them. . . . I lost the poetry of life shortly after *Paolo* was written, and a hunger for the easy pleasant things came in its place. Since then I have written my dramas for money

—only money. And why not? It's the next best thing to love.'

That, I felt, was the truth. He was greedy for life's primitive sensations and his desires were too violent to be controlled. This explained his sudden falling-off in poetry. The desire for the high-sounding phrase had ousted his purely lyrical gift. He wallowed in majestic verse just as he wallowed in strong drink.

The last time I saw him was in 1910, when I found myself by his side at the counter of the Brighton post office. We were both buying stamps and while he was fixing one on an envelope he remarked: 'Disgusting business this stamp-licking! Why can't we run the postal service without filling our mouths with gum?'

Phillips died in 1915 at the age of forty-nine.

It may appear from what has been written above that I spent more time enjoying myself than working while at Brighton. If so, the appearance is not deceptive. Occasionally I signed orders, probably for the issue of petrol or the commission of jobs in the workshop or the hire of cars, but the drivers drove, the fitters fitted, the turners turned, and the retreaders retrod, without much oversight on my part. The proprietor of the business, brother Jack, occasionally put in an appearance and asked how things were going, to which I answered that, though not stationary, they were not exactly speeding, and I may have hinted that they were going in the wrong direction. Most of Jack's time was spent on the racecourse or the golf-links, but he could nearly always raise enough money for the firm's weekly salaries.

As business showed no sign of increasing, our creditors became more pressing, and one day a furious man rang up to demand instant payment of a long-overdue account. My clerk, a jovial fellow, asked for his name, 'Walker,' said the man. 'So's mine,' said the clerk and rang off, whereat I bellowed with laughter. Trade conducted in this fashion was not likely to flourish, and after a year of my management it showed a marked tendency to decline. One of our most accommodating customers had, in the expressive idiom of an ex-naval employee, 'bin an' gone and coiled 'is rope', meaning he had died, and most of the others were peevish when we requested payment of their accounts as soon as their debts were contracted.

At a crucial moment I dashed off to Haslemere, obtained £300 from Aunt Eva, an amazing person whose chief object in life was to give away her money, and temporarily saved the situation. But at last Jack could no longer afford to finance a rapidly decaying business, and he was compelled to liquidate. Following a somewhat uneasy session with the company's debtors, we drank to our demise at the Royal York Hotel.

5

Actor and Secretary

Being almost penniless I was compelled to stay for
several weeks at Bedford. My favour with my father
had, in Shakespeare's phrase, begun to warp, and we
were steadily getting on each other's nerves. He came
out with the pronouncement that 'One can't spend one's
life reading Shakespeare'. I replied that one could,
adding that it was impossible for any Englishman to
pass a day without quoting him. He bridled at that and
said that he, for one, never quoted Shakespeare. I
offered to bet that he would quote or more likely mis-
quote some passage in the plays before the day was
out. He declined to bet, contenting himself with the
remark that I was talking nonsense. Not long after this
he spoke of 'the piping times of peace', on which I
made no comment, but at dinner that night he referred
to someone who was 'more sinned against than sinning'.
I then caught him up on both quotations, and he did
not take it well, exclaiming 'Rubbish!' which sounded
rather thin in the circumstances. A few days later the
subject came up again, and when I declared that
Shakespeare's influence on the common speech had
been far greater than the Bible's, he demanded proof.
I produced Bartlett's *Familiar Quotations* and confounded him by the evidence of 20 pages given to
Hamlet alone, against 12 pages for the whole of the
New Testament, while the works of Shakespeare occu-

pied 122 pages, the entire Bible 38 pages. This did nothing to ease our relationship.

F. R. Benson brought his Shakespeare company to Bedford during my stay, and I determined to try my luck with him. I wrote for an appointment, got it, and after witnessing his production of *Much Ado About Nothing* went round to see him. He was standing on the stage with his back to the curtain discussing something with his stage-manager; but the moment he saw me he came over, shook hands, and courteously asked me to call at the theatre next morning, when I had the devastating experience of reciting Henry V's speech 'Once more unto the breach' in a diminutive chamber just off the entrance-hall of the theatre. He stood a yard away, looking out of the window so as not to confuse me as I shouted the lines in a room where I ought to have chosen 'To be or not to be' and whispered it. He was very nice and said I could join his company if able to keep myself while learning to act, and later he hoped to give me a salary. I need scarcely add that my father displayed no animation and refused to finance me for a year's training. He had a Victorian view of the stage as a sort of licensed brothel, though he never expressed this in words, and he was frankly bored by Shakespeare, much preferring the works of C. N. & A. M. Williamson, diversified by those of Somerville and Ross.

Father would have made an admirable bishop, and if he had entered the Church he would no doubt have achieved that state. He could impose his personality on any conceivable group of people; he had a lot of common-sense, and was an efficient chairman of committee. Above all he was unstumpable; no one ever caught him out; he had an immediate answer for anything. He was a sort of Dr Johnson without genius; that is, he was fully armed for defence, but without the imagination for attack. I recall a few instances at this period of his ability to meet a situation without fore-thought. Someone had been staying with us, and when she left father seemed pleased. 'But I thought you were so fond of her?' said mother. 'However fond one is of people, one is usually glad to see their backs,' he replied. A friend of Jack's came to stay for the week-end without being warned that father had no taste for club-room stories. The women having retired after dinner, the poor fellow embarked on a fairly juicy narrative, pausing for a moment to ask Jack what was the matter when he received a kick under the table. At the con-clusion of the story, usually received with a shout of laughter, there was a pregnant silence. 'Quite so', said father rising. 'Well, I think we'd better join the ladies.' Jack's friend left early next morning.

A relative who asked father an improper question was rebuked: 'I don't think you can be aware of what you are saying.' And he always objected to swearing. I once managed to change 'bloody' into 'bother' as I saw him entering the room. My sister Elsie tells me that at the age of thirty she drove him to church, bumped the curb with her car, and let out a 'damn!' After a pause, father said: 'I'm afraid, Wowsie, from the way you spoke, that was not the first time you have used the word.' A shattering incident once occurred when the workmen were in the house and mother heard them using a word, excessively common in their class but quite unmentionable in polite society. She dropped the bomb at lunch, while her grown-up children gasped and held their breath: 'What is the meaning of the word f——, Henry?' Without batting an eyelid father dismissed the question: 'A vulgarism, my dear, in fre-quent use among the lower orders.' There was, by the way, little of what passes for snobbery in him, because a snob is always aware of someone above him in the social scale, while father could never have imagined anyone superior to himself in any sense. In describing how he had several times been mistaken for King Edward VII, he managed to imply that the resemblance reflected credit on the Royal Family.

On the whole he was a serious person, and the one thing he took more seriously than anything else was sport. He was a bad loser and became irritable if the game were going against him; while I was a good loser, not caring whether I won or lost at any game, however hard I tried to win. I was rather fond of croquet, and though too impatient to study the strategy of the game my roquets were pretty deadly. Consequently, on the rare occasions I played against him, our matches were never finished. He would carefully arrange for his next innings, place my striking ball at the far end of the court, and satisfy himself that all was well for his next break. But I had an unerring eye, and to his annoyance I almost invariably knocked one of his balls out of position, wrecking his nicely-prepared plans. Having done that, I was usually incapable of negotiating more than two hoops before making a hash of something or other. But it all made him testy, and in the hope of disqualifying me he would follow me round the court on the chance of catching me out in a follow-through shot when striking the two balls together. I have forgotten the precise terminology of the game, so this loose description must suffice.

Shortly after he ceased to be captain of the golf club the committee decided that the course should be opened for Sunday play, and I defied him by fixing a match for the Lord's Day instead of going to church. He said nothing when I came in late to lunch, but for several days his attitude to me was morose. Then, in a fit of puerile temper, I did an inexcusable thing. Somehow the subject of Christianity arose in conversation, and I remarked that if Christ were at all like the average

Christian he must have been a pretty poisonous person. Father was horrified, but did not lose his dignity. 'I shall either have to assume that I heard you incorrectly or order you out of the house,' he said. Replying that I would catch the next train to London, I took a sorrowful farewell of mother and left. But he bore no resentment, and after three years of absence I was welcomed back, never again to be on bad terms with him. With the passage of years we got to like one another, and in time I think he became as fond of me as I was of him.

My memory refuses to function at this point. How I lived during the next few months I cannot think, but almost certainly on gifts of money, possibly from Harry, possibly from the aunts, certainly from mother. I shared digs with a fellow I had met during my Hampstead days. He had a tiny flat in a Westminster slum, where a few impecunious actors had gathered together and lived in tenements. His was Flat 2, 81 Regency Street, and consisted of two bedrooms and a kitchen-sitting-room. While at Bedford I had used his flat for occasional meetings with Bella, and at the beginning of 1911 I became a permanent resident. His name was John Beamish. As secretary of The British Empire Shakespeare Society, he had called at Gayton Road to advise me against forming a branch of the Society at Hampstead, his reason being, as I later discovered, that it would add to his labours. He was a wonderful talker, a dash of cynicism added to his native humour making his monologues stimulating as well as entertaining, and he would have been a fine actor in 'character' parts if he had not suffered acutely from nerves at rehearsal. His family disliked his association with the stage, themselves belonging to the army and navy class, and did their best to get him a job as lecturer at a Japanese university, since he loved poetry, especially that of

Shakespeare and Wordsworth. To oblige them he read innumerable books on Japan, and then told them that as he now knew all about the country there was no need for him to go and see it. He had been educated at Haileybury, and on leaving had joined Benson's company. When I went to live in his flat he was acting in Fred Terry's company at the New Theatre, and suffering bouts of profound depression, which only lifted in the excitement of talk. He made a hobby of horoscopy, and under its influence became a fatalist. He was over six feet tall, had an impressive forehead and jaw, humorous eyes, and a slightly crooked nose. Ten years my senior, I often benefited from his advice and became much attached to him, making him the subject of my first pen-portrait, which has since disappeared.

In January 1911 I was of some use to my mother, who had come to London to help Aunt Eva when Uncle Frank died that month. To quote *The Times*: 'in 1909, when he was in his 88th year, tardy official recognition of his scientific attainments came to him in the shape of a knighthood', and incidentally the notice in that paper tardily drew my attention to the biographical value of such compositions. Nowadays one of my pastimes is reading the obituaries of eminent people and deriving much pleasure from the art of lying about the newly dead. Galton was a wealthy man, and left the greater part of his estate to the University of London for the foundation of a Galton professorship of Eugenics and the work of the Eugenics Laboratory which he had instituted in his lifetime with an annual grant of £500. At his wish Karl Pearson became the first Galton professor, and while mother and I were busy sorting out papers and books at 42 Rutland Gate we had many visits from Galton's future biographer. Sad to think of all the letters to Uncle Frank from famous Victorians which passed through my hands, to be carelessly read and dismissed. I would study them with intense interest now.

But Shakespeare was my main preoccupation, and already I had obtained an interview with Tree, who had promised to give me something in his next production, following the enormously successful run of *Henry VIII*. All my memories of that extraordinary personality, and of the three seasons of my engagement at his theatre, are to be found in my *Beerbohm Tree* (1956), so I shall not repeat them here. But I must briefly describe my first two efforts as an actor. Following a revival of *A Midsummer Night's Dream*, in which I appeared as a silent courtier, Tree gave one of his annual Shakespeare Festivals, which opened with *Julius Caesar*. I received the part of Publius, an ancient senator who in Tree's version had three words to speak: 'Good morrow, Caesar', and thereafter held his tongue. With the intention of making my first professional appearance, if not striking, at least effective, I spent much time studying the voice and walk of old men, quietly piping to myself and practising a totter. For two hours before the opening performance I was busy, with the help of a friend, putting enough wrinkles on my face to match the long white beard. I felt confident of my palsied movements but less certain of my quavering voice, and as I stood in the wings waiting for my entrance I practised the falsetto of a centenarian. The great moment arrived; I braced myself to meet it, and marched on to the stage, which was the cause of my undoing. In my anxiety to reproduce the accents of senility, I had temporarily forgotten the motions of senility, and I strode into Caesar's room with the gait of my age. Realizing my error, I stopped abruptly, and was about to return in order to make an entrance more consonant with my make-up when Caesar said 'Welcome, Publius', which in the text followed my words 'Good morrow, Caesar'.

Shattered by the deprivation of my greeting, I collapsed into the palsied condition necessary for the part; but at the same instant I forgot the piping tones that had been so carefully rehearsed and replied with the audibility of a young man whose lungs were in good order: 'Hullo!' Antony, Brutus and the rest followed me into Caesar's apartment, and I tumbled off somehow, horrified by my ghastly exhibition. Naturally I expected instant dismissal and shook in my sandals as Tree came up to me at the conclusion of the scene. 'What did you say to Caesar?' he asked in the rather fearsome guttural tone he put on for special occasions. 'I'm afraid I said "Hullo!", Sir Herbert', was my miserable admission, and I was about to stutter some feeble sort of excuse when he went on: 'Oh! I beg your pardon. My mistake. I thought you said "WHAT HO!".'

That was all. I heard no more about it. But I naturally expected my first part would be my last, and it might have been if I had not impressed the stage-manager Cecil King with the stentorian nature of my voice as a citizen in the Forum Scene, when I had to bawl a question from the back of the crowd: 'What does he say of Brutus?' This earned me the part of Balthazar in a revival of *The Merchant of Venice*, the next play in the Festival. In Tree's production the part was played as a dignified major-domo, so I began to study the carriage and manner of butlers, and soon felt that I could make announcements in an unexceptionable style. This time, I decided, there would be no trouble with speech or walk: I had achieved both to perfection and they synchronized. I would justify my promotion and be the envy of the junior dressing-room, none of my compeers having parts in the comedy. But fate played a dirty trick and I had not the experience to trump it. In Tree's annual festivals about half a dozen spectacular productions were staged in as many weeks, the rehearsals being

necessarily scrappy, and the 'noises off' were often not
heard until the first performance of each play. So when
I made my entrance in the part of Balthazar, ceremoni-
ously carrying my wand of office, I took up my position
with great dignity, planted my wand firmly on the
ground, threw back my head, opened my mouth, and
addressing Portia, commenced a speech that should
have run: 'The four strangers seek for you, madam, to
take their leave; and there is a fore-runner come from
a fifth, the Prince of Morocco, who brings word the
Prince· his master will be here tonight.' But before I
had sent forth three words of this speech, a terrific blast
of trumpets, which, unknown to me, should have
heralded my entrance, made me jump into the air,
completely disordered my thoughts and disarranged
my attitude. The blast ceased and I tried to collect myself. Once more I threw back my head and again I
opened my mouth. But the managerial requirements
were not yet satisfied. I had not uttered a word before
another and closer blast of trumpets, which unknown
to me, should have heralded my speech, finished what
the first had begun. At its conclusion I was speechless.
I was not going to be made a fool of a third time, so I
held my peace. But that second outbreak really had
concluded the programme from a heraldic point of view,
and Portia and I remained for an appreciable period
gaping at one another in dead silence. She was the first
to speak; and as Shakespeare had failed to provide for
such a contingency, she was forced to take a liberty
with the text:

'Well, sirrah?' she said.

By this time I had completely forgotten what my
speech was about; but I had to say something, so I
retorted:

'Well, madam?'

This cornered her but did not advance matters. Sud-

denly I heard an angry hiss from the stage-manager:
'Get off the stage, you bloody idiot!' I did as he
suggested.

A few weeks of rough experience in a repertory company would have enabled me to take both these incidents in my stride. But except for a little work as an
amateur, I was a raw recruit performing on England's
leading stage, a thing that hundreds of well-trained
actors would have given their ears to do.

Something of far greater importance in my personal
history occurred between my first and second seasons at
His Majesty's. I went for a short summer tour of a play
called *The Builder of Bridges* by Alfred Sutro, and
played my first part of more than a few lines. In the
company was a pretty girl named Gladys Gardner,
with whom I promptly fell in love. We visited Scar-
borough, where late one night, sitting on the sands in
the moonlight, I asked her to marry me. She agreed to
do so when we had enough money to live together, and
soon we became sexually intimate, a prudent preliminary to a satisfactory marriage. She and I liked the same
kinds of things, especially reading, walking, music, talking, and the theatre. We appreciated the same sort of
humour in life and literature, and she sympathized with
my Shakespearean mania. Her father, J. C. Bardili, was
a German from Stuttgart, though his name suggested an
Italian origin. Her English mother, Emma Gardner,
had died after giving birth to a sixth child when Gladys
was quite young, and her father had married again, her
stepmother being French. Bardili, whose family were
brewers at Stuttgart, had become a naturalized Englishman, and represented a big firm of German brewers in
England.

The summer of 1911 was an exceptionally hot one,
and on the hottest day in it Gladys and I walked between cornfields from Deal, where we were acting, to

Sandwich, which we thoroughly explored before returning on foot. So excessive was the heat that at Felixstowe we played one evening to an audience of twelve. A summons to His Majesty's compelled me to leave the company after five weeks of the tour, and following the run of Tree's *Macbeth* production I went off to spend a holiday with my brother Harry, who had married Pearl Leahy of Limerick and taken a house at Athlacca in that county. Pearl's sister Dora lived with them and used to accompany me on long rough shooting expeditions to the various bogs in the district, where I shot many snipe and occasionally duck and woodcock. Hunting and shooting occupied most of the days and all the conversation. Altogether I spent three long holidays in Ireland between 1910 and 1912, one of them golfing at Lahinch, and they are among my most pleasant memories, the invigorating company of Pearl and Dora contributing in no small measure to my happiness.

Early in 1912 a wire from Tree's stage-manager offering me a small part in *The Man Who Was*, which was to be given for a month at the Palace Theatre and followed by a revival of *Trilby* at His Majesty's, tempted me to abandon my holiday; but the temptation to extend it was stronger, and I remained in Ireland until Tree produced *Othello*, to be succeeded by the annual Shakespeare festival, my return being expedited by a letter from Gladys telling me that she was enceinte.

We were married at the Westminster registry office on 6 June, but to soothe the two families we antedated the ceremony by two months when making the announcement, our caution being justified when Gladys gave birth to a son who weighed ten pounds, a trifle overweight for a seven-months baby. Our marriage was witnessed by John Beamish and Amy Lloyd-Desmond, an actress-friend known to us as 'Dessie', who lived in one of the Regency Street flats and used to talk with

John and me about Shakespeare and Browning and
Dickens and Thackeray and kindred themes, refreshing
us at intervals with cups of tea, until two or three in the
morning. Our boy was born on 13 January 1913, and
on 29 May of that year, to relieve the feelings of my
Aunt Adèle, our marriage (I quote the certificate) 'was
confirmed by a Religious Service solemnized in the
Church of St Stephen-the-Martyr, Portland Town,
N.W. in accordance with the rites and ceremonies of
the Established Church.' Beamish and Dessie were
again our witnesses, the former having to jump from
one spot to another when it became necessary to give
the bride away, a formality we had not foreseen. To the
consternation of Dessie, my wife and I were practically
incapable of pronouncing the responses, both being
seized by the humour of the situation. However, Aunt
Adèle was placated and paid all the expenses. Fortunately for us, Beamish decided, soon after our marriage,
to leave his job on the Shakespeare Society and go on
tour as an actor. He let his flat to us for three months
and managed to get me appointed as his secretarial
successor. For the sum of £2 a week I held the job for
two years, until the outbreak of war in August, 1914.

I may say at once that I could not have had a better
wife than Gladys from the moment we laughed our way
into marriage until her death nearly forty years later.
Our love and mutual dependence on one another grew
with the years, and despite certain sexual irregularities
on my part, which produced unhappy emotional ten-
sions, we never wished to separate. At the beginning of
our life together she knew very little about cooking, but
she soon taught herself and became an expert. During
my period with Beamish my meals had been few and
innutritious. I did not think I could afford meat, or cook
it, and my pangs of hunger were alleviated by poor
confectionery and an occasional egg. Once I tried to

make an omelet, but somehow it got transformed into a rather heavy sandwich cake, which we ate with jam. It amazed me when Gladys brought home two chops and I found that they only cost fourpence apiece. That was the beginning of rational feeding for me; but I had weakened my constitution by semi-starvation in the City and again just prior to marriage, and the effect soon became apparent.

When we had to leave Regency Street, we managed to find a diminutive flat at 4 Avenue House, Henry Street (now Allitsen Road), St John's Wood, for which we paid 15/- a week. Gladys's father gave her 10/- a week, and we got along on a weekly total of £2-10., which included the salary and midday meal of Edie Neaves, a girl who came daily to help in the flat and take the baby for an airing. Incidentally the night before the baby arrived Gladys and I walked up Hampstead hill to dine with my sister Elsie and her husband in their Frognal flat, after which we walked home, and about two in the morning I had to take her in a taxi to Queen Charlotte's Hospital in Marylebone Road, where after a very painful period of parturition she produced the child who was called after his grandfathers and father, Henry Carl Hesketh, though always known as Henry.

We now lived within an easy walk of No. 8 Clifton Hill, the house of the Hon. Director of The British Empire Shakespeare Society. He was Acton Bond, a handsome, socially charming man with a perfectly produced and admirably modulated voice. I liked him, but we were always on rather formal terms and we scarcely ever discussed anything except the business of the Society. I spent about three mornings a week at his house, when he dictated letters and arranged forthcoming meetings. The Society had been founded by a Miss Morritt, and its first President had been Sir Sidney

Lee, the leading Shakespearean 'scholar' of his day, who wrote a biography of the dramatist from which the reader would conclude that the author of *King Lear* had been more of a respectable tradesman than a poet. There is a story that Edward VII once gave this royal tip: 'Stick to Shakespeare, Mr Lee, there's money in him.' Lee took the tip, backed a winner, and found there was a title in him too. But he was not so successful with Acton Bond, criticizing him for taking too many leading parts in the public readings. A stormy scene took place between the two at a meeting of the committee. Bond won, Lee resigned, and when I became secretary the President was Princess Marie Louise, a grand-daughter of Queen Victoria, while the committee consisted of nearly all the notable actor-managers of the time.

The Society presented readings of the plays at intervals in West-End theatres, and the value of the Princess as a figurehead may be gauged by the fact that almost every leading actor on the stage gladly lent his theatre or read a part on being told by Acton Bond that his services would be appreciated by 'Her Highness'. Small parts for the West-End readings were easily filled by competent players because certain newspapers sent their critics; and so we were able to give professional renderings of the plays by 'stars' and their satellites to packed houses at no cost to the Society. It was not so easy to cast plays for Sunday evening readings at the Passmore Edwards Settlement, for no newspaper critic would come to them and it was the only free evening of the week for actors. On such occasions one or two professional beginners, including myself, would usually have to divide the smaller parts between them, and I recall an uncomfortable reading of *Richard III* when I had to read six parts of my own, in addition to several for which a member of the cast had forgotten his responsibility, while the two little Princes were taken by an actress of seventy and another in an advanced state of pregnancy.

The Society had branches in various parts of the kingdom, and theoretically all over the Empire, but the only one outside the British Isles that we were able to print on our notepaper was at Wellington in New Zealand. I doubt if we really believed in this antipodean branch, though we occasionally corresponded with a fellow who claimed to be the secretary. My own opinion was that he had a small circle of friends who met at his house on Sunday evenings and read Shakespeare together. We were therefore astounded when a gentleman named Joynt called one day and said that he was a Vice-President of the Wellington branch in New Zealand, Bond was the first to recover, and our visitor was clearly impressed by the enthusiasm of his recepttion. Thereafter he was exhibited on platforms as an important imperial representative; he was asked to distribute prizes; he was glad to deliver speeches; and we did not omit to advise the press when he visited Stratford to lay a wreath on Shakespeare's grave.

Occasionally we imported an eminent lecturer from the Continent, and one of our biggest catches was Dr Georg Brandes, the Danish critic, who addressed the Society at the Garrick Theatre. I got the impression that, however much he liked Shakespeare, he loathed Shakespeareans, and he was not in the best of moods when Bond and I received him in the green room before the lecture. Bond's favourite play was *Othello,* and he used to read the leading part very effectively. He now tried to gain the approval of Brandes, who was nursing his pointed beard and gazing coldly into space: 'I was greatly interested, master, in your statement that *King Lear* is Shakespeare's greatest work. But surely you place *Othello* on an equal eminence?' Without a flicker of change in his expression, Brandes replied, spacing the words: 'I do not.' This was unaccommodating, and Bond shifted his position, his eyes meeting mine. Calming himself, he turned again to Brandes and said cheerfully, 'Well, I suppose—ha, ha—I suppose it's a matter of taste.' Brandes, still nursing his pointed beard and gazing coldly into space, spoke with frigid emphasis: 'It is not.' Bond retired to see whether all was ready for the lecture.

Among the many books on Shakespeare that I read while secretary of the Society was one by Frank Harris called *The Man Shakespeare*. After the dreary works by university professors, it was a revelation. Here was a man instead of a mummy, a man with parts and passions, a man one might meet any day in the street. Time has toned down my first estimate, but I shall not easily forget my early excitement over Harris's book, which impelled me to write to the author, a first sight of whom in an underground cabaret was not impressive. But he asked me to his flat in Lexham Gardens; and though his carefully stage-managed entry into the room with his wife on his arm struck me as a trifle overdone, I found his conversation inspiriting. His reverberant bass voice made platitudes sound like profundities. He scorned the moral precepts with which most of us had been brought up, scoffed at our masters and pastors, mocked our respectable backgrounds, derided all our conventions, and proclaimed Love as the be-all and end-all of existence. That sort of thing made a great impression on youngsters brought up in the shade of the Victorian age, and he did not lack disciples. He could quote Shakespeare, Keats and Browning by the yard, the lyrics with trembling voice and tearful eyes, the rhetoric with thunderous majesty of declamation, and his listeners were spellbound.

'By what by-paths and indirect crook'd ways' this undersized, overdressed, lowbrowed, ill-featured fellow

became editor of half-a-dozen magazines and newspapers, and for a time occupied a leading position in
London journalism, no one knew. Certainly the blackmailing of men and the seduction of women had a lot
to do with his success. The yarns he told of his financial
exploits would have made Baron Münchhausen think
again, while his descriptions of amorous adventures
would have caused Casanova to tone up his memoirs.
We were treated to hair-raising episodes in his life as
a cowboy on the Mexican border, but probably it all
boiled down to the fact that he had once milked a cow.
According to his accounts, he had been born in various
countries at different times, and educated at several
establishments at the same time. In his last years he
wore an Old Etonian tie and claimed Rugby as his
school; but it would not be safe to assume that he was
at Winchester. Whatever else he may or may not have
been, he was certainly a character in his own right, and
I liked him and laughed at him simultaneously, though
his company could be embarrassing. I once lunched with
him at Simpson's, where he paralysed a church dignitary
at the next table by asking me in a *sotto voce* that must
have been audible in the Strand: 'Did Jesus Christ wear
gaiters?' I never met him after 1914, but we remained
on cordial corresponding terms for the rest of his life.

My excessive admiration of his two books on Shakespeare led to an awkward incident with Acton Bond.
The B.E.S.S. held an annual elocution competition, the
book-prizes for which were presented by the President
at a public meeting. As a rule the books were of all sizes
and shapes but on one occasion Bond left their choice
to me, and on the table in front of the Princess were two
piles, those on her right of one shape and size, those on
her left of another. The right-hand pile consisted of
The Man Shakespeare by Frank Harris: these were
for the female winners of the competitions. The left-

hand pile consisted of *The Women of Shakespeare* by the same author: these were for the male winners. At the conclusion of the proceedings Princess Marie Louise expressed her surprise at the lack of variety in the books chosen, and Acton Bond told me that I had placed him in an invidious position, since it might be insinuated that the Society would benefit from the sale of works by Frank Harris, a man of no standing at all in the Shakespearean world.

Our committee meetings were usually dry and tedious, the Princess being a down-to-earth practical person who did not like to waste time. But one meeting was, in Acton Bond's view, of a momentous order, and he sent personal letters to various actor-managers requesting their attendance in a room at the Haymarket theatre. For my own amusement I kept a private account of the session which may now be printed, the death of Princess Marie Louise having removed the last of those who took part in it. Up to the age of thirty, when I got a bit of shrapnel in my head, I was blessed with a remarkable memory, and could reproduce long conversations practically verbatim, if I did not let a night intervene between their occurrence and my record. The following report was written within two hours of the meeting it describes:

The Princess was in the chair, and the others present were Sir George Alexander, Arthur Bourchier, H. B. Irving, Lewis Waller and Acton Bond. I might add that Waller was a stranger at our meetings, this being his first and last appearance. He wore tweeds and a red tie; and he entertained us with yarns while we were waiting for the Princess and her lady-in-waiting, Miss Hawkes. The meeting opened with Bond's explanation of its urgency. An inhabitant of Plymouth, Massachusetts, had written to ask whether he could start a branch of the B.E.S.S. in the home of the Pilgrim Fathers, where it would have to be known locally as the Anglo-

American Shakespeare Society. After I had read his letter to the committee, the talk began:

PRINCESS : Well, I'm in favour of it.

BOND : But the title of the Society, m'am?

PRINCESS : What does it matter? So long as they acknowledge the parent organization?

BOND : Your Highness forgets—if you will forgive my saying so, m'am—that we should have to change the Aims and Objects of the Society. Our Foundation was exclusively for the British Empire.

PRINCESS : Well, Sir George, how do you feel?

ALEXANDER : I agree with Mr Bond.

BOND : I only put that view forward, m'am. I do not say we cannot overcome the difficulty.

PRINCESS : What's your view, Mr Bourchier?

BOURCHIER : If your Highness will permit—(*addressing Bond*) how many branches have we outside England?

BOND : Oh, quite a few! Let me see. There's—er—Wellington, New Zealand, and—er—how many are there, Pearson?

PEARSON : Quite a dozen.

BOURCHIER : Where?

PEARSON : Edinburgh, Belfast, Glasgow—

BOURCHIER : Yes, yes, yes, I know, but—excuse me, m'am— how many are there outside the British Isles?

BOND : Is this important, m'am? I mean—

BOURCHIER : I just wanted to know—your Highness will understand me—whether the addition of a branch in the United States would be such a great matter. If we have a number of branches in the Imperial Dominions, surely we needn't worry about this potty little place—whatsitsname?

PEARSON : Plymouth, Massachusetts.

BOURCHIER (*irritably*) : I know, I know . . .

ALEXANDER : What is it our correspondent says about the Pilgrim Fathers?

IRVING : They landed at Plymouth, I believe.

BOND : In the *Mayfair.*

PRINCESS : The *Mayfair?*

IRVING : The *Mayflower*, you mean.

BOND (*quickly*) : I said the *Mayflower*.

PRINCESS : I thought you said the *Mayfair*.

BOND (*laughing*) : Very good, your Highness.

BOURCHIER (*laughing*) : Very good indeed, m'am.

ALEXANDER : Aren't we rather. . . ?

BOND : Quite so. We mustn't get away from the scheme.

BOURCHIER : You say we have a dozen overseas branches?

BOND : Is that right, Pearson?

PEARSON : Oh, quite that.

PRINCESS : But where are they?

PEARSON (*rapidly remembering his geography lessons*) : Sydney, Capetown, Calcutta—

BOND (*interrupting*) : Er . . . hem! Exactly. But, your Highness, may I suggest that the scheme under consideration concerns the United States only. The question before the committee is whether we can consent to a Branch of the B.E.S.S. calling itself by another name.

PRINCESS : Well, I don't think it matters—if they pay their annual tribute regularly.

BOND (*laughing*) : Good! Excellent, m'am.

BOURCHIER (*laughing*) : Admirable, your Highness.

IRVING : What would that be worth?

BOND : It would depend on the number of members.

IRVING : At a rough estimate?

BOND : Perhaps ten pounds a year, or more.

PRINCESS : Couldn't we make them pay extra for the privilege of belonging to the British Empire?

BOURCHIER (*laughing*) : That's an idea, your Highness.

BOND : (*laughing*) : You have a keen financial sense, m'am.

ALEXANDER : We seem to be taking a great deal of trouble for ten pounds a year.

BOND : Ah, but it's the principle, Sir George. It may not stop there. The other leading cities of the States may wish to join us.

ALEXANDER : Then we could alter the name, as suggested, to the Anglo-American Shakespeare Society.

BOND : That would scarcely come within the scheme of the Founders.

IRVING : Who are the Founders?

BOND : Well, to be precise, there was only one Founder : Miss Morritt.

PRINCESS : And she has nothing more to do with the Society?

BOND : Forgive me, m'am, but she is keenly interested in our work.

PRINCESS : Surely the committee can change the rules if it wants to?

BOND (*shaking his head gravely*) : We could obtain legal advice m'am.

PRINCESS : Then what is the feeling of this committee?

ALEXANDER : I should agree to any majority ruling.

BOURCHIER : And I, your Highness. Indeed, I should prefer that you m'am, would suggest a ruling. We would all, I am sure, follow your Highness.

(*A rumbling of affirmatives.*)

PRINCESS : Well, what do you think about it, Mr Bond? After all, you are the General Director and have all the work to do.

BOND : I feel, m'am, that as things are we had better keep to the original scheme. When all's said, Shakespeare is *our* possession. Other nations can and do admire him, but he does not *belong* to them.

IRVING : He belongs to the Americans all right. They speak his language—

PRINCESS : With a different accent, surely?

BOURCHIER (*laughing*) : Capital, m'am, capital!

BOND (*laughing*) : Very clever indeed, your Highness.

ALEXANDER : Yes.

WALLER (*who, so far, has not opened his mouth*) : Will your Highness excuse me?

PRINCESS : Certainly.

WALLER : Thank you. I have an important match this afternoon. (*He bows and leaves the room.*)

BOND (*explaining*) : He plays a lot of golf, m'am.

PRINCESS : Oh! . . . I wondered why he was so silent.

(*A pause, while everyone wonders whether this is a joke. Bond decides it is, and laughs judicially. Bourchier risks it, and laughs boisterously.*)

ALEXANDER : Then, as Mr Bond is against it, we'd better write and say they must form their own Society.

BOND : Please don't make me solely responsible. I assure you—

IRVING : It can be put to the vote.

BOURCHIER : How does your Highness feel about it?

PRINCESS : I really don't think it matters much either way, do you, Sir George?

ALEXANDER : Not in the least.

IRVING : Of course it doesn't.

BOURCHIER : I quite agree.

PRINCESS : So the feeling of the meeting is that the matter should be left entirely to the discretion of Mr Bond?

(*The feeling appeared to be unanimous.*)

BOND : Thank you very much, your Highness. Then you authorize me to turn down the suggestion as not being within the scheme of the B.E.S.S.?

PRINCESS : We authorize you to do whatever you like about it.

BOND : I am very sensible of the trust reposed in me. Your Highness can of course understand that I should scarcely have liked to move in the matter without obtaining the committee's sanction. A great deal may depend on this decision. In fact I cannot exaggerate its importance. Thank you, m'am.

In the autumn of 1912 Tree put on a patriotic show called *Drake*. I was offered a small part, but as my secretarial work was rather strenuous just then I did not feel like facing a month of those strangely unpredictable rehearsals at His Majesty's. The necessity of increasing my emoluments compelled me to find a stage job the following year, and I went to see Granville Barker, who promised me something in the early autumn. By the beginning of August, 1913, I was rehearsing at St James's Theatre in Bernard Shaw's new play *Androcles and The Lion*. Prior to this Shaw had produced his own plays, but the combination of the Fabian Society's foreign politics and Mrs Patrick Campbell's domestic politics left him no time, and he abandoned *Androcles* to Barker, who, in accordance with his invariable practice, toned down the acting. Barker was a perfect producer of his own plays, of John Galsworthy's, and of the modern domestic drama but he failed with Shaw and Shakespeare, both of whose plays call for the flamboyant acting of the old school. No one would have guessed that Barker's nature was expressed by his love of over-production and under-acting. He desired perfection and harmony, both of which he tried to obtain by a finicky attention to detail, a squeamish avoidance of emphasis; and his prose, like his outlook, was over-refined. This explains much of his future career, which displayed a lack of guts in facing failure, a want of strength in grappling with reality. Eventually he ran away from life by marrying a rich woman and becoming a Shakespeare professor. Many men and women fall in love with the symbol of their craving for wealth or fame or social distinction. Barker longed for comfort and security, and these were symbolized in the person of his second wife, to whom he surrendered his spiritual and physical being.

But the Barker I knew in 1913 was a fascinating fellow, with quiet charming manners, who took me by the arm in a friendly way and gently explained how each sentence of my part should be spoken. It was a pleasure to watch him and to work for him, and I was able to understand how he had transformed a brainless spouter like Henry Ainley into a first-class actor. Physically and vocally Ainley had everything in his favour, but before Barker took him in hand his success had been due to his personal appearance and powerful voice. He was simply a wonderful instrument, and Barker showed him how to play his notes which, though modified by the master, were clear and resonant.

My part of Metellus, a short one, did not call for much mental struggle, but I also understudied the Captain, which necessitated a close attention to the rehearsals, and the unconscious biographer in me was stimulated by Barker's method of making the actors interested in their parts, telling them all sorts of things that had happened to them before their appearance on the scene. At the time I was not greatly impressed by the play, probably because of its fabulous content. Never having cared for fairy stories or allegories or fantasies, the Lion prevented me from appreciating *Androcles*. But my later recognition of the comedy's inspiration made it an exception to my usual dissatisfaction with fables, and it became one of my bibles. The 1913 production was preceded by a feeble thing called *Harlequinade*, which bored playgoers and added so much to the expenses that the two plays ran no more than eight weeks. Then came a morbid piece called *The Witch*, wherein I understudied a youth who is seduced by his stepmother, that being quickly followed by a repertory of plays, shortly transferred from the St James's to the Savoy Theatre among which I was cast for the lover in Molière's *Le Mariage Forcé*, Marlow in Galsworthy's *The Silver Box*, Another Gentleman in Ibsen's *The Wild Duck*, and the Exhibition Secretary in Shaw's *The Doctor's Dilemma*, which play was the sole success of the repertory. After the dress-rehearsal of the last-named, Shaw came on to the stage with a volume of notes for the principal players, dismissing me at once with 'You're all right'. This probably brought a look of smugness on my face, because he quickly added: 'But don't let the knowledge that you're all right make you think you couldn't be better.' I felt chastened but not humiliated.

Barker next produced *A Midsummer Night's Dream*, in which I was asked to understudy Oberon, Demetrius and Lysander. But again I felt in need of rest from rehearsals, and declined the offer. Altogether Barker put on three of Shakespeare's plays; and although their novelty of presentation made a sensation, I did not personally enjoy them as much as Tree's productions. Their attraction was largely due to the fact that, since very few people bothered to read Shakespeare, the greater part of the audiences discovered that the plays as written were quite interesting. Those of us who knew them well were not in need of this disclosure and were able to supplement the usual acting versions with our knowledge of what was left out. Nearly all the cuts in Tree's productions were sensible, and enabled him to stage the plays with imaginatively realistic scenery, colourful tuneful music, and superb pageantry. His casts included the best Shakespearean actors of the day, and the verse was delivered with a proper appreciation of its poetry and rhetoric; whereas Barker's players had to speak with extreme rapidity often under-acting their parts, and his scenery, tasteful and impressionistic, was a trifle bleak and arty. If we consider the choruses in *Henry V*, the stage-directions, costume details, processions, masques and marches in so many of the plays, and the splendour of the original production of *Henry VIII*, there can be little doubt that Shakespeare himself would have preferred Tree's presentations to Barker's.

But Barker's distinguished place in the history of the British stage was won by his work for the modern drama, above all for Shaw, whose fame as a dramatist in England was founded at the Court Theatre under Barker's influence. I often discussed the subject with Shaw towards the end of his life, and one night I dreamt about Barker, seeing him quite vividly as I remembered him, and waking up the next morning to read the report of his death. To spiritualists this may signify something, to psycho-analysts Freud alone knows what, to common-sense nothing whatever except that I had been talking and thinking about Barker.

6

Wartime

A stage career is not favourable to lasting friendships, partly because it is extremely favourable to immediate friendships. With their peculiar temperaments actors and actresses are quickly on familiar terms, but as they constantly change their milieu the same thing happens in each play or company of which they form a part. Of the many friendships I made among actors, only three were durable, and each of them dated from my first three years on the stage. The first was with Douglas Jefferies at His Majesty's, the second and third were with Allan Jeayes and Baliol Holloway in Barker's company, the first being founded on a love of talking, the other two on a love of walking. A few friendships that may have endured were closed by death in the war that began in August, 1914.

I joined Kitchener's Army in the early part of that month, and what had been a warning soon became an alarm. For a year or more bloodstains had sometimes appeared on my pillow when I woke up in the morning. As I felt perfectly well, I dismissed the matter from my mind, though Gladys begged me to see a doctor. Five or six weeks of drilling, route-marching, drenching and sentry-go converted the spots of blood into clots; I had to undergo a thorough medical examination, and was invalided out of the army with tuberculosis. There is a snapshot taken of my father, my brother Jack and myself standing at the front-gate of our Bedford home in 1915, in which I look rather like a skeleton covered with skin. While still on sick leave waiting for my dismissal papers, I went to seek the advice of Acton Bond. The B.E.S.S. was on the verge of closing down 'for the duration', and I had to find a job. Bond very kindly wrote a letter to Sir George Alexander, and within a week I was understudying the two leading parts, played by Alexander and Herbert Waring, in a revival of *His House in Order* by Sir Arthur Pinero.

It would be impossible nowadays for anyone to occupy a position like Pinero's in the theatre of his time, and no other dramatist in the history of the British stage has been accorded his contemporary pre-eminence. From the production of *The Second Mrs Tanqueray* in 1893 until the 1914 war he was a playwright-autocrat and actors spoke of *His House in Order* and *The Gay Lord Quex* with bated breath, as if no one on earth had ever approached his mastery of stagecraft and characterization. So great was his prestige that managers dared not decline the honour of presenting his plays, even if convinced that they would be flops. The only notable critics who refused to acclaim him as the high priest of dramaturgy were those irreverent persons Bernard Shaw and Max Beerbohm.

I was told by the stage-manager of the St James's Theatre, Vivian Reynolds, that I might watch the rehearsals from the front if I kept out of the author's sight; so I hid myself in the back of a box and had a good side-view of Pinero, who was sitting in solitary state in the first row of the stalls. His personal appearance was almost as impressive as his reputation: he had a square jaw, determined mouth, beaked nose, bushy eyebrows, bald head and severe expression. Even the confidential tones of his booming bass voice could be heard all over the theatre. He seldom removed his hat from his head or

his gloves from his hands, and he smoked cigarettes perpetually. Later I noticed that he was of middle height,
inclined to be stout, and not unlike Napoleon I in build,
appearance and manner, as he paced the stage with short
quick steps, body bent forward, hands behind back,
stopping suddenly at intervals to bark his commands.
Though he could smile charmingly, the actors saw more
of his minatory frown and were frightened of him. He
treated them like automatons, instructing them minutely
about their movements, gestures, vocal modulations,
facial expressions. 'Scratch your chin reflectively at that
point, Alec,' I heard him say, and Sir George Alexander
dutifully and reflectively scratched his chin. The author
knew his plays by heart and sharply corrected any performer who deviated by a syllable from the text.

I liked Alexander from the start. I had heard that he
was a frightful snob and refused to acknowledge members of his company when passing them in the street,
that if he had been blessed with children he would have
cut those who were not in his set; but as usual with this
class of rumour, generated by envy, I found that it was
based on hearsay. Standing outside Dover Street station
after a rehearsal, I saw him coming and turned my eyes
the other way. He stopped to ask whether I was quite
happy at his theatre, and we had a friendly little chat
on the pavement. Not long after I joined his company
he asked me to be secretary of The Arts Fund, which
invited popular 'stars' to organize concerts at the
Palladium for the benefit of actors, painters, musicians
and writers who had been hit by the war. I remember
stage-managing one of these concerts for Irene Van-
brugh, and having to make an announcement that, the
next item on the programme being the thirteenth, Miss
Shirley Kellogg refused to appear until the figure 13
displayed in electric light was flashed off. A little later
Alexander persuaded me to act as secretary for the

Laurence Irving and Mabel Hackney Memorial Fund. I was cast for parts in every play he did, earning about £3 a week. One of them was called *Kings and Queens*, written by Rudolf Besier, who later made a considerable stir with *The Barretts of Wimpole Street*. Another was *The Big Drum*, a new comedy by Pinero, and a week or so before the first night I had the rather alarming experience of meeting Pinero socially.

Alexander asked me to dinner at his house in Pont Street, and the other guests were Pinero and Austin Brereton, who had written a Life of Henry Irving. I was by many years younger than the others, and felt nervous and diffident. They could talk allusively of so many things about which I was in the dark, and so for some time I was merely a listener. Then the subject of Irving came up, and Pinero said that he had been at his greatest in Shakespeare, mentioning in particular his Macbeth and quoting a line of poetry that had been written on his performances: 'Thou clarion set for Shakespeare's lips to blow!' I could not resist the temptation to correct a man who was so punctilious about the speaking of his own text, and I uttered the word 'trumpet'. Pinero looked at me as if I had just appeared from somewhere and said 'Eh?' Aware that I had the attention of the table, I quoted boldly: 'Thou trumpet set for Shakespeare's lips to blow!' 'Oh!' said Pinero disapprovingly. Alexander asked who had written it. Becoming overbold, I said in a rather challenging manner: 'That genius Oscar Wilde.' An atmosphere of constraint fell upon the table, for although Wilde's name had come back into circulation by that time it was still mentioned with economy. There was a long and pregnant pause. Everyone waited for someone to speak. At last Pinero growled: 'No. Not a genius. No.' 'Clever,' murmured Brereton. 'Brilliant,' suggested Alexander. 'Talented ... yes ...' said Pinero, and then, to settle the question beyond all dispute, he added: 'But *not* a genius. Definitely not.' I had been put in my place firmly and finally, but I would not abandon my position without a passing shot. 'Then who is a genius?' I asked. 'Well . . .' said Alexander, and stopped there. We awaited the oracle and looked at Pinero, who leant back in his chair, folded his hands, smiled graciously, and spoke: 'Perhaps Shakespeare. . . .' We all laughed, and the incident closed pleasantly.

Pinero had no sympathy with the subtle undertones of acting. He wanted every word he wrote to be heard at the back of the gallery. After one of the acts at a dress rehearsal of *The Big Drum* he came on to the stage and paced up and down in a ruminative manner while we waited anxiously, much as Napoleon's officers must have waited for his opinion of them after an uncertain action. Then he addressed us: 'I'm glad you are all enjoying the play. I've heard it's an excellent one, and I'm sure it's too good to keep altogether to yourselves. Don't be so selfish. Let me hear some of it.' He marched back to the stalls, the curtain rose for a repetition of the act and we played it in a less confidential manner.

Not only the actors but his fellow-playwrights were mortally afraid of him. He was the dictator of the Dramatists' Club as well as the stage. In those days the Dramatists' Club was a clique of well-established playwrights who made a point of blackballing everyone whose reputation was not solid and respectable like their own. Bernard Shaw told me that when he and Granville Barker wanted Gilbert Murray to join it, the clique were about to blackball him. Pinero got to hear of it, turned up at the decisive meeting, and in his most imperious manner ordered them to elect Murray. They listened in respectful silence and obeyed without a word. Incidentally Shaw got Pinero his knighthood, though he was very careful to conceal the fact. In going through the private papers of Beerbohm Tree, who was knighted at the same time, I came across a remark made to him by Pinero just before the ceremony: 'Do you not think we might have this done under gas?'

In the autumn of 1915 I tried to join the Kite Balloon section of the army, but the doctors would not pass me. My one chance to distinguish myself as an actor with Alexander occurred in the spring of 1916. Hitherto he had tried me for two leading juvenile parts, but my obvious inexperience had forced him to substitute Ben Webster and Owen Nares, telling me 'Your time will come.' He said that I lacked ease in moving about the stage and advised me to watch Marion Terry, who glided from one spot to another so gracefully that no one noticed how she did it. I was understudying Alexander in nearly every play, as well as appearing in some small part, so I made a close study of his movements and soon picked up the necessary trick. Having rehearsed me for a very good part, the valet in a comedy called *The Basker* by a woman known as Clifford Mills, and decided that I was not equal to it, he engaged Leon Quartermaine and again allowed me to understudy his own part.

The play did well, but Alexander fell ill, and in an acute state of nerves I made my entrance in a leading part with heart-palpitations; but I quickly steadied myself with the thought that no one could stop me and criticize my performance. Indeed I soon felt so much at ease that I had the impertinence to put in a few of my own 'gags', which went well with the audience but not with the authoress, and I made a success of the part because it suited me down to the ground, being that of a naturally lazy man who rises to action when the occasion calls him. There was a moment in the play that called for great self-possession on my part. Following a scene with a girl to whom I had lost my heart, I was left alone, murmuring to myself: 'All little shiny goldy gleams, and dear little blow-away curls', upon which the curtain slowly descended and the less sturdy members of the audience restored their shattered tissues in the bar. Many years later Godfrey Tearle told me that the most trying sentence he had ever spoken on the stage was in Ethel M. Dell's *The Way of an Eagle*, when he brought the curtain down with a brief soliloquy: 'It is not the way of an eagle to swoop twice.' I submitted that my phrase from *The Basker* was a greater strain on the nervous system, and after repeating it slowly he allowed my claim.

Alexander's absence from the cast did not reduce the size of the audiences, and I played his part for a week. No one was more surprised than he, and while still in bed he sent for me. I tried to explain my success by saying that I never appeared at my best at rehearsals, that I was the sort of actor who had to be left alone, and that the character suited me because I was born lazy. He then promised me the part of an Indian Prince in his next production, a comedy by H. A. Vachell, at double my present salary, and assured me that he would not speak to me at rehearsals unless I asked for advice. After that he often dropped out of the cast to let me play his part, the slip in the programme stating that he was 'compelled to be absent on a matter of public importance', and occasionally watched my performance from the back of a box. The Indian Prince was cut bodily from Vachell's play by the censor but Alexander paid me the promised salary for the run of the piece, and offered me the juvenile 'leads' in his next two productions, a revival of *Bella Donna* by Robert Hichens and *The Aristocrat* by Louis N. Parker; but by that time I was back in the army and the parts were played by Leon Quartermaine and Dennis Neilson-Terry.

My triumph in *The Basker* brought one regret: John Beamish was not alive to know of it. He had told me that I had the appearance but not the technique for the stage; but playing a leading part, and getting more 'curtains' than Sir George Alexander had done, proved that technique could be picked up easily enough, and I should have liked to gain John's approval. Like me he had joined the army at the outbreak of war, and had been wounded in France in the summer of 1915. I saw him frequently in a military hospital on Millbank, and when he was fit enough he took a room near us while waiting to rejoin his regiment. We were now living in the upper part of No. 14 Abbey Gardens, St John's Wood, a more commodious place than the flat in Henry Street, which we left in January 1915, and John had a bedroom a few doors away. But something went wrong; we never knew what; and soon after marrying a girl whom he brought to see us, he shot himself in the public lavatory at the juncture of Edgware and Harrow roads, leaving a letter addressed to me in his pocket. A policeman called one evening, and we just had time to identify John at the mortuary on Paddington Green before I was due at the theatre. I was the chief witness at the inquest, but could throw no light on the tragedy except to say that he was liable to fits of depression. All this happened early in November 1915.

It was Beamish who first told me that George Alexander ran his theatre to perfection, and I soon discovered this for myself. He was a born businessman. Actors could rely absolutely on the rehearsal hours, which began at 10.30 a.m. sharp and ended at 1 o'clock precisely. The curtain rose at the moment announced, punctuality and efficiency being enforced in every department. In the same way the committees over which he presided were models of what such things should be, and he had great organizing ability. Early in 1916 he consented to be chairman and organizer of the Actors' Committee for the commemoration of the tercentenary of Shakespeare's death, and he asked me to serve under him as secretary. I agreed, and had the pleasure and pain of watching him grappling with all the details of a mammoth show, pleasure on account of his wonderful tact and skill, pain because he was in the early stages of diabetes, which occasionally prostrated him and eventually killed him. The funniest part of the committee's deliberations was the casting of *Julius Caesar*, the main item to be seen at Drury Lane Theatre on 2 May. All the West-End actor-managers were on the committee, and nearly all of them were eager to play the best part while equally eager to give the impression that they did not wish to do so. They let it be understood that they were working for 'the Cause', not in any way for themselves, but the clash between ideality and reality often placed them in tricky positions, and nothing but Alexander's adroitness saved their faces. He attended to everything, and the whole enormous undertaking, including the musical programme, the Shakespeare Pageant, the play, and the production of a Memorial Volume, went without a hitch, despite the wranglings, complaints and ebullitions of wounded vanity that he had to endure from all who felt their importance had been overlooked.

I regret to add that on three occasions I caused him some uneasiness. His wife, who was running the programme department, wanted special 'uniforms' for the ladies who were to sell them, and bothered me unduly on the subject when I was preoccupied with more pressing matters; in which condition I must have snapped at her, because she complained of my behaviour to her husband, who gently chided me. The second occasion was more serious. For half an hour before the performance started I acted in the capacity of manager and stood in the entrance hall of Drury Lane Theatre, dressed up to the nines, to deal with any questions that might arise. Suddenly I became conscious of a noisy red-faced fellow speaking rudely to Arnold, the box-office manager of the St James's Theatre, who was giving his services for this matinée. I went up to him and said that, whatever his grievance, it was no excuse for impoliteness. He turned on me and asked me in an insolent tone if I knew who he was. I replied that I did not and had no wish to know, adding that if he could speak like a gentleman I would do my best to meet his complaint. He bawled something to the effect that Sir George Alexander should hear of my damned impertinence and stamped out of the theatre. Later I heard that he was the Duke of Something or other, and poor Alexander, telling me sadly that I was not cut out for a courtier, wrote the fellow a soothing letter.

The third incident I thought funny enough to record in my notebook that night. Alexander had said that I must be present at the reception of King George V, Queen Mary, and their children, when they arrived for the entertainment. Receiving royalty is not much in my line, and I did my best to lose myself in the auditorium just before the party was expected; but Alexander spotted me and dragged me into the vestibule where the three old actor-knights, Sir Squire Bancroft, Sir Charles Wyndham and Sir John Hare, were awaiting their monarch, together with another actor, F. R. Benson, who was to be knighted that same afternoon. (Incidentally, Alexander told me that he had pressed Benson's claim to the honour, and that they had never heard of him in the Lord Chamberlain's office.) The door between the vestibule and the street was wide open, and a carpet and awning stretched across the pavement for the royal visitors. It was a filthy day outside, the rain streaming down with monotonous insistence. 'Their Majesties are late', I heard Bancroft growl into the ear of Wyndham, who had practically lost his memory at that time and answered 'Why?', which struck me as funny. My amusement must have been audible because Alexander 'Ssh-ed' me. There was a stir in the crowd outside. 'He's here,' said Bancroft. 'Who?' asked Wyndham. A loud laugh from me, an angry 'Ssh-ssh!' from Alexander, and the royal car drove up to the awning. The King, followed by the Queen, came quickly into the vestibule, shook hands with Alexander and turned to the other knights, being prompted by Sir George before he spoke to each; and thus the scene progressed:

ALEXANDER (*whispering to the King*): Lady Bancroft has been ill.

THE KING (*shaking hands with Bancroft*): How is Lady Bancroft?

BANCROFT: Much better, thank you, sir.

THE KING: I am pleased to hear it.

ALEXANDER (*whispering*): Sir Charles Wyndham's memory is bad.

THE KING (*shaking hands with Wyndham*): It's a long time since I've had the pleasure of seeing you act.

WYNDHAM: Yes, yes, sir; yes, yes. I beg your pardon?

ALEXANDER (*quickly whispering*): Sir John Hare has lately been on the Music Halls.

THE KING (*shaking hands with Hare*): How do you like the Variety audiences, Sir John?

HARE: Tolerably well, sir; they are enthusiastic.

THE KING: My best wishes for your success.

HARE: Thank you, sir.

ALEXANDER (*whispering*): This is Mr Benson, whom your Majesty—

THE KING: Ah. yes. (*Shaking hands with Benson*) I hope to have the pleasure of seeing you again this afternoon.

BENSON: Thank you, sir.

ALEXANDER: This is Mr Pearson, the secretary of our Committee.

THE KING: Oh! (*Shaking hands with me*) Very nice weather we've been having.

PEARSON: A bit damp about the knees today, sir.

I had not meant to correct the King, but I felt that something was required of me, and the pelting rain gave me the cue. For a moment I felt that everybody had been turned to stone. Alexander's eyes seemed to be popping out of his head; but the King passed on, and before I could do more than notice that I had dropped a brick I was shaking hands with Queen Mary and two or three of the royal youngsters. Passing me on the stairs when the show was over, Alexander stopped, frowned, and remarked: 'You should have said "Yes, sir".' I looked downcast and replied 'Sorry.' But the incident must have tickled him because he smiled, put his hand on my shoulder, and said: 'You stand rebuked but forgiven.'

On that note I will leave Alexander, whose kindness to me never varied. Several times I visited his house in Pont Street and the home built for him at Chorley Wood, and when in relaxed mood he occasionally spoke of Oscar Wilde, whose first and last comedies he had produced, telling me some interesting things which ultimately appeared in my biography of that genius (*pace* Pinero).

Within a week of the Drury Lane performance I was again in the army. Knowing I could not get back into the infantry, I joined the Army Service Corps, for which by that time the medical examination was perfunctory. A few questions, a formal heart-tapping, and one was in uniform. All institutions are filled with square pegs in round holes, and in the 1914-18 war the army made a special point of placing people in the jobs that were least suitable for them. If you were an expert linguist, you were put where your knowledge could not be of the slightest use; if you were a coal-heaver, you found your self dealing with figures; if you were an accountant, you were turned into a cook; and so on. To spare the authorities the mental effort of finding me a job for which I was totally unqualified, I volunteered for the Motor Transport, knowing nothing whatever about motor-cars except that they were liable to break down, and was immediately accepted.

My view of the war was fairly objective, for I hardly ever gave way to the spasms of patriotic emotion that afflicted so many of my contemporaries. There may have been moments when I surrendered to the common delirium, but I was never taken in by the slogans of press or platform, and I had long since ceased to feel that there was anything romantic about soldiering. The whole business struck me as sordid, barbarous and horrible, and I believed that with a little courage and common-sense it could have been avoided; though nowadays I am under no illusion as to the essentially primitive passions in human beings that make war inevitable unless countered by the equally primitive passion of funk. On the other hand, the thing having happened, it was no use whining about the rights and wrongs of the case, and the conscientious objectors seemed to me as fatuous as the war maniacs. We may have a conscientious objection to life or death, but we continue to live and die however strongly we object. Once begun, the war was like a house on fire, and it was pointless to ask how the blaze had started. The only thing to do was to douse it and leave the discussion of its origin till after it was out. It really had become a choice between death and slavery, or at least between the misrule of Britons and the tyranny of Germany; and I had no doubt that loss of life was better than loss of liberty. But the propagandists blurred the issue with their stuff about the violation of Belgian neutrality, and the poets wrote blasphemous nonsense denying life and glorifying death, like that of Rupert Brooke's:

> Now, God be thanked Who has matched us with
> His hour,
> And caught our youth and wakened us from
> sleeping.

Which merely showed that Brooke lacked the vitality to face life, or felt that his own life at the age of twenty-six was too futile to face.

Preferring laughter to heroics, I extracted as much entertainment as I could out of unpromising circumstances, and broke every regulation that could safely be ignored. Discipline for the sake of discipline has always seemed to me absurd, and I found the army more ridiculous than school because it treated men like children. But the self-importance of officers and N.C.Os. was extremely laughable, and I managed to get through my eight months as a tommy not without amusement. After an uncomfortable spell at Pennington Camp near Grove Park, afterwards condemned as unfit for military purposes, I was posted to a unit at Shepherd's Bush, put into the quartermaster's department, and given a sleeping-out pass. Gladys brought our small boy to 36 Paddenswick Road, Ravenscourt Park, and there we remained in very pleasant digs for the rest of the year. My office-hours, pure waste of time for the country and myself, were from 8 a.m. till 6 p.m., so we were able to see plays and spend our evenings as we liked.

At that time Frank Harris was bombarding me with letters from New York, which incidentally got me into hot water with the military authorities because he was generally thought to be a paid German agent. I continued to correspond with him, knowing quite well that he was neither pro-German nor pro-English nor pro-anything else except pro-Harris. Among other things he wanted me to gather the opinions of leading English writers on his life of Oscar Wilde, copies of which he sent me for distribution not only to them but to the editors of leading newspapers. I received curt and displeasing replies from, among others, H. G. Wells, Arnold Bennett, Joseph Conrad, James Barrie, Hall Caine, Edmund Gosse and Rudyard Kipling, while two or three papers dismissed the book in brief paragraphs. Bernard Shaw alone behaved with magnanimity, sending me a long letter addressed to Harris describing his personal relations with Wilde. This letter enabled Frank to print a cheap edition of his book which sold in thousands. My friendship with Shaw started at this period. First of all he wired us an invitation to lunch; somehow I got a day's leave, and we made the acquaintance of his wife as well. Then I had two or three evening sessions with him, and we discussed everything from Wagner to the war. I found him generous, kind-hearted, high-spirited, and without a trace of resentment against the friends who were attacking him with the utmost virulence because he had kept his head during the conflict. Nearly everyone goes mad in wartime. Shaw alone among famous writers remained sane, not, as he once told me, because he was objectively Irish, but because he was subjectively Shaw. I thought him a great man at the time, mentally and spiritually far above his contemporaries, and I have since had no reason to alter my opinion.

By the end of 1916 I was getting tired of entering bolts and nuts and blankets and palliasses in ledgers, and decided to get a commission. Princess Marie Louise signed my papers, and early in 1917 I was in an officers' training corps at Grove Park, Gladys moving to digs in Burnt Ash Hill near by, though now I had to sleep in

the military billets. It took six weeks of intensive training to turn a tommy into an officer. Since we were in
the Motor Transport, it goes without saying that we
received no training in mechanics, and our time was
spent in drilling and attending lectures on ballistics and
cognate themes. Having determined to get a commission, I concentrated on the tedious details to which we
were subjected and passed the exams easily. I also got
top marks for lorry-driving and drilling, though I nearly
lost my commission on the parade-ground by giving another fellow a tip:

Having survived my own exam as a drill-master with
success, I was placed as a 'marker', i.e. the post at which
the squad had to be drawn up in a particular formation
by examinees, one of whom was hopelessly nonplussed
and appealed to me for help. He was standing to attention a yard behind me, and I twisted my lips to whisper
what he had to do. Unfortunately my whispers tend to
be audible at some distance, and the examining officer
at once halted the proceedings to demand who had
spoken. The serjeant-major bore down upon me with
menace in his stride, and bawled: "Oo spoke? Did
you?' 'Yes, sir.' 'What did yer say?' I had to think
quickly. 'He had forgotten the officer's order, sir, so I
repeated it to him.' The serjeant-major clearly did not
believe this lie, but he merely said 'Ho!' I fancy my
drilling had softened his heart, because after yelling
that no one must under any circumstances open his
mouth on parade, flatly contradicting this by adding
that all questions must be addressed to himself, he retired
to his place, while our hearts resumed their normal
pulsations.

The top dozen in the exams, of which I was one, were
commissioned and despatched within forty-eight hours
to Mesopotamia. The doctors were so busy inoculating
us against possible diseases that they had no time to

spare for our present states of health, and I was passed
fit on my own word, though my private doctor had
warned me that, short of a miracle, I would be dead
within a year. As death from cholera or heat was just
as likely in the East, I did not let this medical sentence
worry me unduly. The troopship *Kenilworth Castle*
took us as far as Durban, stopping at Sierra Leone and
Cape Town on the way, and during the trip a few of
us amused ourselves by composing, printing and dis-
tributing two numbers of an attenuated magazine called
'The Eastern Enterprise', for which I wrote the leaders
under the heading 'Pot-Pourri from the Poop'. The
publication consisted of gossip, scandalous innuendos,
and equatorial humour. I doubt if it amused anyone but
the contributors. For me the journey was notable for
the beginning of a long friendship with Dick Hammond,
an entirely admirable fellow who managed to make a
hobby of army life and returned home to become a
director of Barclays Bank at Norwich. The journey from
Durban to Bombay was done in the *Aragon*, which was
later sunk. Hammond and I stayed at the old-fashioned
Watson's Hotel in Bombay and enjoyed our freedom
from the ship's restrictions. We arrived at Basra in time
for one of the hottest summers on record, when for two
months the shade temperature varied from 120 to 130,
once reaching 135 in the tents at Kut.

Soon after our arrival I went down with sandfly
fever and colitis, being sent to Beit Na'ama hospital,
where the ministrations of a nurse made my convalescence pleasant and perhaps longer than it should have
been. Following my discharge from hospital I had a
bad bout of septic sores, which might have resulted in
the loss of a leg if I had not disobeyed the doctor and
exercised it by crawling about the tent in unspeakable
pain. The dry intense heat of July cured my tuberculosis, but having survived an appalling summer I nearly

died from a combined attack of dysentery and malaria. All through the scorching days of July and August the M.T. convoys went to and fro across the desert, taking food to the infantry who were resting at their distant posts. Heat-stroke caused many deaths among our men, and sometimes, our *chagals* having been emptied into the radiators to keep the cars going, we were so thirsty that we would have drunk our own water if there had been any to drink. My unit, 784 Company, was posted at Baqubah on the Diala River some thirty miles north-east of Bagdad, and there we were grilled in the summer of 1917. One day in particular was stamped on my memory and recorded in my diary during the next few days in an attempt to keep my mind occupied. It was 2 July. I left camp at the usual hour in the tail of my convoy. Hope, the driver of the van in which I travelled, was just out of hospital. I was getting accustomed to new drivers, having had sixteen in the past eight weeks, all of them admitted to hospital with depressing regularity. Some had returned to camp marked for 'light duty'. Others had been invalided to the Base. The rest had been buried.

The early morning of 27 July was cool and refreshing. There was a kind of 'mystic breathing' over the desert while the sun was yet invisible. The date-palms along the bank of the Diala looked green and inviting. It would have been pleasant, I felt, to wander among them before the delicious fragrance of the morning air was annihilated by the sun.

There were forty Ford vans of provisions for the little post of Beled Ruz that morning; and as the head of the convoy turned the bend of the road beyond the far bank, the tail dipped down to the near bank and disappeared into the cutting that led to the pontoon bridge. Gradually, as the last few cars crossed the river, the rumbling of the wheels on the loose boards ceased, and the convoy was hidden from the camp by the belt of trees which fringed the Diala for several miles on the other side.

For a few minutes we ran between palms, cut off from the road by mud walls; then we turned to the left along a road that had been made to skirt the town, crossed a little stream by 'Cossack' bridge—so-called to mark the spot where the English met the Russians shortly after the fall of Bagdad—and halted for a moment in the desert beyond to pick up two Lewis guns and an armed escort.

Off again, across the lines of a narrow-gauge railway that was soon to knit up Baqubah and Shahroban, and out into the seemingly endless plain that in a few hours would be burning and lifeless. But now, in the still freshness of the early morning, doves and larks were flitting to and fro in search of provender, dropped perhaps by yesterday's convoy. Large crows, some black, some grey, some almost white, wheeled in the air; while here and there, hovering above or stalking on the ground, gigantic hawks, the desert's chief scavengers, were biding their time, waiting for the next dead donkey or camel in which they could flesh their predatory beaks. Occasionally a jackal, that other great scavenger of the desert, started up from the ground on the right or left of the convoy and slunk off to its hiding-place, stopping now and then to look back at the strange machines that had usurped its sovereign right to roam at will.

Sometimes a little group of Arabs passed by, their women and children on donkeys, taking advantage of the lull 'twixt night and full day to cover the ground as fast as they could. They, too, like the jackals, gazed enquiringly at the weird horseless vehicles, distrust in their eyes. These white-faced strangers had entered their kingdom unasked and unwanted, not as travellers craving hospitality, but as potential plunderers. What good thing could they bestow on the children of the sun,

who despised their religion and detested their 'modern
improvements'? So the swarthy desert-dwellers let the
white-faces sweep on, regardless of their doom, with a
shoulder-shrug: for Allah is merciful, Allah is just,
Allah will avenge.... Praise be to Allah!...

In a wealth of golden glory the sun appeared over the
horizon, and the desert gleamed and shimmered under
its first rays. Coveys of sand-grouse rose from the scrub
and filled the air with their rook-like sounds. Plovers
made festive circles high above the tapering line of vans.
The whole of nature, or what there was of it, seemed
to be trembling with ecstasy, on tip-toe with excitement
to greet its Master, full-tongued. For perhaps half an
hour every scrap of discernible life in that colossal level
of dust appeared to lift its voice in praise of the Life-
giver. For perhaps half an hour....

For a while I forgot the convoy, forgot the country
I was in. Leaning back in my seat, I gave myself up to
thoughts of home, to memories of summer days on the
Ouse. I closed my eyes and saw the green meadows of
Bedfordshire and the trees on Hampstead Heath. When
I opened them again a breeze had sprung up and several
miniature whirlwinds, carrying with them the lighter
refuse of the desert, were panicking through the scrub.
The plovers were settling on the ground in a chorus of
shrill cries, and the sand-grouse were calling to one another in low, bodeful tones from the sparse tufts of sun-
dried, dust-blighted vegetation. The larks had ceased to
sing, the hawks to circle. A mirage of palm-trees in a
vast expanse of water appeared on our right, and a
heavy brown pall of dust blotted out the horizon on our
left.

In a minute it was upon us, enveloping us in a blanket
of thick choking grit. Sprawling over the plain, mostly
off the track, the vans blundered on, each driver utterly
cut off from his fellows by a nightmare of moving dirt,

nature's most hideous and isolating curse, each doing
his utmost to reach the little post of Mahrut, a wretched
caravanserai half-way between Baqubah and Beled Ruz.
Desolate though it was, the wall of the *khan* there would
afford some protection from this stinging Niagara of
dust.

I did not attempt to go forward, telling Hope to stop
the engine. Then we sat tight and waited for the storm
to blow over. While we waited every crevice of the
vehicle was clogged with dust. Our eyes, ears, mouths,
were filled with dust. A thick coating of dust covered
our hair, our hands, our clothes. Speech was impossible.
Thought was impossible. We could hardly see one another. Physically we were merged in dust, mentally
cloaked in dust. It was like being buried alive. To
breathe freely was to be suffocated. The world was a
chaos of flying filth. That was the reality. Everything
else was illusive, imaginary, inconceivable. . . .

Bump! A wandering car had struck us and come to
a standstill. It did not seem to matter. No one got out;
no one moved. 'Buried cities,' I soliloquized, the power
to think having returned to me at last. 'Don't you see?
These blasted storms account for all the buried cities
in Mesopotamia.' 'Yes, sir,' said Hope dutifully. I peered
through the curtain of gloom between myself and the
driver. Hope was apparently thinking of something else,
for his eyes were nearly shut and his hands rested limply
on the wheel before him.

Ten minutes went by . . . twenty . . . thirty. . . . It
seemed an eternity of time. Then the storm began to
pass over. A red ball showed through the folds of dirt
ahead. It was the sun. I welcomed it with a shout. Later
I remembered that shout and cursed myself.

It took the best part of an hour to collect the cars and
do the necessary repairs after the storm had blown over.
Some had sunk into sand-drifts at the side of the track.

Others had fallen into *nullahs* and had to be lifted out. Others had collided. Others had tried to scale *bunds* and had nearly been wrecked in the process.

Mahrut was reached and passed. The sand-hills beyond were successfully negotiated, and by nine-thirty the convoy was running easily over the flat stretch of desert that had to be crossed before we came to the *bund*, the road and the rice-fields of Beled Ruz. The *bund* and the road had been constructed by a French engineer, the former to protect the canal from which the rice-fields drew their water, the latter to simplify the transport of local produce.

Now the sun began to assert itself. Already it was hotter than the hottest day an Englishman could experience if he stayed at home. The wan men in their pith helmets knew what was before them. They sat motionless, with grim set faces, in the shade of their matting-covered hoods. The deathly silence of the desert was closing in upon them. Some whistled, to shake off the memory of fifty yesterdays; others sang; the majority made no effort to forget, but clutched the steering-wheels before them and summed up their chances of another day's survival.

Stealthily the sun crept upwards. This was merely a day, an ordinary summer's day, in Mesopotamia; but each dawn for these men heralded a day of doom. Would they, could they, see it through? Yes, assuredly. For now the convoy was through the *bund* and a cool breeze across the irrigated rice-fields renewed them and gave them confidence. What a wonderful, life-giving air-current that was! Every day the miracle happened and every day this wind over the waters, this light fanning of heavenly breath across a swamp of mud, had quickened us and obliterated for an hour all memory of the awful aftermath. No, not quite obliterated, but dulled the memory for perhaps five minutes; and then the contrast between this hour and the following ones would rise up in our minds and strike the brightness from our eyes.

By the time I arrived in the rear van at the Beled Ruz supply depôt half the convoy had off-loaded and the drivers were busy filling their radiators. Little time was lost in completing the business, and shortly after eleven o'clock the men were ready for the return-journey.

After instructing the sergeant who led the convoy to wait for the tail at Mahrut, I watched the vans leave their parking ground. I noticed that most of the men looked as fit as could be expected. I spoke to several whose physical unfitness for the job was obvious and who ought still to have been in hospital, asking them if they had enough chlorinated drinking-water in their *chagals* for the journey, and telling them to fall out of the convoy and stop their cars instantly if they felt un-well. Very often, I knew from bitter experience, a man would drive on until he fainted, with disastrous results, when a little water in time might have saved him.

Every car except my own and Sergeant Stuart's 'breakdown' van had now left.

'That dust-storm has made us an hour late today, Sergeant,' I said. 'I'm afraid we'll have a bad run back.'

But Stuart was an optimist. 'I've got enough spare tubes for as many punctures as there are cars,' he re-plied, jerking his thumb towards the back of his van. The appalling heat from the ground made punctures our first consideration. Everything else, from breakage to engine-trouble, was child's play to Stuart, who was happy if he had a sufficiency of tubes. But 27 July was an exceptional day even for the summer of 1917; and as the dust-storm that morning had made us an hour late, Stuart's optimism was not well-founded.

Everything went well until the convoy had passed the *bund* and was panting along in the desert beyond. Then a wind sprang up and followed us all the way to Baqubah. A following wind in the open desert, on a day when the thermometers in the tents registered 133 degrees, is a thing that cannot be described. When, in addition there is the heat of an engine that converts all the water in its radiator to steam every twenty minutes, words become meaningless. The vans began to fall out of their position with maddening persistence. The inner tubes seemed to have no greater resistence than paper. Even the outer covers could not withstand the heat, and Stuart's stock of spares was running low before we reached Mahrut. Worse still, the men had to use their own too-slender supply of drinking-water for the radiators.

At last it became well-nigh impossible to touch the wheel-rims. Fortunately Stuart had a pair of gloves, but this meant that only one man at a time could do the work. The tyre-levers were so hot that the slightest grip of one blistered the hand that pressed it. The sun streamed down pitilessly on the backs of men engaged in repair-work and drove them fainting to their seats. The wind scorched; the ground threw off sweltering fumes; the men's throats became parched, and they were seized with a fearful giddiness.

The situation at Mahrut was serious. Six men were incapable of facing the remaining fifteen miles. Luckily there were six spare drivers, so the vans of those who were left in the tiny tent-hospital could continue the journey to Baqubah. Every drop of water the post commandant could spare was swallowed up, lukewarm though it was, by the gasping men. Stuart shook his head and 'doubted the advisability' of proceeding. But we had no alternative. It was necessary to reach camp in time for the men to load the cars and have a rest.

Tomorrow, I reminded Stuart, food would be wanted for the troops at Shahroban. Their existence depended on our labour.

During that Mesopotamian summer humour was at a premium between 10 a.m. and 5 p.m. The same old joke got the same helpless grin a hundred times in succession. Men were too weary to think of something new and too warm to protest against a repetition of the old. From sheer mental vacuity, I added: 'At Shahroban we'll join the infantry and lead a quiet life.' Stuart allowed his features to form the necessary grin and the convoy moved off.

The heat now was terrible. A curious idea struck me. I pictured God dancing and clapping his hands and singing a song with the refrain: 'Got you now! Got you now! Got you now!' Another idea crossed my mind. The phrase 'Hell with the lid off' was wrong. This monstrous congestion of elemental horror, this atmospherical strangulation, was Hell with the lid *on*. There was nothing about it that remotely suggested escape, not even an escape from frying-pan to fire. It stifled and choked; its ghastly oppressiveness made one dizzy.

Suddenly I became aware of the man by my side. Hope was speaking to me, but I could not summon up the mental energy to listen. I said 'Yes' vaguely at intervals. Then it dawned on me that he was talking of his family and home. Odd words filtered through the mental vacuum that enveloped me. 'Eight kiddies,' he seemed to be saying, 'and the missus a rare mother to every one of 'em. . . . I'd like to see 'em grow up, I would. . . . They was doin' nicely when I 'ad to join up. . . . John— that's the eldest, sir—'e wanted to come along o' me— only ten years old. . . . It give me the 'ump to leave 'em. . . .'

The van pulled up and I got out mechanically. It was

only another puncture. No one spoke a syllable. Slowly
and painfully the job was finished. Breathing became
an effort. Action was divorced from volition. Every
motion was automatic, unfelt, meaningless. Death and
decay were around us, cutting us off from the living
breathing world. I gave a hand and then leant against
one of the cars, exhausted and half-conscious. A burning
pain shot through me. The heat of a piece of steel that
I was propped against had seared my flesh. I cursed
and staggered back to my van.

The tail of the convoy moved on, stopped, moved
on again, stopped again. I groaned. The weariness of it!
Out and in, out and in, out and in . . . a puncture, a
carburettor choked with dust, a boiling radiator, a
nearly fainting driver . . . and always the endless chatter
of Hope. Why on earth did the man go on talking?
What could he find to talk about? Tormenting though
they were, the halts and exposures beneath the merci-
less sun were almost a relief after the nerve-racking
stream of Hope's raucous repetitions. Perhaps the poor
fellow was suffering from a touch of the sun. Or perhaps
he was trying to forget the miserable present by calling
up memories of the past. Always those 'eight kiddies'—
he kept harping on them—and 'the missus'.

Something began to buzz and sing in my head. The
desert danced before my eyes. The screen in front of
me was twisted into strange shapes. That last exposure
must have done the trick. Damn! Whatever happened
I must not lose consciousness. I gripped the seat beneath me in an agony of apprehension. Then, after an
interval of blackness and whirling spots, consciousness
returned and I saw the date-palms on the Diala. 'Hur-
rah!' I cried, but my voice sounded unearthly, unfamiliar, as though someone else had spoken.

'D'you think they'd give me a month in Blighty, sir?'
Hope was still babbling; but now I listened atten-

tively, because I wanted to make sure that my fainting fit was over.

'I've bin out 'ere the best part of two years, an' they're always writin' to ask me why I don't come 'ome.'

'Well, you see, it's not easy to be sure of anything,' I said, picking my words with an effort. 'The war's not over yet and they want every man that can be spared— Hullo! what's wrong?'

The car had swerved. Hope was leaning over the steering-wheel. His hands were still trying to do their work; but an instant later they shot from under him and his face fell forward. In a last convulsive movement his left foot pressed on the brake and the car pulled up with a violent jerk.

He was dead.

The tail of the convoy stopped for the last time, and Hope's body was lifted into the back of the van. Through the blinding glare of the afternoon sun I drove the dead man into Baqubah. At the entrance of the camp I noticed three enormous hawks wheeling slowly in the airless void above us.

That summer took a heavy toll of our men, and it was a company of semi-invalids who arrived in September for the new push on the Euphrates front, where I saw something of my friend Dick Hammond, as well as the battle of Ramadi, after which I was at death's door for some weeks with the combined attack of dysentery and malaria. Discharged from hospital in November, I rejoined my unit for the Persian campaign.

I got on well with my men, because I hated all the red-tape and discipline of the army and let them do their jobs without interference. Regarding punishment as a confession of incompetence in those who imposed it, I abolished the childish regulations whereby fellows were 'crimed' for misdemeanours; I shared in their labours, and closely attended to their rations; with the

result that we did better work than any other M.T.
unit on the Line of Communication, and whenever anything really difficult had to be achieved we were invariably chosen for the job. By getting food and equip-
ment through very difficult country and keeping up the
supply, we enabled the famous Dunsterforce to enter
Persia; and at the end of it all I found myself mentioned
in despatches 'for gallant and distinguished services in
the Field', which made me feel rather silly, knowing
as I did that every single man under my command
deserved the honour quite as much as I.

As one's life sometimes depended on not being left
in the desert for a night with a broken-down car, and
as I would not subject anyone else to such an ordeal
(there being a rule that cars must not be abandoned),
I made up my mind to learn all about the mechanism of
the things, and did so, forgetting it all when the knowledge was no longer vital. Once, when I had remained
behind to tinker with a fellow's car while the pass we
were penetrating was under fire, a piece of flying metal
caught me on the top of the head and knocked me out.
Some years elapsed before my scalp was properly
cleaned up, and it is possible that the trouble while it
lasted had a slight effect on my brain. All I know is that,
during a legal case in which I was involved some years
later, an old friend, Douglas Jefferies, volunteered to
bear witness that ever since the war I had been a little
crazy, which amused me vastly at the time.

At one time or another there were some sharp interchanges between me and my superior officers, the
acrimony of which may have been partly due to the
pressure of foreign substances on my skull, though I
disagreed with them fundamentally on the subject of
discipline, much of which is merely due to power-mania.
In one case I took a very grave risk. Two of my fellows,
exhausted by overwork, were found asleep on their posts

at night when my O.C., arriving unexpectedly, was not challenged. We were on the eve of an action, so he contented himself with putting them under close arrest, ordering me to repeat the formalities every twenty-four hours until the end of the present emergency, and then to have them court-martialled. I knew that this would almost certainly result in their being shot, and decided to take a chance. In other words I forgot all about it, told my sergeant to do the same; and my O.C's attention was so much absorbed by the battle and its consequences that he forgot, too. Had he remembered, and found that I had failed to remand the men every day, the court-martial might have had to sit upon me.

Occasionally my hatred of unnecessary rules and regulations led to amusing results. Though I had practically abolished 'orderly rooms', criming men, and all the rest of the nonsense, I was compelled by my sergeant-major now and then to take notice of certain misdemeanours, and one day he insisted on parading before me a lad named Tasker, who had damaged his car through carelessness. Having no option, I reprimanded him, King's Regs. making it necessary that the cost of the damage should be deducted from his pay. I did what was required of me in a very half-hearted apologetic manner, afterwards taking the lad on one side and giving him the money with which in my official capacity I had been forced to tax him.

Before the Dunsterforce went into Persia, I was ordered to report on the condition of the tracks through the country as far as Hamadan. A small British force had reached the Pai Tak Pass, which roughly divides Irak from Persia, but General Dunsterville would not risk a journey through Persia to the Caspian Sea until he was assured that the country was penetrable by motor transport. Accompanied by my driver and a Persian guide, I started off one morning at seven o'clock, and found at the top of the Pass that the hills and valleys were covered with snow. At every village through which we passed the inhabitants were in a horrible condition, due to successive occupations by Turks and Cossacks. Those who had not been starved or frozen to death and who had strength enough to stand on their feet were more like famished wolves than human beings. The weaker ones fell on their knees to beg for food and fought one another with all their remaining strength for the bits we could spare them. The stronger ones were dangerous, and to save our skins we had to keep a bright look-out, sometimes firing above their heads to frighten them off. I wished that everyone who thought war romantic could have seen what I saw: a whole people dying off and transformed into animals.

For three days we picked our way between Karind and Hamadan, spending the nights in the open as far as possible from human habitation. There was no proper road, only a rough track that meandered among the rocks of the mountain passes and lost itself in the quagmires of the plain. Several times we were bogged, and more than once I was on the point of turning the car round and giving it up as a hopeless task. But we always managed to dig ourselves out and to find some way round or over the obstacle of the moment; and on the morning of the fourth day we stood, dead-beat and half-frozen, in front of the consul's house at Hamadan. Having despatched my business there, and seen to my driver's accommodation and garaged the car, I started off with my native guide to call on MacMurray, manager of the Persian Bank, with whom I was to spend a couple of nights before returning.

Our way lay through a veritable hive of stinking lanes and depopulated bazaars. In spite of my own acute discomforts, I could not help noticing the frightful sights that met the eye on every hand and the disgusting odours that assailed the nose at every turn. Dead or dying people, mostly very old or very young, lay in corners and doorways. The groans of the sick and dying filled the air, and in many cases the dead had been left for days and weeks to putrefy. The whole of the weak and defence-less portion of the community was being killed off by hunger, and the air was poisoned with the stench of decomposition. The bones of the victims showed bare through their drawn and wasted flesh. I hurried through these pest-holes as fast as their human obstructions would permit, with my guide shuffling along behind me and plucking at my right or left arm when he wished to signify a change of direction. Large flakes of snow percolated through the battered, creviced roofs of the bazaars, and the slushy ground made our progress both slow and arduous.

As we were threading our way through a particularly rank maze of tortuous alleys, each of which looked like a cul-de-sac, I became aware of a long-drawn murmur, which rose and fell like the unearthly cry of jackals in a palm-grove. At first I paid little heed to it. I was too intent on reaching my journey's end and shaking off the all-pervading nightmare of suffering and death to think of anything else. But the sound increased in vol-ume the further we went, and at length I stopped to listen. It was no longer a murmur but a roar—a roar of angry brutal voices. It seemed to encompass us, though that, I knew, must have been the echo. My Persian guide could not enlighten me, but fingered nervously at my sleeve urging me on. There was nothing for it but to continue on our way. The noise was now almost deafening. Yells mingled with hootings, and there was something inhuman in the hoarse hungry monotone that formed a perpetual accompaniment to the devilish din.

At one spot where a lane, wider than most, cut through the bazaar, we stopped again. In a moment, so it seemed, a solid wall of humanity appeared on our left, hurled itself upon us, and swept us along the lane to an open space a few hundred yards further down. Physical force was about as much use as verbal protestation to deal with this impact. It never entered my head to attempt either. I had no time for reflection. But the moment we reached the clearing I bolted for a doorway on the opposite side, turned to face the mob and drew my revolver. I was amazed to see that no one was taking the slightest notice of me, that no one seemed aware of my presence. Having had no time to consider the position, I had naturally regarded the incident up to now as an assault on myself.

The square was full in an instant, but everyone's attention was directed to something in the centre, and the jostling to which I was subjected as I stood on the doorstep was merely due to lack of room. Someone by my side laughed. I glanced round and saw my Persian guide. He too, though only just recovering from a very natural trembling-fit, was staring over the crowd towards the centre of the square. For a while I failed to make out the cause of the disturbance. Standing on the doorstep we had a good view of the proceedings; but beyond noticing the fierce faces and wild gestures of the vociferating spectators, I remained for a few minutes completely in the dark as to their meaning.

Suddenly the crowd began to surge backwards, and I noticed that a clearing was being formed by about twenty men, taller and stronger than the rest, who appeared to be controlling matters in the foreground. Then, down a lane of bawling livid humanity, two half-naked women came running towards the open space. They ran, crouching, their arms over their heads, as if to protect themselves from the blows of the mob. Instantly the crowd closed up behind them and they stood, bent and shaking, in the ring formed by the human wolves, who continued to rend the air with their yells, moans and hisses.

I was so much absorbed by the spectacle, wondering what it was all about, that I forgot everything else, and I was only made conscious of my immediate surroundings by a violent wrench at my wrist. With a shock I discovered that my revolver had gone, that I was now defenceless. The crowd was pressing upon me and forcing me back against the door. 'No good, sahib—pistol gone. Sorry, sahib—I did not see in time.' My Persian guide was speaking. He was still by my side. But the scene in the square still held me spellbound and I could think of nothing else. Without troubling to follow up my loss, I beseiged the fellow with questions. What was going to happen? Why were the people shouting? What was the matter? Why were the two women there? And so forth. In a few words he told me the truth. I gasped and went cold all over. I might have dropped if I had not been held upright by the pressure of the crowd. These two wretched souls had gone mad with hunger and had eaten their own children. They had been dragged here by their fellow-citizens to be stoned to death.

I remained for some time in a dazed condition, overcome by the horror of what I had heard. The fact that I was hemmed in and could not get away made my situation all the more intolerable. A shrill scream from one of the women brought me back to full consciousness. I gazed out over the multitude to where a tall man at the edge of the clearing was lifting a large stone above his head with both hands. A moment of tense silence. Thud. . . . It struck the woman on the breast, and a thin spurt of blood streaked the tattered gown with which she tried to ward off the cruel blow. A demoniacal howl rose from a thousand throats, and the writhing form of the helpless victim was pounded with a hail of bricks and dirt.

I scarcely know what followed. A murderous fit seized me, and had I kept possession of my revolver several in the crowd would have gone to join the miserable object of their wrath. With a strength born of momentary insanity, I fought my way through that obscene gang of brute-beings, and found myself some minutes later, lame and dishevelled, in a large yard, where I sat down to regain my breath. My guide had kept close behind me and now begged me to follow him without a second's delay. Realizing our danger, I did so.

When we reached our destination he handed me a revolver. 'Where did you get this?' I demanded. 'It is yours, sahib. I took it from you. It was safer with me.' I looked at the man's impassive face, but said nothing. He had probably saved my life.

In the middle of 1919 I was furnished with the epilogue to this tragedy. Passing through Persia for the last time, I dined with MacMurray. Several other British officers were guests, as well as the Persian Chief of Gendarmes, and the state of the country before the arrival of our troops became a topic of conversation.

'Yes, they were bad days, bad days,' said the Chief of Gendarmes. 'Your country, gentlemen, pulled us out of a nasty hole. But there are few among you who saw us at our worst. There were cases of cannibalism—dreadful, dreadful! One does not care to think of them. Those women—you remember them, Mr MacMurray?—they were unlucky.'

'Yes, yes, I remember them,' sighed our host, shaking his head and looking at me.

'How, unlucky?' I asked.

'Well, you see, it was so general,' replied the Persian. 'They were caught in the act, as you say; there were plenty more.'

'I suppose they were both killed,' I said, more from a desire to close the subject than from curiosity.

'Killed? Yes. And cooked, my dear sir.'

'Cooked?' I cried.

'Naturally,' he answered, lifting his eyebrows in mild surprise. 'Cooked and eaten. . . . But what would you? The people were so hungry.'

In spite of the horrible scene I had witnessed, my trip made me interested in Persia, and a few months later, following the capture of Kirkuk in which we took part, I managed to get transferred to a heavy lorry unit stationed at Kermanshah. Here I nearly succumbed to a fever that killed off dozens of men in the camp, my own recovery being largely due to the attention and companionship of a new acquaintance, Colin Hurry, who had been sent up the line by G.H.Q. to discover why all the material despatched from Baghdad did not reach its proper destination. Our lifelong friendship commenced at Kermanshah, though I had met him once before at Khanikin. His was the only first-rate intelligence I encountered during my life in the army.

Though I cannot state it as a positive fact, I believe that my recovery from other illnesses was largely due, not to the remedies of the physicians, but to the spiritual medicine administered by Shakespeare, whose *Henry IV* had under pressure of war become my favourite among his works, remaining so to this day. The delight I took in Falstaff and his companions somehow increased my resistance to disease by lifting my spirit and lightening the burden of mortality. I have already written of this queer miracle in the preface to my *Life of Shakespeare*; but since then I have recalled that another curative source was Bernard Shaw's *Caesar and Cleopatra*, which engaged so much of my cogitation from time to time that I wrote to the author asking for autobiographical details of his *Plays for Puritans*. A long letter from him gave me intense joy, and the memory of it as I write prompts me to mention my old debt to him.

The author

The Pearson family. Standing: the author's father (Henry) and Harry; seated (left to right): Jack, the author's mother with Elsie on her knee, and Hesketh, aged five

The author's birthplace: Hawford near Worcester (from a water colour by the author's Aunt Eva)

On his world tour, 1908: Hesketh Pearson, aged 21, at Niagara Falls

The author in uniform, 1914-18 War

On the stage: Godfrey Tearle and Hesketh Pearson (right) in The Fake, *Apollo Theatre, London, 1924*

With his first wife, Gladys, and his son, Henry

Forbes-Robertson

Granville Barker

With George Bernard Shaw in 1945

With Malcolm Muggeridge

Colin Hurry

With Hugh Kingsmill

Hesketh Pearson's second wife, Joyce

My service in the East of two a half years closed with a battle between myself and the authorities. I was asked to lecture the troops on demobilization, and I was expected to fill them up with a lot of nonsense about the difficulties of getting home. Instead I told them the naked truth as I saw it, with catastrophic results at G.H.Q. For a while it looked as if I would have to face a court-martial, but a convocation of colonels thought better of it, and I was taken on the staff as a precautionary measure, becoming a captain when placed in charge of personnel. My time in Baghdad was made bearable by plenty of golf, tennis and bridge, and above all by letters from my men in 784 Company, which showed that, whatever my shortcomings as an officer according to King's Regulations, I had won their confidence.

While on the staff I became involved in an incident that might have assumed international significance if it had not been blanketed by the chaos that followed the war. Early in 1919 the British authorities were asked to oblige the Shah of Persia, whose grandfather had remained embalmed at Teheran for several years awaiting burial among his ancestors at Kerbela, the holy city on the Euphrates. Until the British arrived in 1918 the road had not been safe enough for the orderly conduct of his corpse, but now there were no difficulties in the way, and we at once obliged the Persian Court by arranging a funeral to start across Mesopotamia from Bagdad. A Ford van was sent to Teheran, and the shell containing the late monarch was deposited therein. The driver had received a characteristically laconic order to collect:

Box, one, containing deceased Shah,

but he had received no notification whatever of the possibly ceremonial nature of his duties. Several courtiers, who were to accompany the body to its last resting-

place, were in attendance on horseback. They anticipated a slow and triumphal procession over the moun-
tains and across the plains. They would, they felt certain, be received as honoured mourners at the towns and
villages of Persia and Mesopotamia through which they
passed and share the reflected glory of the royal remains.

But they were doomed to sudden and bitter disappointment. No sooner had the solemn transference
from vault to van taken place than the driver jumped
into his seat and sent the car bounding out of the court-
yard. Before they had recovered from their surprise
and mortification, the van was cutting along the main
street of the metropolis. They tore after it breathlessly.
They drew their revolvers with the intention of firing
at it the moment they got within range. Near the
principal gate of the town the van was momentarily held
up by the traffic. This gave its pursuers time to get within a hundred yards of it. They came racing round the
corner of the street, saw the van, which was just about
to get into top speed once more, and opened fire on the
disappearing vehicle. The bullets flew wide and scattered
the rest of the traffic with startling effect. The entrance
to the gate was clear in an instant, and through it the
courtiers could see the van flying down the road with the
coffin dancing about in the back like a pea on a drum.
The driver imagined that a revolution had broken out
as a direct consequence of his removal of the august
relics, and did not stop to ask questions. He ran for
several miles on a flat tyre.

The courtiers returned to the palace and eventually
managed to get the necessary mechanical transport in
which to continue the pursuit. But the fleet-wheeled
hearse ahead of them had obtained a good start, and
after three days' strenuous travelling arrived at Karind,
where the driver went in search of refreshment. Unfortunately he did not think it necessary to describe the

precise nature of his load to the camp officials at that post, and the N.C.O. in charge of the supply depôt, thinking the box contained bully beef, gave orders for it to be dumped with the other provisions. In due course the driver returned to his van, discovered his loss, reported it, and a hue and cry was immediately raised. At this point the courtiers arrived at the post and were informed of the occurrence. They promptly demanded the execution of the driver. Sensation. . . .

After the telegraph lines between Bagdad and Teheran had been reeling with neurotic messages for several hours, the box on the supply dump was opened for the bully beef it was supposed to contain, the mistake was discovered, the Shah was restored to his distraught countrymen, and, with myself as guard of honour representing his Britannic Majesty's Government, the coffin-bumping was modified for the remainder of the journey to Kerbela.

My own funeral, as prophesied by the doctors, should have taken place long before this; but somehow I survived, leaving Baghdad in November 1919 and arriving home in time for Christmas. My physical appearance convinced my wife that I needed lots of plum pudding, my height being six feet two inches, my weight eight stone eleven pounds.

PART

II

7

Suicide of an Actor

It was a sunny December day as we sailed up Plymouth Sound and I realized for the second time in my life, the first perception having occurred on my return from America eleven years before, that I was an Englishman through and through. The sight of the green fields and hedges tugged at my heart and brought tears to my eyes, this emotion being speedily followed by roars of laughter as we caught sight of a policeman on the quay, and the soldiers on board, many of whom had been in the desert for two or three years and forgotten the existence of such a person, gave vent to a yell of 'Bobbee-ee-ee', which flabbergasted the man in blue, who hurried away from it, his rapid disappearance adding to the general gaiety.

Tree and Alexander had died in my absence, while Granville Barker had deserted the stage for a life of luxury, so I had to find a new employer, the Shakespeare Society having no money to pay a decent salary. I received the usual gratuity for my rank in the army, and soon a small pension for my (apparently) incurable diseases, malaria and dysentery, which returned at intervals until Shaw advised me to try an unregistered practitioner, Raphel Roche, whose treatment put me right about two years after my return, when of course my pension ceased. After a short holiday at Amberley in Sussex with my wife, I wrote for an appointment with

153

Dennis Eadie, who was then running the Royalty Theatre. He asked me to call and see him, and at our meeting said that Alexander had spoken of me in glowing terms. He was about to revive Sir James Barrie's *The Admirable Crichton* and offered me £6 a week to understudy him in the name part. It was just what I wanted: very little to do, and enough to live on while doing it.

Barrie was the most successful dramatist of his time, though he never received the deference paid to Pinero, possibly because the critics felt a little ashamed that he could make them cry so easily. He touched and sometimes twanged the heartstrings to such effect that the hardened occupants of the stalls sobbed audibly. By publishing the fact that he hated publicity, he obtained more of it than any of his rivals except Shaw, whose political views got him a double dose. I had never seen Barrie, guessed from his work that he would be rather foppish in appearance, and assumed during rehearsals that the insignificant little fellow waddling up and down the stall gangways in an overcoat, woollen muffler and bowler was Dennis Eadie's financial backer. He was smoking a large pipe and borrowed a match from me, warning me that he would probably steal the box if I did not keep an eye on him. He seemed a pleasant chap, so I asked if the author ever came to rehearsals. He replied that the author was nearly always present, and then, becoming very mysterious, he said that the author and himself were as like as two peas and that he helped to write Barrie's plays. I displayed incredulity, and he waddled off. 'He must think me an absolute idiot', I said to myself, feeling convinced of it when I discovered that he had taken my box of matches. I asked an actor near by, 'Who's that little blighter in the bowler? He's pinched my matches.' 'That little blighter in the bowler is Sir James Barrie,' said the actor.

On his next perambulation Barrie stopped and said to me: 'I have discovered half-a-dozen boxes of matches in my overcoat pocket. If one of them is yours, you may take it.' I took it. 'Seen Barrie yet?' he asked. 'Yes.' 'Good. I told you he was not unlike me,' and he rolled down the gangway. A week or so later he sat next to me in the stalls and I asked him about his first published book, *Better Dead*, in which the chief character tries to murder a number of eminent people, fails, and is then tempted to crack the skulls of his two lovely babies. I felt that it represented the author's real feelings far more accurately than *Peter Pan*, but it gave him no pleasure when I said how much it had amused me, and he declared that he would like to destroy every copy in existence. I could understand his point of view, for by this time he had become a highly respected member of the community, a baronet who mixed with barons. An early friend of his, A. E. W. Mason, told me that 'towards the end of his life Barrie became very fond of duchesses'. He also began to appear at public functions, such as the burial of Thomas Hardy in Westminster Abbey, at which he acted as pall-bearer along with Bernard Shaw, John Galsworthy and Rudyard Kipling. 'Galsworthy and I were six-footers,' said Shaw, describing the scene to me, 'and Barrie, realizing that he could not stand up to us, made his effect by miraculously managing to look exactly three inches high.'

One wonders what the Barrie of *Better Dead* would have thought of the author of *The Admirable Crichton*, who for his revival tagged on to the play a bit of patriotic piffle which made me shrink every time I had to say it at understudy rehearsals. The real actor should be able to speak any balderdash as if he meant it; but I was always more of a critic than an actor.

During my service in the East, Gladys had taken a house, No. 88 Abbey Road, St John's Wood, in which friends of hers, Ethel and Maud Denny, with their mother and their nephew Donald Gordon occupied the upper part while we had the lower half, remaining there for nineteen years. At the beginning of 1920 our son Henry was a boy of seven, quite transformed from the child I had kissed for the last time, as I then believed, three years earlier. In the state of my health and the precariousness of my income we decided to have no more children, and never regretted our decision, as we were quite satisfied with our own company.

The revival of Barrie's play was fairly successful, and when it came to an end I was asked by Madame Donnet to play the student Trofimov in Tchekov's *The Cherry Orchard*, a production by The Art Theatre. Presumably I gave satisfaction because my friend Violet Dean, secretary of The Art Theatre, told me that Madame Donnet intended to put on *Macbeth* with myself in the chief part. But no more was heard of the organization, and by that time I was sufficiently aware of my histrionic defects to be dismayed at the prospect of acting the most difficult part in the world's dramatic literature.

The autumn of 1920 saw me playing the guardian of the two children in *The Blue Lagoon*, a dramatic version of de Vere Stacpoole's popular novel. With elaborate scenic effects, the show was produced by Basil Dean at The Prince of Wales Theatre and ran for about nine months. Mine was a dreary part and a long run made me play it in a drowsy manner. In two or three months I was repeating the words automatically, and at the end of six months I was scarcely aware of what I was saying. One evening the automatic process broke down. In the opening scene on board ship I had to tell the story of the two children to the captain of the boat, beginning with the words: 'Little Emmeline's father, captain, died before she was born; her mother died in giving her birth.' Instead of that I started off: 'Little

Emmeline's mother, captain, died before she was born.'
Unaware of my error, I was surprised to observe the
contorted look on the captain's face, and anxious to
steady him I emphasized my next remark: 'Her father
died in giving her birth.' The audience might have remained calm if the orchestra had not just filed in for
the music of the storm scene, and knowing the play by
heart a few of them guffawed. Instantly the house took
it up and rocked with laughter, while the captain turned
his back on the audience and shook from bow to stern.
Fortunately the stage-manager was equal to the occasion and gave all the signals for the ensuing hurricane,
when to my great relief the ship went down and the
nature of the joke was explained to me.

Something more important for me than my nightly
appearances on the stage occurred during the run of the
piece. I had a long wait between the first and last acts,
which I often spent with Colin Hurry in some near-by
bar, and one night he took me to a pub which was then
situated in a passage between Regent and Vine streets
and introduced me to a friend of his named James
Mitchell, a Scot of remarkable intelligence, who hid an
affectionate nature under the guise of cynicism, had
a wide knowledge of human beings expressed in the
form of paradox, and loved to argue that if his antagonist could not see that green was red he must be colour-
blind. In the years ahead James and I spent many evenings together, often developing into early mornings, and
our friendship was cemented over innumerable dis-
agreements and many bottles of wine.

My next job was with Nigel Playfair, who opened a
season at the Playhouse, Liverpool, in September 1921,
with Harold Chapin's *The New Morality*, in which I
played the husband, Colonel Ivor Jones. The following
month my first book, *Modern Men and Mummers*,
appeared.

It was the height of irresponsibility. If I had wished to wreck my stage career, I could not have set about it more effectively. The book contained pen-portraits of famous actor-managers and accounts of their doings which were libellous enough to prevent any living producer or manager from employing so rash a chronicler, so indiscreet a critic. I heard from various sources that those who were not furious were frightened. Before publication it was necessary to obtain Shaw's permission to quote some of his letters to me, for which purpose he had seen a few pages of the book in proof. His advice was admirable, and I ought to have taken it. He said that Gerald Cumberland had published a book about living people with just my recklessness: 'The result was that his next book was so ruthlessly boycotted by the reviewers that both the writer and his publisher appealed to me—one of his victims—to say a word for him in public.' Words of wisdom followed: 'The more candidly you criticize, the more delicately you must draw the line between what may be said and what may not. In short, your manners must be as good as your brains if you are to make good your claim to criticize. You must give your man the republican respect that is due to him before you pull his work to pieces. And all criticism of his conduct must start from that basis. Nothing is worse than a sneer, even though it may not incur damages.' Shaw's feelings when I showed him the publisher's contract for my book were strongly expressed:

'Hesketh, you are a dunderhead!' he began.

'Thank you. But why?'

'This contract, man!'

'What's wrong with it?'

'What's *right* with it? If you sign it, you won't make a penny. You are presenting your work to them, gratis; and lest your widow should benefit by it, you are letting them have the profits for fifty years after your death.'

'But it's on a sharing basis.'

'Sharing fiddlesticks! You'll share their overhead expenses—that's all the sharing you'll do. Are you completely devoid of business sense? You should demand £50 down, fifteen per cent on the first thousand copies and twenty per cent on all sales above a thousand.'

'Well, I'm afraid I've practically agreed to sign the contract as it stands.'

'Oh, of course, if you want to give your work away with a pound of tea, no one can stop you. God help you! Anyhow, there's always the work-house to fall back on. The only thing that surprises me is that you aren't paying them handsomely to publish it for you.'

'What do you suggest?'

'I doubt if you're worth saving, though your high opinion of my work shows that you are not altogether a lost soul. If you like I'll refuse to let you publish my letters for a farthing less than £10 a word.'

'I can't ask you to do that; it wouldn't be treating them fairly.'

'Then your wife must make the next move. Go home and tell her to divorce you. She's not safe with you. She must find a man with a large private income, or one who can make four out of two and two. This is a serious matter. You shouldn't be at large. Good-bye; and don't come to me for advice when you're in the bankruptcy court.'

Again I should have taken Shaw's advice, but I had as little commercial sense as I had common-sense, and I went blindly to my doom. At a distance of forty years the whole thing seems trivial enough; but when I say that except for Sir George Alexander and H. B. Irving, all the people named in the following extract from my book were not only alive and important but excessively touchy, the careless nature of my proceeding will be appreciated. This was my description of what happened when the committee of leading West-End actors set about the job of casting the parts in *Julius Caesar* for the Shakespeare Tercentenary Commemoration performance at Drury Lane in 1916:

The first decision George Alexander came to, as chairman of the casting sub-committee, was to cut himself completely out of the cast. He would, as a matter of fact, have played Brutus better than anyone, and he would have enjoyed doing it, but he decided to take no part in it on the ground that the younger men should be given a chance. He suggested Matheson Lang for Brutus and the committee agreed, though without much enthusiasm from one or two quarters. Thereafter it was adumbrated that Mr Arthur Bourchier felt slighted at being passed over, he having already played the part with Sir Herbert Tree at His Majesty's Theatre, receiving high praise for his performance from all those who believed he might again go into management on his own account and be of some use to them. Delicately, therefore, Mr Bourchier absented himself from the next meeting of the casting committee, and the crisis was discussed.

'I can't see him in the part myself,' said Alexander. 'Nor can anyone else,' said H. B. Irving. 'Except himself,' chipped in Gerald Du Maurier. Everyone agreed finally that he was the very last man for the part—and everyone agreed finally that he must be cast for it. 'We mustn't have bad feeling on the committee.' Alexander summed up, 'so I'm afraid there's only one thing for it: give him the part and he'll help us on the committee, don't give it him and we'll never hear the end of it.' The general feeling of the committee being that matters would run more smoothly with Bourchier soothed by Brutus than ruffled by Flavius or Marullus, it was agreed that the part should be offered him. (Note. Thus placated, he literally ate out of the committee's hands thenceforward.)

Next came the question of Mark Antony. Alexander said, 'Henry Ainley.' After the Bourchier episode everyone agreed hastily, almost falling over one another in their excitement to eclipse themselves utterly. There was, for a moment, a perfect craze for self-suppression. 'What about Cassius?' queried Sir George. 'I suggest Harry,' he continued, turning to H. B. Irving. 'Yes, yes, admirable,' murmured the committee. 'No, no, what of the younger men?' risked H. B. It certainly was a risk, because the rest of the committee were beginning to wonder what *they* would be doing when all the fat parts had been bestowed. The committee murmured correct responses, but the post-Bourchier enthusiasm was noticeably on the wane; so, veering to the only safe point on the compass. H.B. asked Alexander: 'Do you really think it would be best?' And, comforted by the latter's reply, he quickly accepted in the following well-chosen words: 'I shall try to deserve the honour you all do me, but I will gladly retire in favour of anyone more worthy than I—and there are many.' No one feeling equal to the occasion, Alexander rapidly went on with the casting. 'I think,' he said, 'that I am not only voicing the opinion of the committee but of the whole theatrical profession, as well as the general public, when I say that Frank Benson should play the title-rôle.' This time there was manifested quite honest enthusiasm, not only because Frank had no enemies, but also because the part of Julius Caesar is the most thankless title-rôle in the whole body of English dramatic art, and everyone knew that dear old Benson couldn't possibly out-mouth Caesar's mouthing. It was a piece of casting both safe and popular. Also no member of the committee hankered after the part. Benson bowed his head gracefully before the storm of eager gratulation, and accepted his fate with becoming modesty and thankfulness.

Mutually complimentary speeches having been given and received, there was a lull, at the end of which Du Maurier asked to be put down for one of the citizens. This terrific act of self-abasement sent a shudder through everybody present. The tension was increased when Charles Hawtrey said that he would 'walk-on'. Everyone was of course thankful they had not suggested themselves for serious parts, but for decency's sake it was generally felt they should have

kept silent and 'let determined things to destiny hold un-
bewailed their way.' But it is a wonderful and beautiful
thing to see a great man humbling himself, for in few other
ways can he be so exalted. Curiously enough, however, the
disease is not catching, and the rest of the committee regarded the action of these two in the light of a joke, quite
characteristic of both comedians. I solemnly entered their
names under the heading of 'Citizens with lines' (i.e. lines
supplied by Shakespeare, not those left to the imagination
of the incoherent if articulate mob) and the serious business
of the meeting was resumed.

Casca was the next part to be cast. Everyone agreed that
it should be given to a corpulent member of the fraternity.
Someone said (I think it was Ben Greet, but my notes do not
help me here) that this was the part Bourchier ought to play.
Sensation. Alexander emphatically intervened. 'That's already settled by vote of the committee,' he said, scenting
the danger. 'We must think of someone else.'

'Who has the larger belly—Asche or Calvert?' asked
Hawtrey. The subject of stomachs was carefully gone into,
and Oscar Asche gained the suffrages of the majority. He
was duly cast for the part.

There now only remained the subsidiary parts. The final
decision as to these was left to Alexander, but a number of
names were definitely pronounced worthy of inclusion,
among others Martin Harvey and Fred Terry, neither of
whom was present.

Finally I read several letters. One of them was from
Godfrey Tearle, begging to be allowed to take any part,
long or short, in the performance, and offering his services
as an assistant stage-manager, or in any other drudging
capacity. Charles Hawtrey promptly objected on the ground
that Tearle was not in khaki. 'I,' said he, 'will sever my connection with the whole affair if Tearle is allowed to do anything.' This virtuous and patriotic sentiment, coming as it
did from a man of such high standing in his profession, was
perforce echoed by his comrades, if somewhat shame-
facedly by the younger ones, who felt they themselves might
be called to the colours if the war went on long enough. But

Hawtrey, in the full security of his age, bated no jot of his martial vigour. The fact that 'Dear Old Charley' had been through the Bankruptcy Courts was a feather in the scale against the immense issues now involved, and Godfrey Tearle was sacrificed by the committee on the altar of Hawtrey's civic morality.

Having thus satisfied their consciences, both by the work they imagined they had done and the patriotic tinge that had been imparted to their disinterested endeavours, the committee broke up. It is hardly necessary to add that George Alexander had guided and inspired all the work except the black-balling episode just related.

In this light-hearted fashion I treated many other notable personalities of the time, and there was 'a libel on every page', as a well-known critic put it. Many angry letters and threats were received by the publishers and myself, and one threat of a libel action would have been serious if the attention of the person concerned had not soon been diverted by more pressing matters.

Horatio Bottomley was a leading journalist, the editor of a weekly paper, a financial gambler, an eminent orator, a Member of Parliament, and perhaps the most popular figure in the country during the 1914-18 war. He was also, like many press magnates and M.Ps., a humbug, and like many businessmen, a swindler. He was paid well for recruiting and patriotic speeches during the war, and at one of them he made a remark that was overheard by a fellow who reported it to me. The scene was the Kursaal at Harrogate. Bottomley always closed his speeches with emotional perorations, and I described the enthusiasm evoked on this occasion as being 'as unprecedented as it always is whenever Mr Bottomley speaks'. I then reported some of his phrases:

'And now, ladies and gentlemen,' he said, 'there are three things that are going to win us this war. One thing is our position in regard to munitions.' At this point the speaker said a few words about the munitions situation generally. He continued : 'The second thing that will help us through this terrible ordeal is that we are Englishmen !' This sentiment was naturally greeted with an immense outburst of cheering. For several minutes Mr Bottomley stood erect on the platform waiting for the silence that patriotism would hardly give. At last he held up his hand and order was restored. In solemn tones the orator proceeded :

'And the last thing, ladies and gentlemen, that will—beyond cavil or question—give us Victory Triumphant is THAT THERE IS A GOD IN HEAVEN !'

At these inspiring words the whole audience rose as one man and nearly lifted the roof off. Mr Bottomley bent before the deafening roar, and then, with a bashfulness that does him honour, quietly disappeared from the public gaze. He was naturally pleased at the success of his efforts in the sacred cause of Humanity, but being a really big man he minimised the true extent of his magnificent achievement by saying to the first person he ran up against after leaving the stage :

'That fetched the buggers—what ?'

Though I toned down the last sentence by changing the penultimate word, Bottomley was disturbed and would certainly have spread himself in the law courts if a more damaging libel had not shortly claimed his attention and caused him to bring an action which resulted in his downfall and seven years' penal servitude, to the unspeakable joy of all the humbugs who had not been found out.

My act of stage-suicide was committed in October, 1921. But before the staggering indiscretion of my book had been fully grasped I appeared in a sketch with Ethel Irving at the Coliseum, and during one performance Nigel Playfair called to see me. He had been asked to put on a play by Bulwer-Lytton called *Not So Bad As We Seem* for a single performance at Devonshire House in Piccadilly, where Charles Dickens and his company had performed it in 1851 before Queen Victoria and Prince Albert. The proceeds of this revival would be used to start a children's library at 13 Johnson Street, Camden Town, where part of Dickens's boyhood had been spent. Playfair's idea was to have the drama acted by authors, as it had been seventy years earlier, and he asked Shaw to play a part. Shaw replied that it was ridiculous to expect authors to put up a decent show and advised him to cast the play with actor-authors if possible, mentioning Granville Barker and myself. Unfortunately the author chosen for the long and important part of the villain could make nothing of it, and Playfair begged me to save the situation. I only had a week in which to learn a part nearly as long as Hamlet and to rehearse with a hopelessly amateurish company while appearing twice daily at the Coliseum. The performance took place on 30 November, 1921, and somehow I struggled through it. Ivor Novello as the hero played his first part of consequence and played it very badly, while the cast sparkled with literary 'stars'. There was no time to change the names on the programme, and the author whose place I took at such short notice was credited with 'a piece of work which did more than anything else to hold a very rackety team together'. He wrote to the papers correcting the error.

But if I had played Hamlet better than Forbes-Robertson, it would have done me no good. In theatrical circles my name was mud, as someone expressed it, and for a while things looked grim. My book, however, earned me a friend whose companionship and correspondence until his death meant far more to me than any number of stage engagements. I received a letter from Hugh Lunn, whose father ran the well-known tourist business, and as he wanted to talk with me about Frank Harris, with whom I had dealt in my book, we met, and talked intermittently for twenty-eight years. When we could not converse we wrote to each other, and after his death in 1949 his widow Dorothy very kindly sent me all the letters I had written to him throughout our friendship. By jogging my memory, these will help me greatly as I proceed with this book.

Characteristically all my early letters, from 1921 to 1926, dealt with literary themes, starting off with a lengthy screed arguing that Shaw's Caesar is a far finer portrayal than Shakespeare's. We expended many words over Frank Harris, whose biography Hugh Lunn intended to write, and whose works I still admired. Our interchanges on the subject of Dr Johnson were hostile. The Doctor's religious intolerance jarred upon me, and I thought that Boswell had practically invented him as a great character. I had been greatly struck by the work of Lytton Strachey, my esteem for whose books was constantly expressed in my letters, wherein I also delivered the judgment that Don Quixote and Sancho Panza could not hold a candle to Falstaff. Most of my opinions have been modified by time. In due course Hugh Lunn changed his name for literary purposes to Hugh Kingsmill, and soon after our friendship began I called him Hughie, by which he will henceforth be known in these pages. Though our temperaments were dissimilar, we shared so many tastes that his conversation never ceased to delight and refresh me, while his humour was so rich and spontaneous, his critical intelligence so acute, that I never spent a dull moment in his company. In 1951 Malcolm Muggeridge and I did our best to portray him in a book of letters entitled *About Kingsmill*.

Mention of Lytton Strachey reminds me that I met him in 1921. While at Baghdad I had read and greatly admired his *Eminent Victorians*, which blew the cob-

webs from an epoch, making it vivid and entertaining.
I wrote him a letter of superlatives after the publication
of *Queen Victoria,* and he asked me to lunch at the
Café Royal. I forget what sort of man I expected to see,
but I am sure I did not see what I expected. Perhaps,
too, I did not fulfil his expectations. In spite of my
admiration for his work we seemed to have nothing in
common, and a Rabelaisian story I told him about
Frank Harris made him blench. We parted with mutual
relief.

The early months of 1922 were exceptionally trying
for Gladys and myself. I had no work, and little chance
of getting any. I wrote a series of war stories, but people
were tired of the war and no editor would look at them.
My father-in-law had bought a Mass car and I drove
it for him at week-ends, occasionally using it for excur-
sions of our own. We went to Bedford in it and took my
parents for a few outings, once to Cambridge, where
father showed us some of the places he remembered,
including his college, St John's. On a different occasion
I questioned him about the functions of the Chancellor
and Vice-Chancellor of a university. He did his best to
enlighten me, but eventually confessed: 'When I was
up there, it was not a topic that exercised me greatly.'
This was not meant to be funny, and he looked surprised
when I laughed. Once, when I told him a story that
Hughie and I had enjoyed, his failure to appreciate its
humour added to its comedy. A certain dean who hoped
for a bishopric destroyed his chances of preferment by
preaching a sermon before an ecclesiastical dignitary in
which he spoke of 'the extraordinary conduct of Judas
Iscariot'. Clearly the Erastian dean belonged to the
squarson class typical of the eighteenth and early nineteenth centuries, and as father did too he merely remarked at the conclusion of the tale: 'But it *was* extraordinary.' I reported this to Hughie, who said that my

father's contribution was as good as the original phrase, and then developed the theme: 'How much more at home Judas would have been in Worcestershire round about 1760 than in Judaea round about 30. Comfortable armchairs, and Archdeacon Pearson and Judas over their port. No ungentlemanly insistence or Boswellianism, but just, with a pleasant smile: "A very singular episode, that of the Crucifixion, I make no doubt from what you have let fall, with attendant circumstances full, I hazard, of instruction for the curious in such matters".'

Only once did I notice my father at a serious disadvantage. The sister of a one-time schoolfriend of mine was coming to tea, and my mother warned me not to ask after her brother because he had got into some sort of disgrace during the war, had been cashiered and killed while serving in the ranks. She could not tell me what he had done, but said that father would know. I sought speech with father in his study, asking him how my friend had disgraced himself. After a great deal of humming and ha-ing father said he would rather not talk about it. But I pursued the topic with a few direct questions: Had he got drunk on duty? No. Had he stolen money? No. Had he been insolent to a superior officer? No. Or struck one? No. Disobeyed orders? No. Absent without leave? No. Disloyal? No. I gave it up. Then, said I, he must have murdered someone. No, it was worse than that, said father. I gasped, thinking he had taken leave of his senses, but said as calmly as possible that nothing could be worse than murder. After a long silence, during which he smoked his pipe and looked out of the window, he broke out irritably: 'Well, if you *must* know! Have you heard of Oscar Wilde? It was that sort of thing.' As I was over thirty years of age, and had sat on half a dozen courts-martial for that sort of thing, my 'Oh, is that all?' must have made him wonder whether his ears had deceived him. He turned slowly towards me, removed his pipe, and was about to speak when I removed myself.

While we were dining one night mother happened to say that their new vicar, whom they liked very much, would be in the pulpit on Sunday and had confessed to her that he felt diffident about preaching before me, as he had read my book and clever people always made him nervous. 'You shouldn't have told him that, Connie,' said father. I dismissed the incident with a laugh, but noticed that father was a trifle fretful, which surprised me until I mentioned it to Hughie, who explained: 'Here is a clergyman whom your father admires saying he didn't care what bilge he dished out Sunday after Sunday to half-wits like your old man, but shrank from submitting his platitudes to a keen satirical intelligence like yours.' I appreciated the point, as no doubt my father had done; but the vicar need not have worried, my keen satiric intelligence always being comatose during sermons.

Father was not much of a laugher, and when he enjoyed a joke his mirth was silent, but I was fortunate enough to amuse him during one of our visits in the 'twenties. A man stopped me in the road and began a long yarn about his inability to get work, his starving family, and so on. Having been stung pretty frequently by this sort of thing, I asked why he did not spare his breath and say quite frankly that he wanted a drink, as I understood that kind of request and would always satisfy it if within my power. I gave him half-a-crown and left him speechless. Two days later, in a different road, I noticed a fellow crossing over to my side. He came straight up to me, held out his hand, and said: 'I want a drink.' It was the same man, and I submitted without protest to ironic justice. On hearing of this, my father shook quietly for a while and then advised me

either to walk abroad with empty pockets or to take an
early train to London.

When we returned home early in 1922 in the comfort
of a Mass car, we were instantly reminded of an uncomfortable overdraft at the bank and no ready cash
for the next week's meals. For a while we lived on credit,
and then we started pawning or selling things. Some
Queen Anne silver that had been left to me by Aunt
Adèle raised enough cash to keep us for a fortnight.
The next things to go down the drain were my oriental
saddle-bags. Then I pawned my Persian carpets, and
finally the gold watch inherited from my old friend
Charles Burt, who had died while in the army. Meanwhile Hughie had persuaded his father to give me some
sort of job in his business at Lucerne, and we were on the
point of borrowing money for our fares when in the
last week of April 1922 I received a wire from Odhams
Press asking if I would write weekly articles on promin-
ent people for a new and reformed *John Bull*, and if so
what my terms would be. Inexpressibly relieved, I suggested seven guineas an article. Had I demanded twenty
I might have got it, for an unknown admirer of my
book, Harold Brighouse, knew a director of the firm and
had reported that I was the right man for the job.

Oddly enough, at about the same period, D. L.
Murray of *The Times* wanted me to do occasional reviews for a literary page he was editing. I cannot now
remember the works that received my attention, but
my career as a literary critic was cut short when I dealt
with a volume of reminiscences by Mrs Aria, all of
whose contemporaries appeared in her pages as charming, beautiful, delightful, brilliant, fascinating, and so
forth, with the single exception of her one-time husband, about whom she wrote caustically; and the gist
of my review was that if she had written about her
friends in the style she had adopted towards her hus-

band, her book would have been more readable. I did not know that she had looked after Sir Henry Irving in his declining years and was a popular figure in the upper bohemian world, where my review was considered sacrilegious. The dramatic critic of *The Times*, A. B. Walkley, took on the job of eclipsing my anonymous pleasantries and reinstating Mrs Aria in a long article the same week. I referred to my labours as a literary critic in a letter to Hughie: 'It's rather amusing in one sense, because I'm not allowed to give free rein to my thoughts, and for the first time in my life I am exercising self-restraint. Very good for the liver, I am told!' But it seems I did not restrain myself with sufficient rigour.

My job with *John Bull* lasted several years, and some of my articles aroused angry passions in Ulster during the Irish troubles. I received cards signed 'Red Hand', threatening me with an early death; which worried my wife; but having been potted at frequently in the East, I did not feel myself seriously endangered. I also provided a page or two of gossip for another weekly paper, *The Passing Show*. Both jobs necessitated a good deal of social life; I had to meet people who could give me the sort of information I wanted; and though I have never been a social mixer by nature, I managed to adapt myself to the demands of my trade, drinking more than was good for me, listening to much that bored me, and talking of cricket, racing, football and politics, instead of Shakespeare, Dr Johnson, Wilde and Shaw. In 1923, sponsored by Colin Hurry, I became a member of the Savage Club where all kinds of people were to be met, especially in those days journalists, actors and painters, among the last being Sydney (usually known as Joe) Maiden, with whom I formed a lasting friendship. In the same year Constable's published a slim volume of poems called *The Last Illusion* by Colin, who managed to combine a successful business career with a genius for light verse and a lyrical gift which may be appreciated when the present fashion of chopping poor prose into unrhymed lines has been superseded by a taste for poetry. Colin also contributed a preface that year to my second book, *A Persian Critic*, four of the essays in which were published by *The Times*. Unlike my first effort, it was a soothing work and received little notice. Even the hero of the book did not acknowledge the copy my publisher sent him, possibly because he failed to recognize his opinions in my epigrammatic interpretation.

Although I had temporarily committed self-murder in the eyes of West-End theatre managers, quite a number of stage folk had enjoyed my book, especially those who were not mentioned in it, and from one of them I received an offer to tour the provinces in the autumn of 1922. I accepted it, and played the husband in J. B. Fagan's play *The Wheel* for a dozen weeks with Phyllis Neilson-Terry, Ion Swinley playing the lover. Gladys accompanied me, and what greatly helped to make the tour enjoyable was our friendship with the manager Walter Havers and his wife Lydia, with both of whom we tramped down the west coast of Scotland the following year, our journey being full of comical incidents, the memory of which entertained us thereafter. At that time the west coast had not been overrun by rich trippers in luxurious cars and poor trippers in char-a-bancs, and we had the wilds to ourselves. The inhabitants were accustomed to small gatherings of fishermen at particular places, but pedestrians were new to them and they did not quite know what to make of us, some of them regarding us with suspicion, like the bailiff at Lochinver who warned us not to frighten the fish, some thinking us mad, like the commercial traveller at Ullapool who regretted that the local doctor was engaged on a distant case. Soon after our return I again toured with Phyllis Neilson-Terry as the wicked peer in Temple Thurston's comedy *A Roof and Four Walls.*

My resurrection on the West-End stage took place in March 1924, when Godfrey Tearle engaged me to play a Harley Street specialist in Freddy Lonsdale's *The Fake* at the Apollo Theatre. Godfrey was under the impression that I had done him a good turn in my book of stage portraits, and near the end of his life he called me his oldest friend on that account. Actually I had done nothing except expose the hypocrisy of a leading actor, Charles Hawtrey, whose hostile attitude had prevented Godfrey from being chosen to appear in the Shakespeare Tercentenary Performance. Godfrey was an extremely nice fellow without an atom of self-importance, and as he was also a sympathetic and helpful producer I liked being with him. *The Fake* was an odd mixture of melodrama and cheap comedy, but it entertained the public and ran for over six months, being revived the following year for six weeks at the Lyceum Theatre. Freddy Lonsdale and Noel Coward were the two typical playwrights of the twenties; they breathed the spirit of the age. Those of us who thought their comedies second-rate recognized Bernard Shaw's *Saint Joan* and Sean O'Casey's *Juno and the Paycock* as the great plays of the decade, but Lonsdale and Coward were the true mediums of their time, as Barrie had been in the generation before them.

During a rehearsal of *The Fake* Lonsdale took me on one side, assured me that I was one of the best actors he had even seen, and asked me to play the part in America later on. Though gratified, I declined the offer, feeling rather perturbed when he told me some time afterwards that the way I had spoken his lines showed my contempt for them. He was an amusing little card, difficult to pin down. More changeable by nature than most people, he could be as tough as hickory one day, as soft as putty the next. His career provides a better instance than Shakespeare's of a man with practically no education winning success in a profession where erudition of a kind seems indispensable; and it also illustrates the melancholy fact that fame and money do not bring happiness. Freddy spent the last twenty-five years of his life rushing hither and thither in a demented desire to get away from himself.

Apparently my personality suited the character of the medical specialist because I had quite a few offers to play leading or semi-leading parts after the run of the piece, from Mrs Patrick Campbell, Marie Tempest, Sybil Thorndike and others. But my laziness got the better of me, and after a brief appearance in another play at the Scala, where I repeated my well-known performance of a doctor for an absurdly high salary, I took Gladys for a long holiday in Devon and Cornwall.

An incident during the run of *The Fake* was curious enough to linger in my memory. Unlike Boswell, I do not think casual sex affairs are any more interesting than less romantic forms of evacuation. They may temporarily excite the performers, but unless accompanied by unusual circumstances they reveal nothing characteristic and cannot sustain the curiosity of intelligent readers. Boswell's constant references to his own sordid habits are the boastings of a man who wishes to feel important or triumphant. My own casual affairs were no more interesting than other people's; and as I feel no pride in having possessed the potency of, say, an average rabbit, I shall keep them to myself. But the incident I am about to relate was to say the least, odd.

A girl I had known at His Majesty's Theatre came to see *The Fake* and afterwards called on me. I was removing my make-up when she entered the dressing-

room, and following the usual salutations she informed
me that I must stick to doctors on the stage as I had 'a
perfect bedside manner'. I remembered her as a pleasant
kid about eighteen years old. She had become a good-
looking woman of thirty, with attractive eyes, legs and
bust. But physically I remained unmoved, and when
she asked me to tea at her flat for a talk about old times
I agreed to go without more enthusiasm than good manners made essential.

A week later I turned up at her flat in Belsize Park,
and we talked scandal over tea. Suddenly, unaccount-
ably, but overwhelmingly, I was seized with desire for
her. Sexual hunger produces one of the same symptoms
as hunger for food, and my mouth watered. I got up,
took her in my arms, kissed her vehemently, and went
on repeating that I loved her. To my amazement she
burst into a passion of tears and for some minutes she
seemed to be sobbing her heart out. I did my utmost
to soothe her, and when she could control her emotion
she confessed that she had loved me from our first
meeting, that she had never ceased to think of me, but
that now it was too late, referring, I supposed, to my
marriage.

Many endearments passed between us; we were soon
in bed together; and half an hour later we were lying
peacefully sated in each other's arms when the front-
door bell rang. I felt her form go rigid and noticed
a look of alarm on her face. 'Do you know who it is?' I
asked. 'My fiancé,' she replied. Now I understood why
she had said it was too late. Her flat being at the top
of the building, she begged me to go out on the roof and
wait until she could get rid of him. I covered up my sense
of being slightly ridiculous by a display of temper and
angrily refused to do anything of the kind. 'If he finds
you here, he'll kill you,' she whispered as we quietly
dressed. 'What a pity!' I whispered back with affected

disdain. The bell went on ringing, she went on urging, and I went on scoffing. At last silence descended; but romance had vanished, and soon I left by the back-garden door.

During the holiday Gladys and I took in the late autumn of 1924 I suffered from headaches, and on our return I happened to mention the circumstances to a woman doctor who was attending our son Henry for adenoids. She noticed a large swelling on the top of my head, said that it was a cyst which may have formed over my old wound, lanced it at once, squeezed out some matter, and told my wife to continue squeezing every day until it had all gone. For some weeks Gladys squeezed; but the supply of matter seemed inexhaustible and I still suffered from headaches; so I went to see our family doctor, Murray Norris, who, though he refused to assist his patients to endure pain by administering drugs, always gave me a good laugh, for which reason and because he never pretended to know anything I liked him. Once I had a nasty whitlow on the middle finger of my right hand. He told the attendant nurse to bring him a pair of scissors. She brought the wrong pair, saying she could not find the other. Norris merely remarked 'This pair is a bit clumsy and liable to slip: however . . .' thrust it in, slit the finger open, and displayed surprise when I let out a 'Phew!'. On the present occasion he said that the swelling on my head was septic and must be opened up. Having shaved the hair all round it, he cut the cyst, and exclaimed as the pus spurted all over the room: 'Good heavens! this is going to be a long job. I should have given you a general anaesthetic. You had better hold tight.' For half an hour I suffered agony as he cleaned out the matter, removed a last microscopic bit of lead which had pushed its way up and no doubt caused my headaches, and dabbed the lacerated spot with iodine, upon which I nearly expired with pain. By the time he bandaged me I was soaked with perspiration. The wound had to be washed and dressed several times over the next few weeks, and when I played in the 1925 revival of *The Fake* at the Lyceum I had to wear a tuft of hair over my tonsured head.

Throughout this period I had been writing a book.

8

⌐◈┐

Suicide of an Author

Having done my best to ruin my career as an actor with my first book, I spent the better part of 1925 in writing a work that was liable to wreck my career as an author. The first was an act of irresponsibility, the second an act of insanity. 'O that he were here to write me down an ass!' cries Dogberry. I need no one's help to write myself down an idiot. As it happened about thirty-three years ago, I am incapable of explaining my behaviour. One's body is supposed to change completely every seven years. If so, mine has undergone nearly five metamorphoses since then, and I can only interpret the nature of the man I was from his actions, which were peculiar. My present attitude will at least be objective.[1]

Clearly my main intention was to make money, so that I could settle down to the kind of writing I enjoyed. My secondary purpose may have been to produce a more entertaining volume of reminiscences than the semi-fictional stuff that was then pouring from the press. My third was probably the sheer fun of creating a

[1] Fundamentally one's character never changes, but experience of life disciplines the less responsible aspects of human nature and so influences action, making one's behaviour as a young man surprising to one's maturer self. A further cleavage in my case lay in the fact that I had not perceived my real vocation at the age of thirty-nine, my natural volatility being uncontrolled by the revelation.

sensation and listening to the comments it aroused. While collecting information and gossip about the social and political figures of whom I had been writing as a journalist, I heard enough about them to stimulate my dramatic sense, and I produced a book in which all the figures were parodied and exhibited histrionically. I called it *The Whispering Gallery, Being Leaves from a Diplomat's Diary*, but by no stretch of imagination could a page of it have been written by a member of the British Diplomatic Corps. I have just read it for the first time since passing the proofs for press a generation ago and find some of it commonplace, some of it clever, nearly all of it entertaining. I certainly had a gift for displaying a man's salient features in dialogue form, but it must have been obvious to the intelligent reader that conversations on that level of familiarity and comical repartee can never have taken place. I will give one example out of many. It was common knowledge that the Prime Minister in the early nineteen hundreds, A. J. Balfour, was at loggerheads with his most difficult and dangerous colleague, Joseph Chamberlain, and this is how I pictured them at a Downing Street garden-party:

B : I envy you your button-holes. Fresh from the hot-houses at Highbury, I presume?

C : No, no. I get these in London. I seldom pick the ones at home.

B : Ah! Fancy in flowers, practice in politics, I see.

C : One must have a fancy for something, you know— for philosophy, if everything else fails.

B : Hardly for philosophy, my dear fellow. One has to practise that.

C : Does philosophy help you in politics, then?

B : More than in anything else.

C : How?

B : Philosophy teaches one for example, that man is not perfectible. If one weren't quite sure of that, no cabinet meeting would be endurable.

C : Indeed?

B : And in word.

C : Well, if I couldn't believe in man's perfectibility, I'd blow my brains out.

B : If Campbell-Bannerman got to hear that, he'd spare no pains to make you a sceptic. But you must not confuse desire with belief.

C : I say, Balfour, I have sometimes had a horrid feeling that the perfect man, when he comes, might be something like you.

B : I, too, have been visited with that feeling, but I shouldn't describe it as horrid. In any case you need not lose your slumber over it; because the conception though beautiful, is, I fear, remote. A world of Balfours! Think of it! No, I dare not. Philosophy forbids. The Fall of Man was final. The most that can be hoped for is that he will worship the right gods.

C : Yourself, for one.

B : How admirably you read my thoughts!

C : They are too obvious to call for exceptional penetration.

B : If you will allow me to say so, my dear Chamberlain, you are becoming a trifle inharmonious.

C : Dear, dear!

B : But your orchids are divine. What an exquisite button-hole!

C : Thank you.

B : It almost makes one jealous.

C : *Could* you be jealous?

B : Only of myself. But if anything else could make me jealous, your lovely orchids, rather than your lurid oratory, would be the cause.

C : I can think of an answer, but it's a rude one.

B : I know. Isn't it tiresome? But I see Lady Randolph waving to me. Have I your permission? Thank you. . . . Some day you must tell me the name of your florist.

It cannot have occurred to me that this sort of thing would be taken *au grand sérieux*, but the antagonism to the book was due, not to its evident and innumerable inaccuracies, but to the fact that I had been granted sufficient percipience to hit on the underlying truth a little too often. I am not defending myself. It was the work of an unbalanced person who, when he realized what he had done, acted like a lunatic. But it is worth recording that after the tumult and the shouting had died down W. R. Titterton in *G.K.'s Weekly* wrote that I had been attacked mainly on account of the truth I had told, and he went on to say that if the book were 'not written by one who participated in the scenes he described, then it is written by a genius.' Or more likely by a man afflicted with what coroners' juries call, in cases of suicide, 'temporary insanity'.

When completed I took the manuscript to a director of Odhams Press, who read it, said he would like to serialize it in one of his papers, and made a handsome offer for it if I would divulge the name of the diplomat. This I resolutely declined to do, a fact he later admitted as a witness in the Police Court proceedings. He then said he would like to send the typescript to a publisher of his acquaintance. I agreed, and the publisher liked it so much that his firm offered £250 in advance of royalties but wished to know the diarist's name. I replied that this was out of the question. Meanwhile another English publisher had seen it, had refused to issue it without the diarist's personal authority, but had disposed of the American rights, demanding 25 % of the royalties for having arranged the contract.

In September 1926 I was staying with my wife and son at the Black Dog and Duck Inn, Bury, Sussex, and a director of the firm that wished to publish the book in England travelled down to see me. I gathered from our talk that his firm merely wished to be in a position to say, if questioned, that they knew who the diplomat was, and would be quite satisfied if I gave the name verbally and confidentially to him on the clear understanding that it would never be revealed. I said that I would give him an answer next day if he would meet me at the Norfolk Hotel, Arundel, where, after his reassurance that it would remain a secret, I mentioned the name of a man about whom I had recently been reading in (I think) *T.P.'s Weekly*. The folly of my action was, I thought, negatived by the pledge of secrecy, and I was under the impression that the publishers attached no significance to it, being indifferent to the name so long as they could claim cognisance of a responsible person. But whatever I thought, my conduct was imbecile to the last degree. Had I acted with any approach to intelligence, I would have given the name of a dead diplomat.

The book came out on a Friday towards the end of November 1926, and that morning's *Daily Mail* printed several columns of attack on it, exposing the many errors of fact. There were several reasons for this. *The Whispering Gallery* contained a reasonable estimate of Lenin, then the villain of the European piece, and an unflattering picture of the Tsar of Russia, then being canonized in the English press. These suggested that it was part of a Communist plot though T. P. O'Connor said that the diplomat's view of Lenin accorded with his own and all the known facts. But the portrait of Lord Northcliffe, picked out by the *New Statesman* as both brilliant and truthful, probably rattled his brother Lord Rothermere more than anything else, and he was the proprietor of the *Daily Mail*. There may have been other reasons for the mammoth onslaught. The evening papers joined in the hue and cry, calling the book 'a fake' and demanding its instant withdrawal with an apology for its issue.

The publishers were naturally delighted; three

editions were sold out on the date of the book's appearance, and orders were pouring in. The talk of Fleet Street, they were informed, was that Lord Birkenhead had written it, for no one less brilliant could possibly ... etc., etc., which may have accounted for Birkenhead's denunciation of it a few days later. But the *Daily Mail* had decided to see the thing through, and continued its attack on Saturday. The publishers were frightened by the menace of prosecution, and withdrew the book from circulation after selling off their stock. The Sunday papers deepened the general hubbub, and J. L. Garvin of *The Observer* wrote or caused to be written a leader under the heading 'Ghouls and Garbage'. There was not a single innuendo against anyone's sexual or financial integrity throughout the book, but doubtless the alliteration pleased him, and he could not resist the temptation to howl with the pack.

That Sunday I was asked to attend a meeting of the publishing firm's directors, and I lost my head completely. The volume and virulence of the press comments had induced panic, and my thoughts and actions were no longer under control. Had I been in possession of my wits I would have told them squarely that I had written the book, and that they could no more have believed it to be the work of a real diplomat than of a real dinosaur. Instead I kept up the fiction of a man behind the work possibly with the confused notion that the director who had negotiated with me would get into trouble if I did not brazen it out. But on this point I am vague, and my behaviour on that crucial day is as mysterious to me now as it must seem to the reader. Later the director in question stated that he had accepted the name in good faith and not as part of a bare formality between his firm and me. Such misunderstandings are unfortunate. I ought to add that a clause in the contract stated that the name had been given to a

director but that it was not to be disclosed. After what
I have written of my behaviour, it is hardly necessary to
say that I had not bothered to read the contract.

Following their talk with me, the publishers went
down to placate the *Daily Mail,* and under the influence
of champagne their tongues were loosened. From that
moment, though I did not know it then, I became the
villain of the piece, and my publishers, like the public,
had been grossly deceived. On Monday their explanation throwing the blame on my shoulders, together
with a short note from me trying to shift some of it
back on to theirs, appeared in the *Daily Mail.*

It so happened that I was broadcasting the leading
part in a play from Cardiff that night, and had left
London before the press reporters could run me to
earth. They got to hear of my whereabouts, and the
fun started during the evening broadcasting. I wrote
an account of it soon after the event, which is printed
here for the first time.

A crowd of reporters from every part of England and
Wales descended upon Cardiff. During the first interval
in the play I was told that a dozen people were urgently
enquiring for me at the doors of the broadcasting
station. By the second interval about two dozen had
forced an entrance and were lying in wait for me outside the door of the studio. The play over, I begged
the leading official to tell them that I had left by another exit. He did so, but the reporters just nodded their
heads and remained where they were. There was only
one thing to be done. I decided to rush them. Another
fellow had a car near by in which he promised to take
me to a place of safety until my train was due. None
of the reporters knew me by sight; so I buttoned up my
coat, turned up the collar, pulled my hat over my eyes,
and walked unconcernedly through the doors, chatting
to my friend with the motor. The reporters occupied

nearly all the standing room on the stairs and corridors of the building. There were quite fifty of them. I pushed my way through the knot that cut off my entrance to the stairs and strolled calmly down the latter arm-in-arm with my friend. Everyone peered at us, but no one molested us. Apparently I did not look like an actor, nor an author. So far, so good. We cleared the building and were well down the street in the car before the reporters realized that I had escaped them.

My friend knew his way about the local hostelries, and into one of them we went, where he got the use of a private room. We remained there drinking whiskies until it was time to leave for the train. Then we drove to the station, got out, and left the car with the engine running. Apart from a few obvious travellers the platform seemed deserted. The actress who had read the leading female rôle in the play was returning to London with me. She was already on the platform, and, thinking the coast was clear, I strolled up and asked if she had seen anything of the reporters after leaving the studio. At that instant there was a shout from the far end of the platform and immediately the station was full of figures closing in upon us. I turned with my friend, darted through the exit, and scrambled into his car. Before he could snap into gear we were surrounded by a clamorous mob and subjected to a barrage of questions:

'Are you Mr Pearson?' 'Don't trouble to deny it.' 'You are!' 'What's that?' 'You aren't?' 'Rot!' 'We've combed every hotel in Cardiff and you aren't staying in one of them.' 'How did you give us the slip?' 'That's Mrs Pearson on the platform.' 'It isn't?' 'Don't you come that over us!' 'Of course it is!' 'Now what about this *Whispering Gallery* business?' 'Don't pretend you don't know.' 'Eh?' 'You go and tell that to the Horse Marines!' 'We weren't born yesterday.'

And so on for two or three brain-whirling minutes. Suddenly my friend shoved in his gear and we began to move with a score of hands pulling at us. We gathered speed. A few of them clung on, but by the time we were in top gear they had dropped off, and we heard their voices registering strange emotions behind us.

The idea was to run down the road for about half a mile, turn sharply to the left, cross the line, and return on the other side of the station, from which I could regain my platform through a subway. As we reached the station the train steamed in. I shot out of the car, bolted through the subway, emerged on the platform, made a dive for the nearest carriage, and tugged at the door. A yell, a clatter of feet, and the whole covey of reporters came bounding after me. My mind worked quickly. Almost before they were at the door that had just banged behind me, I had glided rapidly down the corridor, entered the lavatory and locked myself in. This manœuvre, when detected, was greeted with a howl of despair. They kicked the door and exhorted me to come out. One of them shouted at the top of his voice: 'It is forbidden to use the privy while the train is in a station.' Several of them spotted my unfortunate travelling companion and put her through a severe inquisition, refusing to believe that she was not my wife. At length the train moved. But the last carriage had reached the end of the platform before one persevering gentleman dropped off the board, his final words to the lady being: 'Well, I take my hat off to your husband. He's the first person who's ever done me in the eye at this business. Good luck to him!'

I was surprised to see no reporters at Paddington station on our arrival in the early hours of Tuesday morning. But the papers soon enlightened me. The publishers had gone to see the diplomat whose name I had so crazily used; he of course had repudiated all connection with the work and its author; and the *Daily Mail* had a leader headed 'A case for the Public Prosecutor'. I cannot blame the publishers who were badly frightened and jumped at an opportunity to put themselves right with the Press. I do not know what else they could have done. Had they sat tight and done nothing from the first, and if the agitation had moved the Public Prosecutor to act, they might have ended up with me in the dock. Their only alternative was to accuse me, which they did, and a warrant was issued for my arrest on the charge of 'obtaining or attempting to obtain money under false pretences'. The words 'attempting to obtain' were put in to cover the fact that I had already returned them the cheque for £250.

Handled properly, this charge should have been quashed at the first Police Court hearing; but by now the feeling against me had been worked up to such a pitch that the case had left the region of law for that of pathology. I felt utterly crushed by the avalanche that had descended upon me, and would have made no defence at all if it had not been for my sister Evelyne's husband, Colonel Hamlett, known to his relations and friends as 'Dane'. I was at his house explaining the sequence of events in halting phrases when we heard of the warrant. Consequently the army of reporters and photographers which assembled round my house in Abbey Road when the detectives arrived to arrest me was disappointed. Dane took my whole case in hand immediately, and carried it through with an energy, capacity and unshakable conviction as to the issue, for which I have no adequate words of admiration and gratitude.

We drove down to Marlborough Street Police Court, where I surrendered to the law, and Dane bailed me for £1,000, the sum being blazoned forth by the press, perhaps as presumptive evidence that I meditated flight.

Then came the hours and hours of prostrating boredom with lawyers, viewing and reviewing my case from every angle, and Police Court proceedings once a week, which dragged out the case for a month. Walter Frampton, my junior counsel, ably cross-examined the publishers, comparing passages in the book with the sketch of the 'diplomat's' career given in *Who's Who* and showing conclusively that he could not possibly have been identified with the putative diarist. As a result we won the first round in the fight, my counsel having little difficulty in getting the magistrate to send the case to the London Assizes instead of the Old Bailey, though counsel on the other side ruthlessly opposed this.

All my friends rallied round me and helped me in innumerable ways, while many unknown people sent me sympathetic messages. One bright and comical spot was a letter from Frank Harris, who wrote words of encouragement from Nice and advised me to state when giving evidence that 'memoirs are a well-known form of fiction. Say that a widely known literary man told you this. It will make the Court laugh.' My friend Hughie approached Bernard Shaw, who took the view that I had asked for what I had got. 'Poor Hesketh (damn his folly!) has to choose between the heaviest sentence the Court can give him, and a lenient one,' said G.B.S., who urged me to throw myself on the mercy of the Court and say that 'difficult though it may be for anyone to believe a man could be such a fool when it's easier to think him a knave', yet I never imagined the thing would be taken seriously, 'or that the publishers really believed it was anything worse than the fictitious memoirs and travels that have so often been published as genuine.' That, said Shaw, was about as near the truth as I could get, and what I had to do was to ask the Court 'for no more consideration than to be treated as a fool instead of a scoundrel.' My confession, he concluded, must be consistently handsome or it would be thrown away.

I was much touched by the chivalrous action of a man who only knew me as an actor in a play of his. I recorded what follows at the time and have just discovered it among my papers. Freddy Lonsdale rang me up one day and said: 'I want to tell you that I have never in my life seen or heard of anything so scandalous as the way you are being treated. You have all my sympathy, and if you want any help, financial or otherwise, you have only to say the word. I don't care a damn what you've done, and I don't wish to know. If you were the worst criminal in the world, you couldn't have been treated more shamefully. Come and dine with me to-night at the Embassy.' I could not dine with him that night but arranged to see him the following day. The first thing he said when we met was:

'I've just read *The Whispering Gallery*—a brilliant book. The dialogue is marvellous. You ought to write a great play.'

Though he again protested that he did not want to know the facts, I insisted on giving him a résumé of them in order not to get his friendship and support on 'false pretences'.

'My dear fellow,' he said when I had finished, 'I don't care what you've done. We're all criminals more or less. I'm sorry to hear you aren't one. You're only a bloody fool. However, I dare say you'll remedy that in time and become like the rest of us. D'you know the story of Charles Brookfield?'

'No.'

'Charlie was walking down the Strand one day when he recognized a bloke he'd known in the past who'd just done "time" on Dartmoor. The bloke looked at him, then looked away and hurried by. But Charlie turned and called out: "Have you forgotten me, old man? I'm

Brookfield." They shook hands and the ex-convict said, "I didn't think you'd want to know me after what has happened." Charlie replied: *"Know* you! I take my hat off to you. You've done *your* seven years!" '

Freddy again offered me money, which I refused, as my family had been prompted by Dane and was backing me. He then asked me to dine with him at the Embassy. But I told him that Lord Birkenhead and the rest of his acquaintances might be there, and the moment they recognized me it might be awkward for him.

'Rot!' said Freddy. 'I'll introduce you to all of 'em, and we'll have great fun watching their faces.'

But I declined, and at length it was agreed that we should go elsewhere. Two or three days before my case came on at the Assizes I dined with him and Ronald Squire at the Savoy grill. All through the meal my mind was on the ordeal of the next few days, but Freddy did his best to amuse me and keep me from thinking of my troubles. After it was all over he told me that I had behaved 'like a hero' on that occasion; but that was only his kindness; I never felt less heroic in my life.

When I tried to recall our talk shortly afterwards, all I could remember was Freddy's remark that 'Oscar Wilde ought to have a statue in Trafalgar Square for writing *The Importance of Being Earnest*', and that 'A cynic is a disappointed sentimentalist'. I remembered too that Ivor Novello had come up in the course of the meal, shaken hands with me, and wished me luck. After dinner we adjourned to the Green Room Club, where Freddy played poker for an hour or two, and we finished up at Lyons Corner House in Coventry Street, where we ate kippers and drank coffee at about three in the morning.

Between the last Marlborough Street hearing and the London Assizes trial some rival publisher provided evidence against the firm responsible for my book in

the form of three works of a so-called pornographic
nature which had appeared under their imprint. I think
they were Ovid's *Loves*, Balzac's *Contes Drôlatiques*
and *The Golden Ass* of Apuleius, all suitably illustrated.
The point was that if produced in Court they would
discredit their publishers by showing that they jumped
at anything of a sensational order. I was against this
ruse, partly because I thought it had nothing to do with
my case which should be fought on its own merits, and
partly because I detested legal judgment on literary
matters. Moreover Shaw had warned me, through
Hughie, that I must avoid the slightest reflection on
my publishers or the least insinuation that they were
no better than they should have been. But my view was
overruled on the ground that the more my publishers
were discredited the likelier my chances of acquittal.

On the evening before the trial I was subjected to
my sternest test. Dane and I were called to a final conference in the Temple chambers of my senior counsel,
Sir Patrick Hastings. What had happened in the interval to make my advisers change their minds, I cannot
say, and I had the impression that Walter Frampton,
though silently acquiescent, was not wholly in favour of
what followed; but Hastings painted my case in its least
attractive colours and to all intents advised me to plead
guilty, while declaring that if I decided to fight they
would do everything in their power to secure a verdict
in my favour. He assured me that a plea of guilty would
almost certainly cause the judge merely to bind me over,
but that if I fought and lost I might have to face anything from three to six months' imprisonment. Dane
exploded, but Hastings reminded him that it was solely
a decision for myself and my wife, as we would have to
suffer if things turned out badly, and he thought I had
better go home and talk matters over with her. I knew
quite well what she would say, and I said it for both of

us: 'I am not guilty of the charge, and I will fight.'
Dane was very silent as we walked back through the
Temple, but I could sense his indignation..

The trial took place in the last week of January, 1927.
Sir Patrick Hastings opened with a terrific onslaught on
the publishers, and cross-examined two of the directors
on the 'obscene' books they had produced, all three being exhibited. While claiming that the works were
classics, they refused to read certain marked passages
in open Court. The judge looked at the illustrations
through the fingers of a hand which covered his face,
and the jury (barring the two women) inspected them
so closely that I felt their interest was temporarily
abstracted from the case.

I was examined by Hastings and then cross-examined
by counsel for the prosecution, Sir Henry Curtis Bennett.
Owing to the fact that the defence had suddenly been
converted into an attack, I found it impossible to give
my evidence under examination, since my counsel did
not put the right sort of questions to me; and I had to
tell my story under cross-examination, which caused
the judge to remark: 'This is a new position.' When
I frankly admitted that I had told lies, Curtis Bennett
asked: 'Do you realize what you are saying?' I replied
that I had probably told far more lies than he was likely
to tax me with. The Court, I heard afterwards, gasped;
and Bennett was so taken aback that he only put one
more question: 'Why did you keep up the pretence of
there being a diplomat after the newspaper exposure?'
I did not have to pause for the answer: 'Because I was
mad.'

While the jury were absent I discussed Shakespeare
with a poetical warder on my right, and Shaw with a
philosophical warder on my left. But they were not
absent for long, and in answer to the usual question the
foreman announced with pleasing emphasis:

'Not guilty.'

I went up to congratulate Hastings on his success in getting me off. 'Nonsense!' said he. 'You got yourself off by your evidence in the witness-box.' A few minutes later we ran across some members of the jury in a near-by pub, and they informed us that the prosecution never had a leg to stand on, though my engaging candour under cross-examination had won their sympathy.

The view that I was not guilty must have been shared by the publishers, who decided, after a short consultation with Dane, to pay me the entire profits on the sale of the work. The publisher who had placed the book with an American firm had rung up in agitation during the rumpus to renounce his 25 per cent of the royalties, had begged us not to mention his name during the legal proceedings, and had washed his hands of the entire affair. But when he received a cheque from New York the amount was sufficient to make him change his tune, and he wished to retain his stipulated share in the royalties. Dane having advised him that as he had washed his hands of the entire affair he had better keep them clean, he forwarded the total sum, which, with the English receipts, covered all my legal expenses and enabled me to repay the members of my family who had backed me, leaving something over for Gladys and myself.

At the same time as my trial, by an interesting coincidence, the proprietor of the *Daily Mail* was defending an action which involved exactly six thousand times the sum I had received from my publishers as an advance on royalties. I am happy to say that Lord Rothermere, too, left the Court without a stain on his character; though this cannot have meant quite as much to him at it did to me, since his action did not receive so much publicity as mine.

Interested to see how my account of what happened would strike an intelligent member of the modern generation, I asked my young friend Michael Holroyd to read it. He did so, and wrote: 'I do think it possible that you have been a little unfair to yourself over the trial. You stress your apparent lack of mental balance, but as most other people seem to have been reduced to a state of hysteria I cannot see that this stress is needed. In fact you appear to have stood up to what must have been a distressing time with commendable fortitude.'

If I do appear to have stressed my lack of mental balance, it may be that I am conceited enough to be surprised and shocked by my own stupidity, whereas I expect irrational behaviour from other folk. The failure of the literary critics to talk a little horse sense on the stream of lunacy let loose by my book might have irritated me if I had not been aware that these outbreaks of mania are due, not to their ostensible cause, but to the annoyance with life felt by the majority of people, whose accumulated disappointments generate resentment, the expression of which is held in check by conventions and circumstances until released by the creation of a public scapegoat, on whom they can vent their baffled fury and join in the hue and cry without forfeiting their social respectability. I had read of these epidemics in the cases of Byron, Oscar Wilde, Parnell and Dreyfus, and I had personally observed them when Bernard Shaw and Frank Harris aroused the delirious hostility of their fellow-scribes during the recent war. Like Sir Walter Scott, my reactions are dissimilar from those of the multitude, and all my instincts are against what Kipling calls 'the law of the pack'. I naturally warm towards scapegoats. But it is not pleasant to be one, and I did not think it funny at the time. Fortunately for myself, I cannot nurse a grievance, and it appears from a duologue I wrote on 20 May, 1928 that I was already laughing at the whole affair. The chief literary critic of the day, Sir Edmund Gosse, had just died and I read his obituary in *The Sunday Times* for which he wrote. Touring the provinces at the time, I glanced at the paper on Sunday in the train, and promptly knocked off this *jeu d'esprit*, a fitting epilogue to the ridiculous rumpus caused by my book:

Scene: Heaven. Enter St Paul, doyen of Christian dialectics, leading Sir Edmund Gosse, doyen of English critics, by the hand.

ST P : Let me introduce myself. I am Paul of Tarsus.

SIR E *(nervously)* : *Saint* Paul?

ST P *(confidently)* : The same.

SIR E : Then I am in—?

ST P : Precisely.

SIR E : You know me?

ST P : We know everyone.

SIR E *(confused)* : Of course, of course. You must excuse me. It takes some time to—

ST P : Naturally. It is difficult, even for a critic of your eminence, to comprehend Omniscience.

SIR E *(pleased)* : Tell me : am I, then, appreciated in . . . in . . . *(coughing slightly)* . . . here?

ST P : We take in *The Sunday Times*.

SIR E : Good ! *(Saint Paul frowns.)* I mean . . . well . . . it's not a bad paper.

ST P : We have formed our own opinions as to that.

SIR E : Of course, *of course.* I have no wish to influence—

ST P : Don't be a fathead !

SIR E *(stupefied)* : I beg your pardon !

ST P : You needn't. In heaven, when a thing's said, it's said. No one takes the slightest notice anyhow.

SIR E *(relieved)* : Then we *are* in heaven.

ST P : Where the hell d'you think I'd be ?

SIR E *(distressed)* : Forgive me, I—

ST P : Rubbish ! Have you read your obituary notices ?

SIR E *(trying to conquer his eagerness)* : No; who has written them? Did Jack Squire. . . . I mean , may I borrow—?

ST P : You'll find them all in the waiting-room.

SIR E : Waiting-room?

ST P : Yes; first to the right, second to the left; next to the lavatory.

SIR E *(fretfully)* : But I thought you said we were in heaven? *(Saint Paul frowns.)* Sorry. *(Saint Paul makes a hissing sound between his teeth.)* But you mentioned the lavatory . . . rather a shock, you know. . . . I mean, does one . . . in heaven?

ST P : If you think you can hold your water for eternity, you'd better think again.

SIR E *(crestfallen)* : Please don't be peevish. I am only too willing to learn.

ST P : Ah, that reminds me! I've been detailed by Gabriel to ask you a few preliminary questions.

SIR E : The Archangel?

ST P : Naturally.

SIR E : I am honoured.

ST P : Wait till you hear them.

SIR E *(weakly)* : What sort of questions?

ST P : Well, to be exact, only one question of moment. SS Peter & Co will ask you the less important ones—about dogmas and so forth. But it is my duty to warn you that not a little of your future comfort up here will depend upon your answer to this major query of mine.

SIR E *(faintly)* : Go on.

ST P *(touchily)* : At my own leisure, thank you. *(An awkward pause during which Sir Edmund commences an apology, remembers it is useless, and subsides into silence.)* Now attend to me, please. *(Sir Edmund makes an affirmatory gurgle.)* What is, or rather was, your honest opinion of the works of Hesketh Pearson?

SIR E *(holding up his hands)* : My dear sir!

ST P : I am *not* your dear sir! Be so good as to answer my question immediately.

SIR E : Are you referring to the scurrilous author of *The Whispering Gallery*?

ST P : Don't hedge! You know perfectly well who I mean. Incidentally, *The Whispering Gallery* is thought very highly of in heaven. Our librarian, Luke, complains that he is always having to replace stolen copies.

SIR E : *Stolen* copies? Look here, are we in heaven or h—?

ST P : Take care! We don't allow people to question our credentials.

SIR E : But I didn't.

ST P : You did!

SIR E *(plaintively)* : Pardon me, but—

ST P : Be quiet! You are wasting time. Answer the question.

SIR E : About Hesketh Pearson?

ST P *(firmly)* : I am waiting.

SIR E : Well, to tell you the honest truth—

ST P : I should strongly advise you to tell it.

SIR E : I never seriously considered his claim to be regarded as an author of standing.

ST P *(sarcastically)* : You only seriously considered him as an author of lying, I presume?

SIR E *(stung to retort)* : Is that the best you can do in the way of repartee?

ST P : No, sir, it is not! Repartee with us takes a more concrete form, as you shall find to your cost presently.

SIR E : I'm sure I didn't mean to be rude.

ST P : I don't care a damn whether you did or didn't! As I said before, that sort of thing cuts no ice in heaven. Do you wish to amplify your statement with regard to Hesketh Pearson?

SIR E : I assure you, on my word of honour, that no one on earth takes the smallest interest in him; and, if I may say so, I can hardly believe that the Archangels—

ST P : Gabriel reads him every night before turning in, and has copies of all his first editions.

SIR E *(triumphantly)* : For that matter I very much doubt if even he could obtain any second editions!

ST P : A fact that does not redound to *your* credit, sir! Why did you never write about him in *The Sunday Times*? What's the use of being a critic if you don't pick out the master-minds of the age?

SIR E *(on his mettle now)* : *Master*-minds! Huh! Come,

sir—Saint, I mean—let me have the names of these masterpieces; they have escaped my memory.

st p : *Modern Men and Mummers.*

sir e : Ghoulish garbage !

st p : *A Persian Critic.*

sir e : Wish-wash !

st p : *The Whispering Gallery.*

sir e : Garbish ghoulage !

st p : *Iron Rations.*

sir e : Wash-wish !

st p : Very well. It is clear that you have a long way to go.

sir e : But—

st p : But me no buts.

sir e *(brightly)* : That's Shakespeare !

st p : Yes, he ties with Pearson in our *Bible of Familiar Quotations.*

sir e : Well, I'll be damned !

st p : You shortly will be. You are going to hell, from which you can only graduate by becoming an M.P.

sir e : Dear me ! This is very odd. Are there M.Ps. in—

st p : The Master of Pearson's works degree is the highest we have to bestow. Wait here a moment. I'll send Satan to show you the way.

sir e : Goodness-gracious ! The Devil in heaven !

st p : That's the silly term you've been taught to use for him. Satan has his faults, which Michael is always pulling his tail about, but we think well of him, and he is employed as liaison officer with the other place.

sir e : I refuse, I absolutely refuse, to meet him.

st p : The question is whether he'll refuse to meet you. He's a highly cultivated man, though I regret to say that he admires the sort of books you praise so highly on earth.

sir e : What books, may I ask ?

st p : Oh, all the sycophantic stuff about saints, so-called religious poetry, books about eminent men minus their faults, and so on. We keep a special shelf of that kind of rot for Satan. No one else ever wants to borrow them.

SIR E : Look here ! *(A bell rings.)*

ST P : I have no time to look there. You must excuse me. The Evangelists get quite testy when I'm not there to mix the morning appetizer.

(Exit St Paul. Sir Edmund, left alone, sniffs and then sobs.)

9

Self-Portrait

Painters frequently try to see themselves and produce self-portraits. Writers unconsciously portray themselves in their works but usually jib at a conscious attempt to achieve an objective picture, possibly because it would make them feel self-conscious. They may excuse themselves by saying that 'modesty forbids', meaning mock-modesty forbids, for if they were really modest they would not be aware of it. At any rate I am immodest enough to essay a likeness of myself, and this seems to be the right moment in my life, as I reached the age of forty a month after my acquittal.

Readers of the last chapter may find it difficult to believe that the whole tendency of my mind is towards the truth, but if they look back they will find that I made a fearful hash of mendacity. 'You really are a rotten liar,' Freddy Lonsdale said to me. A natural or self-trained liar would have managed the job far more skilfully. The moment I reverted to my normal self in the witness-box, I emerged from the mess my silly deceptions had created. We all suffer from our weaknesses. 'It is not in our stars but in ourselves that we are underlings', as Shakespeare put it, and again:

> The gods are just, and of our pleasant vices
> Make instruments to plague us.

My pleasant vice has always been laziness, which

200

breeds thoughtlessness. I did not take the trouble to think what the result of a casual word might be, in my sloth caring little how the business deal was completed so long as it was behind me and I could forget it. Caught in a maze of misunderstandings by sheer indolence, I tried to push my way out with a series of panic-stricken lies. Sluggishness, followed by foolishness, resulting in fright: such were the ingredients that put me in a tight corner, from which the unblushing truth helped to deliver me. I should perhaps add that my laziness vanishes when I am really keen to do something, as will later be proved, but the range of my interests is restricted and there is very little that I want to do except enjoy myself in my own way.

I will put the first touches to this self-portrait by defining my interests, beginning with my indifferences. As already stated, mine was a case of tardy growth and my character took a long time to develop. Most men do not change much after thirty, but I had reached forty-two before feeling that my personality was, so to speak, set, or almost so. Many people retain their youthful enthusiasm for sport and games throughout life; I had abandoned mine soon after leaving school. Though I still played a little golf and tennis up to the age of forty-one, and when staying with my brother Harry frequently went shooting in his Welsh valley for a few more years, my concern with such things was faint, and my curiosity in the physical feats of other people amounted to nil. In a family of sportsmen I was, biologically, 'a sport'. Of course I could talk about golf, cricket and the rest, the alternative in England being a socially isolated life, but the words of my mouth did not represent the meditations of my heart. As time went on, I also lost interest in politics, a subject that engrosses the conversation of Englishmen next to sport and money-making. I suddenly perceived that politics constituted the game of grown-up children, who loved to exhibit themselves, to tell fantastic lies and to exercise power, just as they had done in the school playground. At the same time I retained an interest in particular politicians, whose independence or comicality made them singular as characters. Though not in the least cynical by nature, I came to the conclusion that nobody, least of all a politician, acted mainly from disinterested motives.

I have never been much interested in religion, another subject that frequently crops up in conversation, and am quite incapable of believing that any one religious institution speaks with the voice of God, who must be polytheistic. Indeed I consider my attitude more religious or at any rate more reverent than that of professing Christians because I have never committed the blasphemy of attributing to God the childish moral judgments of humanity, as promulgated by man-made creeds and institutions. Long ago I decided that credulity is the distinguishing feature of my fellow-mortals, the large majority of whom believe whatever they hear on the wireless or read in the papers. The most up-to-date form of gullibility relates to what is miscalled science, a word that means knowledge or ascertained truth, not, as commonly supposed, invention or experiment. Nowadays the scientists have taken the place of the priests, and their Sinaitic pronouncements are accepted without demur. I personally do not believe that so-called science can tell us anything that really matters, even though it enables us to establish contact with the planets. Finally I am out of sympathy with another illusion of my age, for I do not consider businessmen as a class the least bit more efficient than the members of any other class.

It would appear from the foregoing that in many respects my kingdom is not of this world. But such a

conclusion would be false. I am excessively fond of this
world and find a great deal more delight in it than do
many people who share its interests. I never tire of the
mere spectacle of human beings going about their
business. I cannot take a walk in town or country without being entranced by the novelty or beauty of my
surroundings. I seem to see everything for the first time,
though I may have seen it a thousand times. Life is
always miraculous to me and for ever fresh. I can sit
for any length of time in a pub watching people with
intense interest, and I can sit for any length of time
doing nothing in a garden or on a hill, quite contented
whether my mind be active or empty. I enjoy everything I do and am never bored except in the company
of bores. Innately sensual, I love good wine and good
food, and am inclined to drink too much of one and
eat too much of the other. Up to the age of fifty odd I
was amorously sensual as well, and, though selective in
my tastes, quite incapable of resisting temptation whenever my feelings were excited. I am pretty certain that
my pleasure in life and my inner felicity have been
largely due to good health and a sound constitution,
because I have noticed that men who suffer from
indigestion or some other physical defect have a pessi-
mistic outlook, can never forget themselves in external
circumstances, and usually depend on self-assertion in
order to feel alive.

What commonly passes for religion is not necessary
for my happiness or peace of mind. I derive my
spiritual sustenance from art and nature, and my own
moral sense, inborn and acquired, is sufficient for me,
though I do not expect others to share it. No one was
ever less of a proselytizer than I. The diversity of people
and their ideas is one of the charms of existence, and
the more alike they appear the less interesting they
are. I have never wished to change the world, which is

funny enough as it is. Should it be objected that the Creator did not mean to make it funny, the less Creator he, and I would prefer his mistakes to his intentions. But a creator without humour would be an impossibility, a monstrosity. The whole of creation is riddled with comedy, without which it would be diabolic, not deific. Humour reconciles us to our fate, and for me at any rate some of the great wits and humorists whose gospels I have written have more of the divine in them than many a prophet or saint, though I have never attempted to convert readers to my view. My attitude of indifference to the opinions of others is partly due to a lack of vanity. The meaning of that word should be defined. A man is vain when he accepts the world's estimation of himself, conceited when content with his own. I have more conceit than vanity, as I am quite satisfied with my opinion on any subject that absorbs me and think little of the world's. If not an endearing quality, there is much comfort in conceit: one is wholly unaffected by fashions in taste, the momentary feelings of the community as well as the opinions of individuals: one is free to like what one likes and dislike what one dislikes. Socially, too, conceit is preferable to vanity, because the conceited man does not need to talk about himself, whereas the vain man cannot help doing so. It may be said that no one would write books except for money or fame. But mine are written primarily because I enjoy writing them. If I had mainly desired money, I would have remained on the stage and written plays or some more lucrative type of work than biography. If I had mainly desired fame, I would have written my books in a less individual and more mollifying manner. I am glad that I have made a little money with my pen, because it has enabled me to do the work I like; and I am glad that my biographies have been appreciated by certain critics, because it is more agreeable to be esteemed than abhorred; but my impulse to write has been sufficient to itself and quite unrelated to worldly considerations.

I am only momentarily affected by unfavourable criticism, and forget it within a few hours. I remember being introduced to a fellow at my club who seemed a bit diffident when we shook hands. A drink or two made him suddenly blurt out: 'I thought you wouldn't want to know me after my disparaging review of your latest book.' I assured him that hostile reviews went out of my head as soon as they went into the wastepaper-basket. For some queer reason this made him rather testy until another drink or two had established our fraternity. Was it Samuel Butler who said that he wrote his books in order to have something enjoyable to read in his old age? I can think of few better returns for the travail it entails.

But indifference to the opinions of others does not imply moral or physical courage. In my commerce with the world it merely implies that I am too lazy to bother about hostile judgments, which means that I am incapable of bearing malice. I simply forget what is hurtful, and one cannot be malicious without an object. Cowards and heroes only exist in the romantic fancies of novelists and dramatists. No man is wholly one or the other. I have seen a fellow separate two large and ferocious dogs locked in a death-struggle, and the same fellow quail at the word of a woman. I would not have had the hardihood to attempt the first, and would have laughed at the second. Probably I am like most human beings, brave under certain circumstances, craven under others; but on the whole I should describe myself as cowardly, because I dislike being involved in anything disagreeable, and nearly always seek the easiest way out of a difficulty, being by instinct of a placid disposition, hating rows and loving idleness.

On the other hand my temper, which has much improved since the operation in 1946 removed a large cyst over the old wound, is always liable to lesser eruptions when I am excessively vexed, and on these occasions bravery is in the ascendant. One such incident occurred soon after the collapse of the case against me at the London Assizes. I can give it in detail because I wrote an exact account of it at the time to Hughie, and my letter was among those returned to me after his death.

An emissary of Scotland Yard called at my house while I was out for a walk. My unfortunate wife had not recovered from the distressing period of my trial, and was in a highly nervous state when I got home. Alone with me in the sitting-room, he opened fire. It had come to the knowledge of headquarters, he said that I had received the third and fourth volumes of an autobiography by 'a man called Frank Harris'. I replied that his headquarters had been correctly apprised, though their informant had forgotten to mention that I had also received volumes one and two of the same work. 'Do they wish to borrow it?' I enquired. 'It is well worth a perusal.' He answered that I was committing a grave offence.

'Against what or whom?' I asked.

'Against the law of the land.'

'I am unaware of a law expressly forbidding Englishmen to read the works of Mr Frank Harris. Will you please tell me when it was placed on the Statute Book?'

'The law says that pornographic works must not be procured or distributed in this country.'

'I have neither procured nor distributed such works.'

'But you have received this book?'

'It was sent to me, gratis, by the author. See for yourself.' I showed him the inscribed copies, and continued: 'I cannot prevent him from sending me his works. Nor would I if I could. He is a personal friend of mine, and his books amuse me. I have got more laughter out of his autobiography than from the pages of our greatest humorists.'

'Then you don't think it a disgusting book?'

'Certainly not. I think it highly entertaining and edifying.'

'Edifying? Are you serious?'

'Never more so. No writer should be without it. I regard it as a standard text-book.'

'A text-book!?!'

'Yes. And the text is: "How Not To Do It".'

'I must ask you, Mr Pearson, to treat this matter as important. You are in possession of a filthy and pornographic work, and it is my duty to warn you that you are liable to prosecution.'

'Then it is my duty to warn you that the work is only filthy and pornographic to minds of that description, and that if you prosecute me you will also have to prosecute Mr Bernard Shaw and Mr Winston Churchill (who, I am told, *procured* it) and every other politician and man of letters who has received it in this country. May I ask whether you have approached Mr H. G. Wells and Mr Arnold Bennett?'

'I can't argue with you—'

'I know you can't.'

'Please, *please*. I repeat that I can't argue with you; I can only warn you.'

'Waste of time. You can warn me till you are blue in the face and the entire staff of Scotland Yard is in the last stages of apoplexy.'

'Am I to report to my chief'—he spoke severely—'that you decline to hand those books over?'

'Are you seriously suggesting that I should do so? Is that the object of your visit?'

'Yes.'

At this point I lost my temper and started ranting, the essence of my declamation being reported to Hughie an hour later. Mixing a few oaths with it, this is roughly how it went:

'Then you may also tell your chief that I flatly decline to recognize Scotland Yard's right to issue an *index expurgatorius*, as I don't believe in the Holy C.I.D. I regard his interference as an Inquisition more damnable than the Spanish one, of which he may have heard; and you can inform him that his barbarous and dictatorial methods resemble those of the Bolshevik "Cheka". I repudiate his self-appointed function to institute a bureaucracy of blockheads in a supposedly free country; and you may add that if he wishes to take anything from my house, he will have to do it by force and with the assistance of a special Act of Parliament. Can you remember all that, or shall I repeat it?'

'The gist of it will no doubt be sufficient.'

'That's the best thing you've said yet. Cheers!'

'May I ask whether you have known Mr Harris long?'

'Private interest or public duty?'

'Duty, I'm afraid.'

'Then you'd better write to him and ask.'

'You are not very helpful, sir. You see, it is my job to find out—'

'Then chuck it!'

'What?'

'The job. It's a lousy one.'

He rose and took up his hat, remarking, 'I don't think I can do much more here.' My rage had evaporated and I felt a little remorseful. 'Oh, yes, you can,' I said. 'You can do something that'll make you feel your time hasn't been wasted.' 'What's that?' 'You can drink a bottle of Bass's No. 1.' 'A Pale Ale would go down better, sir, if you have one.'

While we were drinking together in mellow mood I asked him if the Yard really wanted to stamp out pornography, because if so I could give him the names of several well-known firms that published and even advertised works of that nature. He was keenly interested and brought out his notebook, but after I had mentioned the leading University presses he wanted to know what I was getting at. I replied that the brothel scenes in *Pericles* and not a few episodes in *Troilus and Cressida*, both by Shakespeare and both included in editions issued by our leading publishers, made the improprieties of Frank Harris appear like the scratchings of a naughty schoolboy on a lavatory wall. When I was seeing him off, he murmured, 'Well, I haven't got much change out of you.'

But someone else got a good deal of change out of me. I never discovered who he was, but the sound of my name must have appealed to him, and banking on the publicity I had received in the course of my trial he went about the country passing himself off as me, dining with people, staying with them, borrowing their money, and even in one case seducing the daughter of the house. His pockets were filled with newspaper reviews of my books, which he produced and read aloud. He was arrested several times, giving my name, which at first was printed in certain papers; but after a while the police and the local pressmen got wise to it and rang me up to find out whether I was at home or in gaol. It was all very annoying, especially when I received letters demanding the return of loans or continuing the subject of a conversation in which I had taken no part; but I was too heedless to run the fellow to earth. I fancy that my impersonator managed to make a better living out of his borrowings than I did out of my books.

What helped him was my relatively hermitical life.

Few people had seen me except as a character on the stage. I have never cared for society, either with or without a capital 'S', and avoid social gatherings like the plague. They bore me with their noisy chatter and increase my claustrophobia. I love the society of my friends, but when twenty or thirty people are gathered together I am not to be found in the midst of them. My natural place is my home, where I have never known a moment's boredom, and I don't care for congregations, whether of penmen or players or peers or plebeians, no doubt likeable enough individually but too much alike socially. My friends and relations regard me as anti-social, which I am not, but I like to choose my company. I simply abhor crowds and would run a mile to get away from them. It has often occurred to me that such knowledge of human beings as I possess is due to the fact that I do not mix with them indiscriminately. The man who knows everyone knows no one. Also I am distracted at large parties and find myself watching people instead of attending to the talk around me. The result is that my conversation becomes silly, or, as my present wife once put it, I say what I think without stopping to think what I say.

It may in part be due to my apathy, to my not caring for the opinions or company of cliques and social circles, that I have never been ambitious, except when I was young and wanted to play Hamlet. My lack of this attribute, the possession of which implies a competitive nature has helped me to be satisfied with life. Expect nothing, and one cannot be disappointed. All I need add is that, by the kindness of fate, I have done better than the master who gave me nought for an algebra paper would have predicted.

The variety of life is so fascinating that one could spend years studying and enjoying each aspect of it. One of the joys of my life is music. Sometime in

the nineteen-twenties I made the acquaintance of
Beethoven's work, which quickly supplanted Wagner's in
my estimation, and ever since he has been my favourite
composer. There are occasional works I put on a level
with his symphonies, such as Elgar's 'Falstaff' and
Schubert's Ninth, but on the whole Beethoven is for me
second only to Shakespeare in the world of creative art.
I am fond of certain works by Sibelius, Tchaikovsky,
Mendelssohn, César Franck, Handel, Mozart and
others, but I find Brahms constipated and Bach a bore.
As however the last two have countless admirers, they
can get along quite well without my approval. With
regard to warbling, the song of a thrush never fails to
give me pleasure, but the song of a human being seldom
fails to give me stomach-ache. It took me twenty-four
hours to recover from Melba and Caruso in *La Bohème*
at Covent Garden, while Wagnerian singing puts me on
the rack.

I deeply lament that a proper appreciation of painting has been denied me. I am interested in portraits
because I am interested in people, but I cannot get
the thrill out of great landscape pictures which certain poetry and music can give me. I admire, but
remain unmoved. On the other hand I am enchanted
by architecture, both ecclesiastic and domestic. The
exterior of Salisbury Cathedral and the interior of St
Mary Redcliffe at Bristol have the same effect on me
as a great symphony, while Canterbury, York, Ely,
Durham, and the interior of King's College chapel at
Cambridge, appeal almost as powerfully to my imagination; though I detest the choir screens, however beautiful in themselves, that destroy the harmony of some of
our noblest buildings. One of the pleasures of walking
about London and other cities is the sudden detection
of exquisite houses dating from William and Mary or
Queen Anne or George III, and by experience or

instinct I can usually place their period within a decade. The Regency houses of Brighton, too, are a limitless delight. Enough to say that my existence would have been gravely impoverished without music and architecture.

But of all the arts I put literature first. Life must have been strangely barren before books were written or plays performed. The greatness of a people lies in words, not deeds, and even its deeds can only live in words. The theatre opened my eyes to the glory of literature, and to this day the writers I read most frequently are Shakespeare and Shaw. I am still a regular playgoer, and there is nothing for me more enjoyable than a good comedy. With age my taste for tragedy has abated, unless the plays of Tchekov may be so regarded. The novelists whose works have given me most pleasure are Scott, Dickens and Dumas, while Boswell's *Johnson* and Hazlitt's essays are books I dip into year after year.

By reflecting or interpreting life the arts help us to live more abundantly. Without them nations would have no soul, religions would die, and the memory of mankind would perish. Those whose senses are shut to their revelation are only half-alive, as if they were the victims of an incurable disease which preoccupies them to the exclusion of everything except themselves. Personally I would rather be dead than half-alive; and I have enjoyed the experience of living so much that I now ask nothing of life but a quick death.

PART

III

10

Interlude

For a year after the successful issue of my trial we lived on what was left of the sums earned by the book, and during that time I wrote all sorts of things that have never been printed. I had to overcome obloquy and found that the hostility of my fellow-journalists had stimulated me. My subconscious principle seems to have been: not to resist is not to exist. But I made the discovery that those who could have helped me in one or other of my professions would not do so, while those who would have helped me could not do so. Taking a tip from Plutarch, I composed a series of 'Parallel Portraits' in which I tried to show that certain modern writers had their counterparts in politics. 'A publisher is sitting on the book like a frightened hen', I wrote to Hughie, 'hardly daring to hatch yet longing to bring it out . . . my own opinion is that he'll funk laying what may cause a bit of a stink.' Several publishers must have funked it because in due course the book was cremated. I produced a sort of autobiography which also perished.

But most of my time was spent on plays. I went to Colin's house nearly every Sunday and together we managed to construct four of them: a farce, two comedies and a drama. Some of the best episodes in the farce were pinched by a management to which it was sent and introduced into a show by someone else, but before this appeared on the stage our farce had been returned with the usual managerial apology. Sybil Thorndike showed interest in the drama, but apparently something more interesting displaced it. One of the comedies would have been done by the firm of Reandean if we had been sensible enough to place it with an agent who happened to be one of their directors and whose influence was used against it. The other, *A Writ for Libel,* was favourably considered by several 'stars' who wanted to play the leading part: Marie Tempest, Eva Moore and Mrs Patrick Campbell, the last of whom did her best to raise the necessary money, but her star had set and no one seemed anxious to back her. About twenty years later I sent it to the B.B.C., and their drama department broadcast it one Saturday night, after which it was done by several repertory companies, Pilton Wilson arranging for its production at Bexhill, and Arthur Brough making a success of it at Folkestone.

Another playwright's job I undertook was with Floryan Sobieniowski, Shaw's Polish translator, who asked me to turn his literal translations of certain Polish plays into idiomatic English. Three of these, each in one act, called *Peace, War and Revolution* by Waclaw Grubinski, were produced by Robert Atkins for the International Theatre at the Royalty on Sunday, 17 February, 1929. Then there was a comedy, the title of which I have forgotten. And, finally, a poetic drama by Stanislaw Wyspianski known as *The Wedding,* which I struggled with for many weeks. Sir Barry Jackson seemed anxious to put it on, and incidental music founded on ancient Polish tunes was supplied by Sir Arthur Somervell. It would have been a giant undertaking and an almost certain flop, though I believe that if audiences could survive the second act they would be thrilled by the last, which creates an atmosphere of suspense unique in drama.

By the end of 1927 my wife and I had begun to live on borrowed money and it looked as if we would again have to face the conditions we had known at the beginning of 1922, when succour came from Godfrey Tearle, who was about to tour the provinces with *The Acquittal*, politely described as 'a new modern play', and, at the suggestion of my friend Walter Havers, engaged me for the part of the villain. We opened in January 1928 at the Theatre Royal, Portsmouth, and by some fluke, for I have never collected newspaper criticisms, the notices of this and one other play in which I appeared have survived. I must have sent them to my mother because I have recently come across them among certain letters she kept. Actors are rather fond of quoting tedious testimonials to their remarkable performances. Since I never considered myself as an actor, I shall quote both these notices, at whatever cost of personal suffering to the reader, merely to show that I was able to convince at least one member of each audience to the contrary. Here is the first, from the leading Portsmouth paper: 'The man himself' (i.e. the wicked husband) 'is played by Hesketh Pearson, and his reading of this unsavoury character is a triumph which has not been achieved without careful study. His is the most difficult of all the parts in this play, and Mr. Pearson's work last night will be remembered in Portsmouth for a very long while.' That must have been pleasant reading for me over breakfast, but I fancy it merely meant that I was enjoying the change from playing myself, scarcely disguised as a doctor or army officer, to revelling in the part of a murderer. Villains are much more interesting than heroes, even the unnatural blackguards in such third-rate melodramas as *The Acquittal*.

Perhaps a word or two about myself as an actor will

not be out of place at this point; and the first thing
to be said is that I was not at any time an actor. I could
have put up a good show in certain parts, e.g. Cassius in
Julius Caesar, Master Ford in *The Merry Wives,*
Caesar in Shaw's play, but I had neither the self-
absorption nor the technique of the born player. The
actor's art is a combination of study and spontaneity.
I was not sufficiently interested to learn the job, and
not exhibitory enough by nature to encourage inspiration. I echoed from my heart a remark made by that
unequalled elocutionist and natural performer Johnston
Forbes-Robertson, who wanted to be a painter: 'Never
at any time have I gone on the stage without longing
for the moment when the curtain would come down on
the last act.' The man with the true actor's nature feels
exactly the opposite, and spends his days longing for
the curtain to go up on the first act. Laziness, combined
with a love of Shakespeare and an admiration of Beerbohm Tree, sent me on the stage; and as I happened
to have a presentable appearance and an audible voice
I could have remained on it as a 'type' actor, picking
up cash trifles from the films while so engaged. But as
time went on acting bored me so much that I could
not even retain the words of my part, and this made
me decide to abandon the business. Shortly before I
did so a perceptive critic plaintively enquired whether
I mistook sleep-walking for acting.

The tour with Godfrey Tearle lasted throughout
1928, with a short break in September. I formed a
friendship with his stage-manager, Leonard Trollope,
a delightful, easy-going, absent-minded fellow, keen on
reading, and we still see him and his wife Cecily, though
our meetings are too rare owing to their residence in
Minehead. I played my last games of golf with Godfrey
on that tour and have never had a club in my hand
since making two air-shots and topping the ball at a

third on the first tee at Eastbourne before an appre-
ciative audience of about fifty players who were to
follow us round the course. In the spring of 1928 my
book of short stories, *Iron Rations*, was issued by Cecil
Palmer, a pleasant intelligent person whose only fault
as a publisher was that he scarcely ever paid royalties
to authors. About twenty years earlier he had brought
out Frank Harris's *The Man Shakespeare*, and if I know
anything about Frank that would have been an
occasion when the royalties were paid. My war stories
had been written about seven years before they were
published, their chief merit being that with a single
exception they were absolutely true in substance and
detail, their chief defect being that the satire was
laboured and juvenile. I doubt if they sold well, but
that was a secret the publisher kept to himself. As far
as I remember the large majority of newspaper critics
followed his example and remained mute. During the
tour I wrote a book of essays on the art of biography,
which the firm of Lippincott brought out in America.
'This means that I am on my hobby,' I reported to
Hughie. The slightly fictional quality of Lytton
Strachey's work had attracted me, and in *Ventilations*
I had not shaken off the feeling that some fancy was
allowable in biography. But this quickly evaporated,
and before writing my first work of that kind I was
wholly of Dr Johnson's opinion that truth alone is
valuable and interesting, as far as a human being is
able to apprehend it.

The tour over, my main interest in literature could
no longer be satisfied by reading the works of others,
and I decided to write a Life of my maternal ancestor,
Erasmus Darwin, having already collected material
while I was travelling about the country, especially
the Doctor's Commonplace Book which had been lent
me by the Reverend Darwin Wilmot, whom I had

visited in Leamington. Various other relations and connections had contributed, my mother having written to all of them. The problem was: how to keep my family during the six or eight months required to finish the work now that I had absorbed all the available books and documents. The solution was simple. There happened just then to be a craze for Shaw letters and first editions, which were instantly snapped up by American collectors at remarkably high prices. I had a budget of his letters, all his first editions, and some of his plays privately printed for actors in the original productions. The lot fetched about £200, and on that sum we were able to live in 1929 while I wrote my first biography, *Doctor Darwin*.

Everyone to whom I mentioned his name assumed that my reference was to Charles Darwin, grandson of Erasmus, and an American publisher cabled an offer for it on that assumption. But I was not interested in Charles, and no one else appeared to be interested in Erasmus, though I struck a spark of encouragement out of G. K. Chesterton, who said: 'A much better man than his grandson Charles. I like these credulous sceptics: a disbeliever is finer than a no-believer.' I had met G.K.C. several times before, but on this occasion, January 1929, I was a guest at a dinner given in his honour in the committee room of the old Savage Club, of which I was a member, in Adelphi Terrace. Hilaire Belloc was there, with about forty friends or contributors to Chesterton's paper, myself being one (unpaid). I did not belong to the Distributists' League, or whatever his political cause was named, but then I have never belonged to a party or a creed because I am constitutionally unable to swallow the whole of any doctrine.

But I was fond of G.K.C. himself, one of the great 'characters' in the history of English letters. He loved

company, enjoyed a rousing song, relished a vulgar
joke, drank good wine and beer when he could get it,
and preferred bad wine and beer to none at all. He
chatted to everybody he met, whether in a pub or a
drawing-room, talked sense or nonsense according to
mood or atmosphere, and seemed unconscious of time
or place. A sort of Falstaff in bulk and wit, his laughter
could be heard several houses away. He could play
with words so dexterously that his dialectics often consisted of verbal acrobatics. 'Man is a biped,' he
declared, 'but fifty men are not a centipede.' I once
parodied his style, saying that Shaw's most serious
limitation was that he preferred potatoes to potations.
He chuckled over this; and when some years later I
published an imaginary conversation between him and
Shaw, giving him the phrase that had amused him,
he wrote to say that as I could imitate his mannerisms
so well perhaps I would like to produce his next book.
He took no interest in making money, selling his books
for a song. For one of the best, *The Napoleon of Notting
Hill*, he received £100. Even his pugnacity in print and
on the platform was unworldly. He loved disputation
and enjoyed a fight for its own sake, not for any kudos
to be got out of it nor for the pleasure of scoring off
an opponent. He probably never wanted to win because
that would have meant the end of an argument. He was
once asked to stand for Parliament and replied that he
would be delighted to do so if it were absolutely certain
that he would be defeated.

His absent-mindedness was proverbial. An old friend
of his, H. T. Muggeridge, told me that G.K.C. had
arrived late at an Ethical Society meeting, and had
apologized by saying that though his wife always saw
him into a train she was not there to see him out of
it, and on this occasion he had alighted at a station
further down the line. In the middle of his speech he

was taken short, briefly consulted someone on the platform, descended therefrom, walked through the audience which somehow managed to control itself, and after a few minutes' absence returned to the rostrum without a word of explanation, starting off with 'Let me see, where were we?' Many men would rather have faced a firing-squad.

In almost every respect he was the exact opposite of his friend Hilaire Belloc, who went into battle to conquer, was punctilious in all his arrangements, prudent over money, selling his work for as much as he could get, and wholly conscious of what was going on around him.

I used to see Belloc in a bar near Ludgate Circus, debating, reciting in his high-pitched voice, laughing, telling Rabelaisian stories, and improvising lines of poetry that would not have been received with such tumultuous mirth in a company of tea-drinkers. He was what is commonly called 'a man's man': that is, he liked what most men are supposed to like: alcohol, argument, songs, jovial company, bodily exercise, ribald merriment, and rowdiness. Some of his verse impromptus raised howls of delight in bibulous circles. He once started intoning a Shakespearean sonnet: 'Shall I compare thee to a summer's day?', answering the question in his own more direct style: 'Not if I know it, you disgusting bitch!' He wrote a sequence of verses on the pictures in some Dutch gallery, most of which I heard him recite, though only one has remained in my memory. This particular picture represented Mark Antony lying flat on the floor in a drunken stupor with Cleopatra leaning her elbow on his prostrate body, her eyes on the horizon; which inspired Belloc with this quatrain:

> Watchful beside her slumbering Antony
> Great Cleopatra gazes out to sea,

And sighs, and not without a pang recalls
Imperial Caesar's memorable balls.

In appearance Belloc was short, stoutish, thick-set, and might have passed for a red-faced mediaeval cardinal with mutton-chop whiskers. His habitual expression was severe, his conversation precise. In telling someone how to go from one place to another, his instructions were so detailed that unless his companion had an equally ordered mind he could not possibly follow them. I heard him once lay down a plan for reaching Paris from Sussex that so completely bewildered me that I would have found it easier to walk there. He was egotistical, fanatical in his religion, often abruptly rude and indifferent to the feelings of others, but a delightful writer of essays and travel-books. Towards the end of his life Hughie and I visited him at his Sussex home and were surprised to hear that he thought more of being a gentleman than of being an author. We did not deem it advisable to tell him, as Voltaire had told Congreve in a like situation, that we would not have travelled so far merely to meet a gentleman.

It may be that in the years to come Belloc will be remembered as the author of one of the most delightful books in the language and quite the silliest book ever written by an intelligent Englishman. *The Four Men* will be enjoyed as long as people take pleasure in good-fellowship. On the other hand his work on Oliver Cromwell was intended as a blow struck for his religion, a design which exposed him at once as a bad biographer. He tried to prove that the man who had paralysed every Continental nation with fear and whose greatness was admitted by Johnson, Milton, Marvell, Mazarin, Voltaire and Carlyle, was in reality a feeble and futile fumbler.

After that dinner at the Savage Club I wrote to

Hughie: 'G.K.C. frequently referred to little gems of satire written by "Hilary", and Belloc as frequently returned the compliment by mentioning the pearls of wit manufactured by "Gilbert".' In fact it was a homely party. When G.K.C. was not indulging his elephantine laugh, he looked dejected; and when Belloc was not smiling to himself, he looked smug. Colin sat next to Chesterton, and knowing his fondness for good wine ordered bottle after bottle of a particularly fine claret which he knew to be in the Club cellar. Colin assumed that as a member of the Savage he was in a position to stand G.K.C. drinks; but when he later wanted to settle the account, he found to his discomfort that as a guest at the dinner he could not be responsible for the bottles of expensive claret with which he had plied his distinguished neighbour.

Following the food there were speeches and recitations, one guest having the temerity to deliver G.K.C's famous poem with the refrain 'I don't care where the water goes if it doesn't get into the wine'. In a slightly bibulous condition I urged Colin to give the epitaph on G.K.C. which had appeared in his volume *Premature Epitaphs* by Kensal Green a year or so before. At length he surrendered to my importunity and spoke the lines, which have been misquoted and misattributed many times since:

> Place on his hand the jewel, on his brow the diadem,
> Who in an age of miracles dared to believe in them.
> > Chesterton companion
> > > His companions mourn.
> > Chesterton crusader
> > > Leaves a cause forlorn.
> > Chesterton the critic
> > > Pays no further heed.
> > Chesterton the poet
> > > Lives while men shall read.

Chesterton the dreamer
Is by sleep beguiled;
And there enters heaven
Chesterton . . . the child.

I could tell that G.K.C. listened with pleasure, mixed with some embarrassment, while the expression on Belloc's face was a trifle sardonic, as if he felt it presumptuous of anyone but a Roman Catholic to prescribe the qualifications for entry into heaven.

While engaged on my biography of Erasmus Darwin I kept up a vigorous correspondence with Hughie, then living at Thonon-les-Bains on Lake Geneva. Our main theme was Shakespeare, on whom he was writing. The result of his labours, *The Return of William Shakespeare*, appeared in September 1929, and I reviewed it in *G.K.'s Weekly*, describing it as 'the best piece of creative criticism in the language. . . This is as near to Shakespeare as we are ever likely to get with his own works and a first-rate critical intelligence to help us.' I have not altered my opinion. It is one of those rare books I can pick up at any moment and read with undiminished pleasure.

Towards the end of 1929 it became necessary to keep the tradesmen at bay. Hearing from a friend that John Galsworthy's last play, *The Roof*, was being rehearsed, and that the fellow they were trying for the part of the Major was not considered suitable, I went down to the Vaudeville Theatre, read the opening scene, and was passed by the author as well as the producer, Basil Dean. At an early rehearsal Galsworthy came up to me and said: 'You remind me very much of an actor who once played Marlow in *The Silver Box*.' Collecting my wits, I replied: 'That's odd, because you remind me very much of the author of *The Silver Box*.' Displeased, he answered loftily: 'But I *am* the author of *The Silver*

Box.' Grateful for the opening, I pursued: 'And I am the actor who once played Marlow in it.' Shaw would have enjoyed this interchange, but from the look on Galsworthy's face I derived no feeling of fraternity. He seemed a nice fellow, but strangely reserved and a little suspicious.

The show opened at the Golders Green Hippodrome, where the fire effects were spectacular without being suffocating, and it did well. But the Vaudeville is a small theatre and in the last act the smoke caused the first-night audience some discomfort, there being much coughing and eye-watering. After the necessary damping down on subsequent nights, the blaze was never so effective, and this may have hurt the play, which was anyhow a poor one. The short run of eight weeks or so did not affect me, as I was out of the cast during the last fortnight and on my way to America. I had been offered a part in *The Matriarch* by G. B. Stern. With Mrs Patrick Campbell in the principal character it had been a success in London; but our leading actress, Constance Collier, good within her limits, was not good enough for a drama that depended on her performance, and the success was not repeated in America.

We played for a month at Chicago and a month at Philadelphia before starting in New York, where we ran for three weeks. Nearly every author who goes to America writes a book on it. I shall content myself with a paragraph. 'There being a law against drink', I informed Hughie, 'it stands to reason that there is more drunkenness here than in any other country in the world.' That was a striking aspect of life under Prohibition. Like everyone else I was dumbfounded by the view of New York from Hudson River, when the setting sun turned the stately business buildings into a cluster of cathedrals seen in a dream, and by Michigan Avenue, Chicago, viewed from the Lake. I was soothed by the

park and squares of Philadelphia, and kept awake by
the never-ending din of New York, compared with
which the traffic sounds of London are those of a quiet
village. For a relative recluse like me, American hospitality was overpowering. Also the natives seemed
capable of enduring boredom to an unlimited extent.
They love information for its own sake, information
about anything and everything, and when an American
mounts a platform or gets on his feet after dinner he
is permitted to exude facts in a way that would arouse
protest in England. At one gathering a speaker had
already spent an hour churning out stuff of no conceivable interest, and when my turn came I merely
expressed a wish for a cup of tea and left it at that.
There should be a ten-minutes time-limit to all speeches.
If the Americans do not take care, they will weary the
rest of the world with their passion for talking and writing like encyclopaedists.

I again experienced an ineffable relief on returning
to my home country in April 1930. That autumn I was
at the Cambridge Festival Theatre playing Sir Philip
Francis in Lion Feuchtwanger's *Warren Hastings*, and
playing it rather badly I think; in spite of which I was
asked to return there later to appear as Wolsey in
Henry VIII, Hannibal in *The Road to Rome*, and in a
part Ivor Novello had acted in some Austrian or Hun-
garian play. I agreed to do so if they would substitute
Caesar and Cleopatra for the Hannibal drama, as
Shaw's Caesar was one of the few parts that had always
attracted me; but they wished to do the other.

While at Cambridge I went over to Bedford one
Sunday. Remorseless and uncharitable time had dealt
harshly with my dear mother, who was not only almost
blind from cataract, an attempt to remove it from one
eye having failed, but had just undergone an operation
for colotomy at the age of seventy-five. She was in a

nursing home, as cheerful as ever, and delighted with my *Doctor Darwin*, which had recently been published and dedicated to her. The Press had not yet recovered from the names they had called me four years earlier, and the reviews were scant. I had to wait till December 1931, when the bicentenary of the Doctor's birth was celebrated with a front-page article in *The Times Literary Supplement* and my book was praised as 'one of the models of sensible ancestor-worship'.

A few short stories, one of which Leonard Huxley accepted for *The Cornhill Magazine*, occupied my time in the early part of 1931; and then I took the leading parts in two plays touring the provinces, the last being Noel Coward's *The Young Idea*, for which I only had a week to rehearse and learn the words. The result convinced me that I had better quit the theatre and earn a living in some other manner. Owing to my lack of interest I could no longer concentrate, and when I walked on the stage of the Empire (I believe it was) at Edinburgh, and beheld an auditorium about the size of the London Coliseum, the realization that I would have to pitch my voice so as to be heard at the back of the gallery drove the words out of my mind, and I had to conduct the opening scene within hearing of the prompter; which had a desolating effect on the poor girl who played my wife and whose rehearsed movements had to be adapted to the new position I had taken up. Every morning that week I walked round Arthur's Seat repeating my words parrot-fashion, and by the time we reached Glasgow the author would have approved the textual accuracy of my utterance. Whether he would have approved of my performance is another matter. Earlier I threatened the reader with a quotation from the only other surviving Press notice of my acting. It appeared in the chief Brighton paper and was, I hope, written by a woman: 'The other principal character, that of the father, is finely realized by Hesketh Pearson. So charmingly lovable is he that it is difficult to understand how he quarrelled with the adorable Jennifer and afterwards loses his hold on his second wife.' In spite of such appraisals I determined to make this my swan-song, and though I acted the following May at the Gate Theatre, London, in a three-week run of *The Challenge* by David Higham, I consciously took leave of the stage in December 1931 on the last night of *The Young Idea* at Birmingham.

In the early part of 1932 I polished off the last short stories for a volume that has not been published, though several have appeared in magazines or newspapers, and in February took part in a film as a police inspector, writing to Hughie that it was 'a frightful waste of time and a dreadful bore,' and adding: 'For utter incompetence commend me to the film industry. It beats anything in my knowledge, not excepting the Staff during the war.' I spent two tedious days hanging about doing nothing, about half an hour being spent on the set, but the price of my boredom was £12. I never saw the thing, as in those days I scarcely ever went to films, and all I can remember is that Jack Hulbert played the leading part. Then, in July 1932, my new profession was settled for me by Colin Hurry.

He ran an advertising business, in which I did odd jobs at a regular salary for six or seven years. The salary was just enough to keep my family while I spent all my spare hours working in the British Museum reading room and writing my early biographies. My labours for Colin were very irregular; but he knew of my wish to do something else and never called on me to earn my pay unless he really needed me. In short I found my most intimate friend a most accommodating employer. As I had to meet a good many people at lunches and dinners, and make myself agreeable to them, Colin was taking a risk, and he knew it.

Once, in the early 'twenties, when he was editing *The Organiser*, I accompanied him to the Cecil Hotel, where he had to interview the first of the American Rotarians to visit this country, a healthy-looking fellow with a mass of white hair and a bland expression. He greeted us warmly in a private sitting-room, and Colin started proceedings by asking why he was visiting England. He replied simply: 'We come over here . . . to be loved.' I cannot now explain why that artless remark shook me to my foundations. From a man of business it was unexpected, and from him in particular it came too promptly. The slight pause before the last three words may have added to the shock. Whatever the cause, I burst into peals of laughter. The amazement on his face did not help me to self-control. I simply rocked on my chair. Colin, always in command of his emotions, grasped me by the arm, led me from the room patting my back sympathetically, took me to the long bar, ordered a drink for me, and hurried back to the Rotarian, whose astonishment he assuaged by saying that I suffered from shell-shock, upon which the other expressed much sympathy and the interview concluded harmoniously. Returning to the bar, Colin found me in a state of collapse and the barman solicitous but apprehensive.

Vividly recalling that episode, Colin nevertheless hazarded his business and let me loose on prospective clients. On the whole I behaved pretty well, though he must have experienced some anxious moments. I cannot endure bores gladly, and many business people ooze tedium. A bore uncovers a multitude of vices, and the trivial complaints, childish self-pity, stupid bigotry and irritating habits that one does not mind in an interesting person are insufferable in a bore. I cannot remem-

ber giving way to my impatience more than once, but
that occasion probably cost Colin a tidy sum. I was
sitting at lunch next to the publicity manager of a
famous group of papers. He had just returned from
Germany where he had been much impressed by
Hitler's Youth Movement. The whole subject bored me
stiff, but I choked down my feelings and made the
necessary sounds of affirmation and appreciation. He
went on to say that something like it was needed in
England, and then he described it all over again with
many details he had been too enthusiastic to supply at
the first narration. After half an hour I became conscious of clenching my teeth and holding myself in with
an effort. At last he paused, gulped his wine, and turned
to me with the comment: 'Makes yer think, eh?' My
reply was out of my mouth before I knew it was on
the way: 'Nothing could make you think.' Thereafter
his attitude to me cooled, and I fear he showed less
cordiality to Colin, who however refrained from cursing
me.

When first I joined the business Colin's artistic director was Bill Berry, who was followed by Joe Maiden,
and there can never have been such a jolly and friendly
group as ours in any commercial concern. The day's
work finished, Colin, Bill, Joe, myself, Freddie Andrews,
and one or two others, used to drink together at the
Connaught Rooms in Great Queen Street, almost next-
door to our office, and from our shouts of laughter we
might have been mistaken for a troupe of comedians.
Colin usually led the revels, but Freddie was a 'star
turn'. He was the director of a bill-posting firm, though
in his time he had touched many professions, of which
he told the most amazing and amusing stories. With his
deep full voice, grave demeanour, eye-twinkle, and the
always-active forefinger of his right hand, he could keep
us entertained by the hour. I had known him for some

years before he made the surprising disclosure that he
had once run a Shakespearean company in the provinces with Henry Baynton in the leading parts. I
wanted to hear more, and noted down his replies the
same day, as I was then collecting material for a sketch
of him:

'Why on earth did you choose Shakespeare?' I
asked.

'Because we didn't have to pay royalties to the Bard,
and we didn't have to ask the Bard's permission if we
wanted to cut his favourite passages and put in a few
topical "gags".'

'Well, many of *his* "gags" were topical.'

'So bloody topical that no one can understand them
today; so we helped him with a few fruity bits of our
own.'

'How did you get the public in?'

'Schools. That's the secret. Rows and rows of little
bastards of all sexes. We circulated the heads of every
educational establishment wherever we went, saying
that the Bard depended on them. If they didn't support
him now, they'd never get another chance. We gave
them the impression that the Bard would personally
benefit. And we gave 'em a baker's dozen of seats for the
price of twelve.'

'What was the acting like?'

'Bloody awful. No author would have stuck it. But
the Bard, being dead, had no option.'

'What sort of scenery?'

'Rotten! Bought for a song and given away with a
double whisky.'

'Any good points about the shows at all?'

'One damned good point, Hesketh. They paid us
handsomely. The Bard touched the dough every week.'

I should like to have been in that company. The
salaries, I gathered, were small, but the laughs, when-

ever Freddie was behind the curtain, must have been great.

Such was his ability as a humorous raconteur that he made us oblivious to time. I once took him across the road from the Connaught Rooms to the Kingsway Theatre, to see a drama by Emil Ludwig, *Versailles*, since Freddie displayed a passing interest in politics. I was a sort of literary adviser to an organization called the Independent Theatre Club, which had taken a lease of the Kingsway to produce interesting plays. As my advice was never followed, I cannot pretend to have influenced the Club's policy in the least; but my services were more than repaid by the formation of a friendship with the secretary, Basil Harvey, which has endured. I have just been glancing at his extremely lively autobiography *Growing Pains* (1937), in which he quotes a letter from me: 'Having realised that humanity is thoroughly shoddy, laugh at it, don't scream at it; and let your laughter be rich like Shakespeare's, not withering like Swift's. Perhaps the ideal stage in human development is that at which one is always "taken in" by humanity, and always aware that one is being "taken in".' More than twenty years later I find that there is nothing much to add. But Freddie Andrews was not interested in my philosophy; nor was he concerned with Komisarjevski's production which we had come to see. We sat drinking in the saloon while he told stories until the play was over and the lights of the bar went out.

All through the early 'thirties I was troubled by the condition of my mother, and my wife and I frequently spent week-ends at Bedford. In her last years she was completely blind and incapacitated by the horrible operation she had endured. Yet she never complained, and when Gladys had a talk with father, whose osteo-arthritis had immobilized him, she could say with truth that mother's sole worry was that she could not look after him and attend to his comfort. 'That's just as it should be,' he observed. On another occasion he told his nurse: 'I am thankful that my dear wife does not have to suffer as I do.' However ill she felt, he insisted on reading a chapter of the Bible to her every day. He had been so thoroughly spoilt by her that the most trivial deviation from routine evoked his comment, as when one of us failed to tear the toilet paper in the W.C. along the dotted line. My sister-in-law Pearl told me that when staying with them in Ireland she heard father wake mother up at two in the morning merely to inform her that she had packed a red candlestick instead of a blue one. Years later, in Wales, when he had gone out to survey the sky, Pearl asked him whether it would be a fine day. He replied: 'If I were in my own county, I could tell what the weather is going to do.' He could not travel without a thermo-meter and every room in his house was provided with one, another being hung outside his dressing-room window. He consulted at least three of them every morning, every evening and every time he went out, noting the temperatures and the state of the weather in his diary. It was a sort of religious rite. Another of his peculiarities was a conviction that wherever he resided the best of everything was obtainable. At one time Worcester, and then Bedford, contained the best shops, the best doctors, dentists, etc. in the universe. His newspapers too were the most reliable in the country, and he read *Berrows Worcester Journal*, the *Bedford-shire Standard*, the *Church of England Newspaper*, and the *Daily Telegraph*, from beginning to end, though in his later and less active years *The Times* displaced the *Telegraph* and became the most reliable daily paper in the country. His experiences were also of a super-lative order. As he had once been in Australia, it seemed obvious to him that no other place suffered such extremes of heat and cold. It was also the wettest and driest of continents.

Up to the age of seventy-five he remained fairly active, though it must have irritated him when he began to slice and top more golf-balls than he hit straight and clean. He still walked up to the links, played his round, walked down to the Town and County Club, played his game of billiards, walked home, had a hot bath, and started dinner at nine, which lasted till ten. How mother managed to keep her servants was a mystery. He had never lacked for anything, accepted everything as his due, and was not even aware that during the 1914-18 war mother had sacrificed her butter ration to spare him the unpleasantness of tasting margarine. Having a thoroughly conservative mentality, he hoarded things. When no longer of the least personal use, he kept some fourteen suits of clothes; socks, vests etc. by the dozen; guns, bats, rackets, clubs, mallets, and so on. He still cherished the knitted ties he had worn on his honeymoon. No innovations in the house were permitted, no electric light, gas-stove or geyser; and he only allowed a telephone because my sister Elsie paid for it when she was running the home and sometimes needed a doctor at short notice.

As he gradually became crippled with osteo-arthritis he moved with the aid of sticks, later with crutches. The vicar of St Martin's Church begged him to discontinue reading the lessons, but he went on doing so until the choir audibly gasped as he negotiated the chancel steps and for a dreadful moment it seemed certain that he would fall. When no longer able to read the lessons, he ceased to attend morning service and read them to mother instead. At last the stairs at home were too much for him and he decided to remain on the first floor, going along a corridor divided by three stairs from his bedroom to 'the den', formerly our schoolroom. None of us could understand why he chose the first floor, because he could easily have lived on the ground floor, and by his choice he missed three glorious summers, 1933-5, which he might have spent sitting in the garden. It may be that he did not wish to have a water closet constructed downstairs, which could have been done without the least difficulty. Anyhow he had made up his mind and nothing could shake him. He never knew that mother gave his study to the nurse as a private sitting-room, all his relics being stowed away somewhere; and occasionally mother had nightmares when she pictured him coming downstairs and entering the study. His contentment, not her own suffering, was her main care, and I remember her expressing a hope that father would not live to see a Labour Government in power, as it would be 'so awful for him'.

11

Resurrection

Having committed literary suicide, it took me seven years to accomplish my resurrection. My biography of Erasmus Darwin had brought in no money and had been practically boycotted by the Press. But it had shown me what I intended to do henceforth. While writing it at the age of forty-two my vocation was revealed to me for the first time in my life, and I perceived that the writing of biography was the only occupation that could ever completely absorb me. Money or no money, reputation or no reputation, I would go on writing it until, as Hamlet says, my eyelids could no longer wag. Like an actor I would express my own personality by re-creating the personalities of others, which meant that my choice would be restricted to the sort of person who appealed to me. I may say here that in the years ahead I received innumerable offers from publishers and appeals from relations to write the Lives of eminent people, among them a Prime Minister, an Archbishop of Canterbury, a Lord Chief Justice, a famous Ambassador, and a Governor of the Bank of England; but as the subjects failed to inspire me, they do not appear among my works. The qualities I admire above all others in life and letters are good nature, good humour, good sense and good nonsense, and my favourite characters in history as well as my favourite works in literature embrace all four virtues.

I was singularly fortunate in my choice of a second
subject, Sydney Smith, who possessed them in un-
excelled abundance.

The Smith of Smiths was finished in the spring of
1933, when it started on a round of leading publishers,
all of whom turned it down with various excuses: it was
about an unknown man; no one wanted to read the
biography of a clergyman; there was no love-interest;
it lacked drama; it was too full of quotations; the con-
troversial matter was out of date; it was too factual;
and so forth. One publisher was honest enough to say
that it lacked 'the Strachey touch'. This was true,
because I had already reacted against the Strachey
method, which was being cribbed by all the biographers
of the 'twenties and early 'thirties. My work went
against the prevailing fashion of letting the fancy run
free and turning a biography into a novel. With
imagination one perceives the truth, with fancy one
perverts it. Such was, and is, my opinion. Another publisher said that Sydney's frivolity jarred upon him. I
replied that frivolity is founded on a recognition of the
comical asininity of the human species, that if the
majority of people were not fools the world would not
always be in a deplorable condition, and that Sydney's
frivolity was based on clear thinking. The correspondence then ceased, but the book came back. At length
a publisher, Hamish Hamilton, shared my view of
Sydney, and agreed to issue the work if some leading
literary figure would write a preface assuring the reader
that the subject was worthy of his attention.

I sent the typescript to Professor G. M. Trevelyan,
O.M., who had written to say that he had enjoyed my
biography of Erasmus Darwin, and who, though
plastered with degrees from every leading English,
Scottish and American university, had written an
extremely readable and intelligent History of England.

He thought well of the work, though he advised me to call it 'Sydney Smith' because the book was fundamentally serious, my playful title failed to do it justice, and he always feared the use of a title obscure to fools. He further suggested that if the publisher wanted me to cut down the length I should omit many of Sydney's sayings, not my own 'admirable biographical parts'. And he supplied a Foreword which ran as follows:

'This book will enable a generation which has forgotten Sydney Smith, except as a name, to sample his wit and to realize the nature of his very unusual personality and character. Like Swift, he was in the wrong profession; he, too, though conscientious in his performance of the duties of a clergyman, had other gifts and a different mentality from the clerical, a fact which adds piquancy to the story of his life and opinions.

'His qualities as a political and social thinker and as a wit can be fairly adjudicated by those who read this book. For Mr Hesketh Pearson, though as a biographer he exercises his right to agree with his hero perhaps more often and completely than his reader will always be able to do, belongs to the class of honest biographer. He never tries to make a case by concealment. Here is Sydney in his habit as he walked—and talked. The numerous quotations are fair samples of his thought, writings and speech. An honest Englishman is here honestly portrayed. One of the world's most singular and gifted men is here allowed to stand and unfold himself.'

On the strength of this Hamish Hamilton agreed to publish the book; but a week or two later Trevelyan wrote that he had just heard I was the author of *The Whispering Gallery*, and as the diplomat who had been named in that case was a personal friend he felt compelled to withdraw the Foreword. On reading his letter my wife burst into tears. This upset me, and I made a not very polite rejoinder. But Trevelyan had kindness,

if not guts, and said he would give me £300 as compen-
sation for the disappointment. I was delighted, since
the advance on book royalties was only £100, and
extremely gratified when the Professor insisted that the
money was a gift, not a loan. But I still had to find a
leading figure in the literary world to sponsor the book,
and I asked G. K. Chesterton to do it. He read the
script and provided the Introduction, thereby earning
my lasting gratitude.

Publication took place in the first week of January
1934, and if the critics still found it difficult to swallow
me they could not resist Sydney Smith. A sentence in
one of my letters to Hughie suggests that some of them
remained a bit sticky: 'The *Morning Post* has quite a
good selling notice, though the writer seems to assume
that the book was immaculately conceived—that is to
say, he doesn't mention that it was written by anyone.'
I also heard from my publisher that a leading paper
was about to print a long and laudatory review of the
book when its editor identified the author as one who
had committed the crime of being found innocent by a
British jury, and the review was promptly withdrawn.
But on the whole the notices were long and good, and
the work definitely secured me a place on the literary
map. Many people appear to think that a successful
biography means a gold-mine for the author. I will
merely say that *The Smith of Smiths* was considered a
successful biography, that it sold about 3,000 copies, and
that it earned me about £300. Cheaper editions have
since been printed, but I doubt if I have yet touched
a total of £600 on a book that came out twenty-five
years ago.

My next book did not sell enough copies to cover
the £100 advance on royalties. Had I been sensible I
would have followed Sydney with another wit, but my
actions have never been governed by common-sense, and

I was busy writing a Life of William Hazlitt some months before the publication of its predecessor. There were three reasons for my choice: the first was purely personal and will be explained later, the second was my interest in the character of the man who wrote my favourite essays, the third was the repugnance displayed by previous writers to his *Liber Amoris*, which I found fascinating and more revealing than all his other works put together. But the puritan streak in Britons was still strong enough, when my book *The Fool of Love* appeared in June 1934, to make the critics feel uncomfortable, and the reading public showed no eagerness to buy it. I question if more than 700 copies were sold. Had Hazlitt's great passion been inspired by a duchess, or at least a female of respectable social position, instead of his landlady's daughter, my narrative might have been more acceptable.

Most of that June was spent by Gladys, myself and our son Henry at Alcombe, near Minehead, and we had many long walks in the Exmoor country. A delightful holiday was spoilt towards the end by an explosion from me on the subject of Communism, which caused the coolness which afterwards subsisted between Henry and myself. He had done very well at his private school, and still better at St Paul's, where he won a scholarship to Oxford and another to Cambridge, choosing the latter because it was an 'open' one. My Aunt Eva had given him £300 a year while at Cambridge, and he was now in his last year at Clare College, where he could easily have obtained a 'First' in classics if he had not been suddenly side-tracked by the wave of communistic propaganda that swept all the young idealists off their feet in the 'thirties. The trouble with communists, as with all fanatics, is that no subject can be raised in conversation without the dragging in of their particular 'King Charles's Head', which turns them into bores of the first water; and when wandering in lovely weather through the glorious countryside of Somerset, I found it difficult to agree with Henry that life was intolerable in a capitalistic society. I should have had more patience; I should have been content with my inner enjoyment while he drooled on about the doctrines of Karl Marx; I should have remembered my own warning that when people are old enough to know better they are old enough to do worse. In spite of my seniority and paternity I allowed my natural impatience to come uppermost when Henry implied that Shakespeare would have been a finer poet if he had been able to read *Das Kapital*. The idea was so childishly absurd that my sense of humour should have functioned and sent me into gales of laughter. But I had controlled myself for too long, and, as so often happens after a period of boredom when my feelings have been repressed, something internal seemed to burst. I boiled over, my language being violent and personal. Having relieved myself thoroughly, I forgot what I had said within an hour. But our old confidential relationship had melted in the heat of my momentary fury; he no doubt felt that he could never again tell me what was in his mind without exposing himself to another insane outburst; while I found his aloofness exasperating and became incapable of a decent approach to friendliness. Often though I have cursed myself for my preposterous behaviour, I am well aware that, I being what I am and he being what he was, the same situation would be repeated if we had our lives over again.

Returning from Somerset, I went with James Mitchell to Guernsey for a few days while Gladys stayed a short time at Bedford, where she read aloud to mother, who was now bedridden. Towards the end of August I heard that, in a semi-conscious state, mother constantly spoke my name, referring often to 'Hesketh's book'. I am unable to say whether she was still worrying about the book that had resulted in a lawsuit, or about my Life of Hazlitt, which she cannot have liked even if father had censored certain passages when reading it to her, or about a volume of short detective stories which she knew I intended to knock off in order to earn enough to keep us while my next biography was being written. Anyhow, my sister Elsie thought I had better see her in the hope that my presence would ease her mind; so I went down to Bedford for a day, most of which was spent by her bedside in floods of tears. Drugs had been administered to relieve her pain, and she was scarcely conscious. She knew I was there, but had not the strength to speak. Once, during the afternoon, I tried to control my feelings by getting up and standing. Suddenly I found myself pushed roughly to one side by my father, who had entered the room without my knowledge, aided by his sticks, which he placed against the bed. Lifting one of mother's hands, he kissed it passionately, and then the other, and turning with tears in his eyes he hobbled wordless from the room. Towards the evening I left. Just before going I leant down and kissed mother on the forehead saying 'Good-bye, darling'. A strange, deep, ghostly voice which I scarcely recognized answered 'Good-bye, darling', and it comforted me greatly that I had her blessing in that homely phrase.

She died on 27 August 1934, at the age of seventy-nine. In the necessary arrangements that immediately followed her death father sat alone in 'the den', and when at last someone went to see whether he needed anything he said in an aggrieved tone: 'I thought you had forgotten all about me.' Every night after dinner Elsie played a card-game called coon-can with him, and the result was duly noted in his diary. My other sister Evelyne was staying there at the time, and on the night of mother's death, as I discovered later, his diary mentioned three things: the state of the weather, the issue of the game, and within a pencilled square 'Connie died'. Nothing could upset the routine of his life; yet he felt the loss deeply. The bed she had occupied in her illness, fully made up, was never removed from the foot of the four-poster they had shared for nearly fifty years; and whenever he spoke of her to me his voice broke.

Some people seem to enjoy funerals. I detest them. If one has loved the dead, they are unendurable; if one has been indifferent, a mockery. The convention of wearing black is unthinkable if one is upset, meaningless if otherwise. However, I obeyed the conventions, went to my mother's funeral, and could not use my eyes. Afterwards, at lunch, we all did our best to shake off our feelings, becoming somewhat hysterical in the process. Poor Uncle Walter, who had travelled from the New Forest, did not understand that our noisy laughter cloaked our grief, and I found him in the drawing-room sobbing his heart out. I tried to make him understand the situation, but all he could do was to repeat mother's name, saying he had loved her all his life and we could not feel as he felt. Mother would have understood his sorrow's need as well as ours, and father was fortunately deaf.

But not quite so deaf as he was supposed to be. 'Which is your hearing ear?' the doctor once asked him. 'Both,' he replied. 'I can hear quite well, but as people persist in bawling at me, I don't make any effort to listen.' After mother's death Gladys and I spent occasional week-ends at Bedford and a fortnight every year in order to give Elsie a chance to get away. Father refused to have a hearing instrument, so we had to speak loudly to him, spacing our words. On one occasion the servant, carrying the tray containing his dinner things downstairs, tripped and fell the last part of the flight, smashing a good deal of crockery. Since he was deaf, we decided to tell father nothing of the mishap when we went upstairs for coon-can that night, as it was a good distance from the hall to 'the den', a flight of nineteen stairs, if my memory serves me, and a considerable corridor. Our greetings over, and the first hand of cards dealt, father took up his, saying, 'Well, is no one going to tell me about the great crash?' Startled, Gladys asked, 'What crash?' 'Oh, were there two?' he enquired. Recovering quickly, Gladys described the incident. 'What has she broken in the way of crockery?' he wanted to know. But I feel pretty certain that the next time she appeared he asked whether she had sustained any injury, because he treated servants with invariable courtesy, and they all thought highly of him.

When mother died her nurse stayed on to look after father; indeed during her life mother had insisted on father receiving most of the nurse's attention. Nurse Nicholls was a very good masseuse, and as she had a lively nature father enjoyed her company and told her things he would otherwise have kept to himself, for example that he had been personally present at the births of all his children, and that the only proper marriages among his children had been Jack's and Elsie's because he had been present at both. But he never told her that he had secret stores of Cockle's pills, a purgative he had read about in Burnaby's *Ride to Khiva*, and it took her a long time to discover the places in which they were concealed, until which he was affected by incontinence, with deplorable results for her. He insisted that she should go to church regularly to provide him with reports of the sermons. Anxious to know whether any form of self-sacrifice had entered into his religion, she asked if he had ever fasted. 'I wouldn't think of depriving myself,' he said. But signs of religious feeling in others always gratified him. When she showed him a couplet during the Abdication crisis in 1936:

> Hark the herald angels sing
> 'Mrs Simpson's pinched our King',

he expressed pleasure that the lady was in any way connected with religion.

During an epidemic of influenza he said that nurses should consider their patients and not visit other people in case of germs. Having told him of a film she had seen about Florence Nightingale, she complained one day that she could not go out because of his penchant for pills. 'Florence Nightingale wouldn't have complained,' he remarked. It was his considered opinion that 'every woman should learn nursing because it develops the loyalty, carefulness and unselfishness necessary for a wife.' He laid stress on these virtues; and when she stated her intention to take two aspirins as she felt a cold coming on, he cautioned her: 'Nurses should never have drugs in case they are fast asleep when their patients need them.' However she wanted a good night's rest after a heavy day's work, and told him that a dose would help to stave off her cold. She took the aspirins and went to sleep, being awakened at 4 a.m. by a prolonged peal of his bell. She jumped out of bed and rushed to his room. But her alarm was unnecessary: he just wanted to see if the bell would wake her when she was under the influence of a drug. Once she asked permission to go home to Lincolnshire, as her mother and brother were down with pneumonia and needed attention. Speaking of this to Gladys, he grumbled: 'In my young days all servants were orphans. They stayed for life.' It did not escape his notice that the wages of servants were steadily rising, and he protested: 'Why, you've got to pay them the salary of a curate nowadays!'

In his active days he was punctually unpunctual, but as an invalid he demanded rigid punctuality from others, the parson who came to give him Holy Communion, the doctor who came to prescribe his medicine, the members of his family, visitors, and everyone else. His oldest friend was leaving Bedford and came to bid farewell, but because he was five minutes late father declined to see him. However Elsie put her foot down and he had to give way. Elsie also had to be very firm about her second marriage. Having looked after mother and father for eleven years, she hoped he would not take it amiss if she looked after herself, especially as her husband's business and her future home would be in Bedford and she could continue to run father's house, see him every day, and attend to his needs. But he took her announcement very badly, said he was distressed to hear it, could not imagine why she wanted to get married again, and asked who was going to look after him. Directly she let him see that his attitude was selfish and that nothing could affect her resolution, he changed the subject and asked questions about his income-tax paper which she had to fill in. She was much upset that he never wished her happiness or good luck. Fortunately parental benedictions are not necessary for marital felicity. Elsie's married life was a very happy one. Her husband, Horace Deacon, known to all his friends as 'Deak', was one of the kindest-hearted fellows I have known, and one of the most entertaining. It was impossible to feel down-hearted in his company: he radiated geniality, and his humour was infectious.

Gladys and I continued our visits to father until the outbreak of war in 1939 placed difficulties in the way. The routine never varied from day to day. For half an hour after lunch Gladys had a session with him, from

six to seven my turn came, and from nine to ten we
played coon-can with him. Never much of a talker
at the best of times, he had become less so, and I found
it heavy work to keep the conversation fluid. Sport was
his main topic, though occasionally I prompted him to
speak of politicians he had met or heard. As a boy at
Hereford he had seen Palmerston addressing a crowd.
At shooting-parties he had become acquainted with
Lord Rowton, who had told him several stories of
Disraeli, which he passed on to me. Father always spoke
with a smile about Disraeli, whose photograph adorned
our dining-room mantel-piece at home for as long as I
could remember. In his county cricket days father had
known and played against W. G. Grace. It was amusing
to hear that 'the county' had never called on Stanley
Baldwin's father, who was an ironmaster, until my
father proposed him as a Conservative candidate; and
still more amusing to hear that after a musical evening spent at the house of his friends, the Winfields,
father had graciously consented to be introduced to
the leader of the quartet, whose name was Edward
Elgar. His mind could not remain long on one topic,
and I recall that after saying he did not much care
for Elgar's oratorios, in comparison with Handel's, he
drew my attention to two of his pipes which had been
broken when he tried to scrape them clean with a knife.
I said that I would bring him two new ones, on which
he commented, 'One of them had a silver band,' apparently oblivious that half-crown pipes were similarly
adorned. Lest this picture of my father should seem
one-sided, I must add that he was liked by nearly everybody and adored by women. He had perfect manners,
a disarming smile, a soft engaging voice and gentle
restrained speech. Incapable of hatred or malice and
almost invariably kind, he was the sort of man whose
absence made the heart grow fonder. His company

was neither stimulating nor boring, and his iron egotism was amusing when one was not inconvenienced by it. My thoughts of him are almost wholly pleasant.

He never displayed the least interest in my works, an attitude for which I did not blame him, and the only subjects in which we took a common interest were cathedrals, scenery, the stories of P. G. Wodehouse and the operas of Gilbert and Sullivan. He had seen the original productions of the Savoy operas, *Iolanthe* being his favourite, and I rather hoped he would show some curiosity in my biography, *Gilbert and Sullivan*, when it appeared in 1935. But his sole reaction was to draw Gladys's attention to a book on George V which had just been rushed out to meet the demand of a public excited by the Silver Jubilee: 'That's the sort of book Posh ought to write.'

But 'Posh' did not care for that sort of book and went his own obstinate way. *Gilbert and Sullivan* regained the goodwill of the reviewers who had frowned over Hazlitt, and the leading critic of the day, Desmond MacCarthy, gave it a tremendous send-off in *The Sunday Times*. But somehow, in spite of extra advertising and innumerable notices, it did not sell as well as *The Smith of Smiths*, and my publisher Hamish Hamilton, could not account for this until he met another publisher who expressed no surprise, declaring that the vast majority of Gilbert and Sullivan addicts were illiterate. Shortly after this I received an offer from a weekly paper to be its theatre critic. I had already done some dramatic criticism in the 'twenties for a paper called (I think) *Theatre*, and it was a job that appealed to me; but I could not spare the hours from my biography-writing and declined. A little book-reviewing for *The Observer*, which did not interfere with my other work, was my only journalistic output in the 'thirties.

My next book, *Labby*, appeared in the spring of 1936 and scored a critical hat-trick, being reviewed by *The Times*, the *Telegraph* and the *Morning Post* in the week of publication. Yet, though universally praised, I do not think it sold above 4,000 copies. Several politicians who had known Henry Labouchere were then alive, and I interviewed the lot. But they were useless for my purpose. They could rattle away about his politics and their own until I was yawning my head off, but of the man himself they could say nothing of interest. This scarcely surprised me, as I was well aware that the trade of politics dehumanizes people, making them more interested in plots than in personalities. At last I had what I thought a stroke of luck. Lloyd George wrote that he would tell me all he could remember of the famous radical, and as he had begun life as one of Labby's disciples, and was not himself notable for reticence, I congratulated myself, arriving at his club in a state of suppressed excitement but doing my best to look calm on the surface. He gripped my hand, took me into the smoking-room, ordered drinks, said 'Come, now let us talk about Labby', and began a sketch of his own career which lasted all through lunch and carried us as far as the coffee, when, quite by accident, the subject of my study cropped up. Pouring his diminutive jug of cream into his coffee, he idly remarked: 'Labby never wasted the cream. First of all he emptied it into the cup, and then he rinsed the cream-jug with coffee and poured that into his cup. Millionaires never throw anything away. Of course Labby's ancestors were French. Now I always say. . . .' He went on saying it until he had finished his cigar; after which I was well equipped for writing the Life of Lloyd George but had learnt nothing of Labby except that he was frugal, which I already knew.

Having made a selection of Anna Seward's letters

and prefaced the volume with a brief biography, which Hamish brought out in the autumn of 1936, I set to work on Tom Paine, for which Joe Maiden did a very fine 'jacket', having already displayed his gift as a cartoonist on the covers of my two previous biographies. I fancy Tom was good for some 2000 copies. My book of reminiscences, *Thinking It Over*, followed, but already I was meditating an alien theme. From early in 1938, when Hitler absorbed Austria, I realized, along with several other people who did not pretend to a knowledge of contemporary politics, that war was inevitable. It seemed to us that the only people in the country who failed to assess the situation were the professional politicians. This fact alone dictated the choice of my next biography, the only *pièce d'occasion* I have ever produced. I searched history for a man who symbolized the virtues we needed if we were to survive, and found him in John Nicholson, a ruthless fighter with a single idea. The Indian Mutiny had been caused by the same sort of stupidity, incapacity and cupidity from which we were now suffering, and we needed the same sort of man who had saved us in 1857 to get us out of the present mess. Unfortunately Hamish thought the subject off my beaten track, as indeed it was, and refused to handle the book, which after some delay was published by Collins in September 1939, when, though we had declared war on Germany, our rulers still hoped for a miracle which would produce a change of heart in Hitler and his friends. Nicholson's methods were rather too drastic for the mood of the moment, and the British Press fought shy of the book, which was completely ignored by the papers of India and the rest of the Empire. A solitary correspondent wrote to suggest: 'You ought to persuade our war ministers to hand out *The Hero of Delhi* to each conscript. Perhaps it has by now become a textbook at Sandhurst.' In the Battle of Britain a year later Nicholson's methods would have been approved.

Perhaps I had been too busy working and enjoying myself during the 'thirties to take much notice of outside events, but I have always found politics, the fight for power, money, position and so forth, excessively tedious, though some of the humorous personalities in the dog-fight have appealed to me, Labby and Dizzy for example. All through that decade I walked and worked and talked and drank and laughed and dreamt and lived in the moment. In the early 'thirties Gladys and Henry and I spent our holidays together, once at Bovey Tracey in a house called Moor View, where the view of the moor was invisible. We did terrific tramps on Dartmoor, going so far one day that darkness came down when we were still ten miles from our lodgings and we got a lift back on a van piled high with potatoes, whereon we perched. Henry and I developed a taste for draft cider, and as our taste for Devonshire cream was already fully developed we made pigs of ourselves. At least two of our holidays were spent at Arundel, once above a bun shop in the main street, another time at a small newly-built house on the road to Ford, where Henry and I were too large for the rooms and the bill for breakages was greater than the cost of keep. On that occasion I was tired and needed a lot of sleep, thinking on my way down in the train how peaceful it would be after the roar of London. But it was Maytime and we were awakened at four every morning by the chorus of birds, which made more noise than a convoy of lorries. Most days we all managed to sleep for an hour or two on the downs after a picnic lunch. In the 'thirties Arundel was an ideal walking centre, but I went there a few years ago and found that the sound of the jets as they screamed over the lovely park had converted the place into hell with the lid off.

There used to be a pleasant public-house-cum-hotel called the Bridge Inn, which had a glass-covered verandah on the first floor overlooking the Arun. Here we enjoyed the occasional drink, and here I once stayed some days with Colin, forcing him to complete a poem on God by removing the whisky bottle and telling him firmly that his next drink would follow his last line. He had a marvellous power of detachment and could produce lyrics and sonnets in odd hours snatched from business. Here is one:

> Give life its due
> And leave so little over
> That death, your last great lover,
> In taking you,
> Holds not love killed
> Nor love surrendered sadly,
> But to his dark heart gladly
> Clasps love fulfilled.

I also put in a week at the Bridge with James Mitchell, who preferred the town to the country and showed some discomfort when, on our walk by the Arun from Littlehampton to Arundel one day, he observed what he called 'the horned herd' bearing down upon us in crescent formation and refused to accept my statement that they were solely moved by curiosity. One afternoon we strolled to Swanbourne Lake and were soon asleep on a bank in the sunshine, being roused by a sound like the cracking and crashing of timber. Starting up, we found ourselves in close proximity with two belligerent stags whose antlers were momentarily interlocked. James somersaulted down the bank and fled, leaving me helpless with laughter; but I soon followed him as it occurred to me that the rutting season had commenced. After that James refused to stir from the Bridge Inn, where we played billiards for the rest of our holiday.

Another jaunt I am not likely to forget was taken with Hughie to Scotland, for the month of June 1937. We had suggested to Hamish Hamilton that a pilgrimage in the footsteps of Johnson and Boswell would provide an entertaining book, and he had commissioned us to make the pilgrimage and write the book. The result disappointed him because it was utterly unlike what he had been led to expect. We never went on foot when there was an alternative method of travelling by train or motor coach; we ignored the route taken by Johnson and Boswell whenever it suited our convenience; and we dropped them clean out of the narrative when other matters aroused our interest. I found Hughie the most stimulating and restful of companions, his mind always active, his personality tranquil, and the things I chiefly remember of our holiday were the bursts of laughter and the bouts of laziness. We described every incident exactly as it occurred, and accurately reported whatever was said to us, the substance of our longer conversations on the way being written at the end of each day's journey. I fancy that my high spirits and uninhibited speech appealed to him, because the inscription he wrote in my copy of his Shakespeare book runs:

A merrier man,
Within the limit of becoming mirth,
I never coped an hour's talk withal.

He placed the second line within brackets and wrote 'delete' against it in the margin.

Like Dr Johnson, except on rare occasions, Hughie was strangely unconcerned over his personal appearance, and when I did my best, through my friendship with the librarian, J. V. Kitto, to get him the job of assistant-librarian at the House of Commons, I sent him the following:

1/2/38

Dear Hughie

A few hints for your forthcoming appearance at the House of Commons :

Hair cut
Shave
Hat
Respectable lounge suit
Socks to match ditto
Shirt to match ditto
Tie to match ditto
Collar fastened to stud
Shining shoes with laces to match
Soft-speaking voice
False teeth in position
No satchel or book encumbrances
Remember you once held His Majesty's commission
Clean vocabulary.

Yrs
H.P.

But more exalted strings were pulled, and the Speaker gave the job to Hilary St George Saunders.

In the autumn of 1937 our efforts, entitled *Skye High*, were rewarded by enthusiastic reviews from three leading critics, Evelyn Waugh, David Garnett and Harold Nicolson, the last of whom said that we had produced 'a book which will, I know, for long remain among my favourites' and described it as 'a very brilliant study. How agreeable is their companionship! It is as if Samuel Butler had managed to discard Mr Festing Jones and had gone off with Belloc.' This pleased us, but our labours received no other reward, and in due course the book was 'remaindered'. Possibly one feature that failed to entice the reading public was that the main subjects were completely forgotten when other themes claimed our attention. For instance, my enthusiasm for Hazlitt caused us to locate spots associated with him, and at the end of our tour we discovered the inn, now a large private house off the main road, where he had partly written a volume of *Table Talk*.

I have said on a previous page that I had a personal reason for writing a Life of Hazlitt. This was a love-affair that lasted for nine years and was the most vital part of my life throughout the 'thirties. She was an actress less than half my own age, and as she was a virginal twenty when we met I did not at first wish for an intimate relationship. But she did, and no man who is sexually attracted to a girl can resist her beyond a certain point. That point was reached after about six weeks of a gradually weakening resistance, and the relief was immense when I abandoned it altogether. No man feels for what he possesses as he does for what he desires, and most men cool by degrees when their longing is satisfied. It was not so with me. My appetite grew by what it fed on, and not a little of my passion was expressed in my picture of Hazlitt, though his desire was frustrated while mine was fulfilled. Of course she wanted me to leave my wife, and there were moments when I felt the urge to do so and others when I could not face a separation. Now I was dragged one way by my sexual craving, now in an opposite direction by my fondness for Gladys and my sense of loyalty to her who had bravely helped me through all my trials. It was a perpetual see-saw, and anything like an equilibrium seemed impossible.

At last Gladys discovered what had happened and there were agonizing emotional scenes, when I swore I would never leave her and did my utmost to convince her that the affair was a passing phase and would soon be over. And indeed I several times tried to end it by cowardly correspondence, repeating to myself over and over again two disconnected phrases of Shakespeare's Antony:

> I must from this enchanting queen break off,
> Or lose myself in dotage.

But my will was at the mercy of my impulses and I felt completely lost without my enchantress, who by the way resembled Cleopatra in so many respects that whenever I read either of the two plays now I picture her in the part. In fact she made me realize that Shaw's child-Cleopatra is, as Wordsworth would put it, the mother of Shakespeare's woman-Cleopatra; because this girl of mine had the youthful tricks of the first and the mature guile of the second. Her hair was dark, her expression vivacious, her body lithe. She could be alluringly lovely in one mood, and ruthlessly hard in another. She had the 'infinite variety' which Enobarbus ascribes to Cleopatra, revealing a dozen aspects of herself with breathtaking rapidity. Women are changeable, like men, but she could encompass more sudden changes than anyone I have known. Fascinating, infuriating, seductive, aloof, shameless, sensitive, cruel, tender: she could play all the emotional notes in quick succession, and leave me quivering with lust or quiescent with love or tingling with admiration or coldly critical.

Once she wrought a miracle, at least it was a miracle to me. As my sole wish in life is to be independent, I am comparatively free from the envy and jealousy that accompany ambition, and my normal mood is one of vacuous or serene contentment. But occasionally, perhaps because my liver is out of order, I have a fit of melancholia such as attacked me when ill with malaria. While rehearsing at Cambridge I was subjected to one of these fits. Life seemed hopeless, everything in it futile, the mere sight of my fellow-beings sickened me, a load of misery weighed upon me, and even the autumn beauty of 'the Backs' was obliterated by the cloud of my depression. Unexpectedly she arrived. We walked down the Newmarket road together, bought a few things for lunch, ate them in my 'digs' in John Street, and after an hour in one another's arms my mood changed so completely that I could not believe I had spent that morning and the previous day in the slough of despondency. For the first time I fully understood how people could apparently be changed by a moment's revelation. We walked in 'the Backs' late that afternoon and they had never looked so beautiful. My spirit was free, careless, happy, confident. I remembered a passage in the Book of Job: 'When the morning stars sang together, and all the sons of God shouted for joy.' On my return to the theatre that night the evening stars were singing, the world was transformed and my soul shouted for joy.

Incidentally I had skipped a rehearsal called for that afternoon, and the producer Tyrone Guthrie complained of my absence; but so seraphic was my mood that I forgave him. To me it did not matter in the least. That is the strange thing about passion. When under the influence of love or lust, nothing else is of the smallest significance. If the world stopped revolving, one would sail into the blue with blithe indifference. It is not a case of the world being well lost for love. The real point is that the world is well found when in love and ceases to exist when in lust. I was in the dual state of benevolence to all and indifference to everything.

Strange how intensity of feeling can photograph and retain images in the mind, can vividly picture someone at certain moments for no obvious reason and make each picture unforgettable. After twenty-five years and more I can still see her coming through the entrance door of the Criterion Restaurant, dressed in some silvery brown confection, and wearing a small feather-trimmed hat; and again as she crossed a road outside the Caledonian Hotel, Edinburgh, dressed in blue; and again as she waved farewell to me from the far end of a passage in the underground station at Camden Town; and yet again when she alighted at a bus-stop in Finchley Road and kissed her hand to me from the pavement. We met some three times a week for the greater part of those nine years. When I was on tour in 1931 she joined me for several days at Brighton (twice), Eastbourne, Torquay, Taunton and Glasgow. Later we had a room in some part of London, mostly Pimlico, and we spent a wonderful week together at the old Bridge Inn, Arundel. Perhaps my most vivid memory is of an evening at a party where she wore a long white silken creation which clung to her limbs and set off her figure to perfection. For hours I felt as if my body were burning, every mental and spiritual aspect of my nature being wholly subdued by carnality, whence I learnt that no man in my condition is responsible for his actions.

The inevitable crisis came at the beginning of 1939. For years she had done her best to make me leave my wife; and though I found it well-nigh impossible to ask Gladys for a divorce, it was just as difficult not to promise my girl that I would soon be free to marry her. Human beings are not to be judged when in the pathological state produced by sexual passion. At last she got tired of my evasiveness and vacillation, and became engaged to a man I did not know. In a mood that can only be described as sex-ridden, I then asked Gladys to release me. She had recently suffered a terrible blow. Our son Henry had left us without warning for Spain, where he fought in the Civil War as a foreign legionary for the republican government, and news had recently filtered through that he had been killed in the final fighting on the Ebro. The loss for her was irreparable, but in her unhappiness she thought of my happiness and said I could go. It had taken me several days to brace myself to the ordeal, and when I broke the news to my girl (now a woman of twenty-nine though I always thought of her as a kid) she told me tearfully that she had lost confidence in my promises and that her marriage had definitely been fixed. Several hours of agitating scenes and mutual recriminations followed, and late that night I left her angrily outside the church in Woburn Square, walking many miles of streets to gain some measure of calmness. When I reached home early in the morning Gladys gave me more sympathy than I deserved. My behaviour to her was unforgivable but she forgave it, and the rest of our life together was relatively harmonious. My request for a divorce at that particular time was the only action in my life of which I am wholeheartedly ashamed. I have said and done many deplorable things in my life, but I have forgiven myself for everything except this.

12

᛭᛭᛭᛭᛭᛭

Success

Incomparably the most remarkable character of the age in which I lived was Bernard Shaw, and in my opinion its greatest writer.[1] He was an ideal subject for a biography, though he suffered from the curious illusion that men of action provided the best material for that art; and when I pointed out that all the best Lives in literature were about writers and talkers, like Dr Johnson, Socrates and Jesus Christ, not soldiers and explorers, like Wellington, Caesar and Livingstone, he dropped the subject. I had often thought that I would like to write Shaw's biography, but had funked tackling him about it for various reasons, one of them being my lack of interest in politics and economics, to which he attached great importance. But what if I could make him supply a description of his activities in those fields? In August 1938 I discussed the idea with Hughie, who favoured it and mentioned it to Shaw in the course of a letter he was writing about something else. Shaw did not raise any objection, but when I put forward my plan in detail he replied on a postcard 'Don't', adding that

---

[1]The quintessential Shaw, his singular nature and unique genius, may be found in his critical essays, *London Music in 1888-9* as heard by Corno di Bassetto [G.B.S.], *Pen Portraits and Reviews*, and *Our Theatres in the Nineties*, 3 vols, in addition to his two Roman plays, *Caesar and Cleopatra* and *Androcles and the Lion*.

261

the books by Frank Harris and Archibald Henderson contained all that could be gleaned, and that 'I shall dissuade you personally any time you like to see me.' Knowing full well that there was far more to be gleaned than had appeared in the books of Harris and Henderson, I called at Shaw's flat in Whitehall Court on 21 October 1938, and we had a long talk. He raised innumerable objections to the project, and I demolished them one by one. After he had given his consent he turned to his secretary, Blanche Patch, and asked if anyone else intended to write about him. She thought that St John Ervine was collecting material for a book, as he had frequently pumped her for information.

'Oh, Saint John!' said Shaw, pronouncing his name like that of the evangelist. 'You needn't worry about him. I dare say he'll write something one of these days, but it won't be a biography. He was one of my early Fabian disciples and used to worship at my shrine, but now he probably thinks he can write plays as good as mine.'

I floated on air from Whitehall Court, hugging an inscribed copy of his 'Corno di Bassetto' essays on music, and going straight to the agent who had placed my book on Nicholson with Collins. In a day or two he rang me up to say that Collins would give me an advance of £1,500 on royalties for my book on Shaw. This took my breath away, my usual advance having been £100. I recalled Sydney Smith's comment on Murray's offer of £3,000 for the entire works of the poet Crabbe—'a sum which Crabbe has heard mentioned before, but of which he can form no very accurate numerical notion. All sums beyond an hundred pounds must be to him mere indistinct vision—clouds and darkness.' I broke the news to Hughie, who inherited some of his father's business caution and advised me not to tell Shaw. But I felt that Shaw would like to hear of a publisher's reaction to his name, and in any case he had a right to know it. So when next we met I began with some trepidation:

'I've had a very large offer for my biography of you. I hope you won't think I've promised more than I can perform.'

'How much?'

'An advance of £1,500 on royalties.'

'Well, you've got to live.'

That was all. But to make me feel comfortable he wrote a letter in his own hand for the benefit of the English and American publishers and Press:

> 4 Whitehall Court, S.W.1
>
> 2nd December 1938.

Dear Hesketh Pearson

Unfortunately I cannot prevent anyone from writing about me, from the briefest scurrilous paragraph to the most pretentious biography.

But no sane publisher will touch a biography or essay unless *(a)* he has some assurance that I am not going to be unpleasant about it, and *(b)* the author's name is a guarantee of readability.

So you may go ahead with my blessing. There is no one else in the field.

> G. Bernard Shaw.

One of Shaw's main characteristics was perseverance with whatever he had undertaken to do. From the moment he accepted me as his biographer he gave me the freedom of his company, together with a word of advice: 'I need inbunking, not debunking, having debunked myself like a born clown.' As the work progressed he became more and more interested in it and wrote me many letters and postcards between our talks. Whenever he was staying in his London flat I called about once a week and we conversed for an hour or

two at a time. I always had plenty of questions to ask
and he always had plenty to say in reply. Our business
was conducted by correspondence if either of us was
in the country. He was unceasingly generous with help
and advice. Though the busiest writer of his time, he
never failed to see me when I wanted an interview,
and he dealt with all my letters fully, mostly by return
of post. A man in his position receives thousands of
letters from strangers, and his morning mail was so
considerable that postmen were known to whistle light-
heartedly after delivering it. Once a letter arrived with
the simple address 'G.B.S. London.' The writer asked
for information about entries for the dog-races, and
'G.B.S.' stood for Greyhound Breeding Stud.

I spoke with many people who had known him,
including Beatrice and Sidney Webb, Lady Astor and
H. G. Wells. The liveliest of the lot was Lady Astor. I
called to see her on 26 April 1939, and my diary gives
an account of the visit:

> She does not admire Shaw's brains but his character.
> 'He has a good heart,' she said; 'he's really kind and vir-
> tuous; he's good through and through; he has a beautiful
> nature.' She thinks him an essentially simple man; he has
> no interest in royalties (except cash ones) or the aristocracy.
> She had been able to introduce him to a circle of intelligent
> people who were neither actors nor socialists. Above all she
> had been able to get *The Times* to publish his letters, which
> was the only sort of official recognition he cared about. To
> know that *The Times* would print his letters was far more
> to him than a dukedom or the Order of Merit. His weakness,
> she thought, was vanity; he was vain about his figure, his
> youth, his brains; but he did not care what people thought
> of him. 'You mean then that he is conceited,' said I, 'for
> vain people *are* concerned with their effect on others.' She
> agreed that conceit was perhaps the right word. She wants
> him to mention her in his will. 'No one remembers politi-
> cians after their deaths, and my one chance of immortality

is to be mentioned in his will. Besides, I need the money.'
I was chatting with her in a vast mansion in St James's
Square, and knew of her large house in Plymouth, of
another at Sandwich, and of Cliveden. Somehow I did not
see how any sum Shaw might leave her could much increase
her comfort. . . . After that we corresponded, and when I
informed her that her best chance of immortality was to
appear in my book she sent me all Shaw's letters to her.

I started a daily record on 13 January 1940 keeping
it up till 6 August 1945, and this will be useful for my
present purpose as there are no letters from me to
Hughie between August 1940 and January 1948, his
constant changes of address no doubt being responsible
for their loss. It was the only period in my life when I
managed to keep a regular diary, my early attempts
having broken down after a few days, and on reading
it now I find it quite remarkably uninteresting. Whatever my qualifications, I cannot claim to be a passable
diarist. But I shall quote a few of the less commonplace
entries from now onwards.

Lady Astor gave me an account of an interview with
Stalin when she, her husband, Lord Lothian and Shaw
visited Moscow together in 1931. According to her,
Stalin did not much relish her question: 'When are you
going to stop Tsarist government?' Asked to explain
her meaning, she did so: 'Shooting your opponents.'
Stalin replied that they were living in a state of war,
and would stop it when peace came. In the course of
their talk Stalin made a remark that struck me as highly
characteristic of a disgruntled dictator: 'People want
so many things. They even seem to want silver watches.'
I showed my report of what Lady Astor had told me
to Shaw, whose comment was emphatic: 'This is what
Lady Astor now imagines she said. Not a word of it
actually passed. Obviously we could not have asked

Stalin for an interview to insult him in his own house.'
Yet Shaw's description of what happened, as given in
my book, included the statement that Lady Astor's
behaviour 'rocked the Kremlin to its foundations', for
she told Stalin that in discussing the proper treatment
of children he did not know what he was talking about.
This was probably more insulting to a fellow like Stalin
than her remark about shooting opponents, because the
Soviet prided itself on the way children were cared for
and brought up to be good communists, while the
liquidation of hostile elements was a mere matter of
routine. I think it more than likely that both her report
and Shaw's were true, because H. G. Wells discussed
the matter with Stalin and afterwards recorded that
'she certainly annoyed him thoroughly, and his memory
of her rankled'.

Shaw never changed his opinion of the Soviet régime,
and when he read all the quotations I had culled from
his own works which taken together made an unanswer-
able case against Stalin's police state (e.g. 'Progress
depends on our refusal to use brutal means even when
they are efficacious') he stated that I had got all my
notions from the English papers and closed our
argument by saying that he did not depend on a hostile
Press for evidence. 'I would as soon expect a completely
objective account of a mongoose by a cobra,' he
remarked.

In my biography I gave his own account of his
attitude to Communism and his trip to Russia, but I
led up to it with some of those anti-institutional quotations which he thought beside the point.

Having obtained all I could from a tory, Lady Astor,
my next authority to be tapped was a communist, H.
G. Wells. It is the nature of a prophet to contradict himself, but few sages can have issued so many irreconcilable assertions as Wells, whose concern with humanity

had completely vitiated his understanding of human beings. He could not endure praise of his early novels, which alone are likely to survive. Once I said how much I had enjoyed Kipps, Polly and Bungay. He brushed them aside, calling them 'Tentatives, holiday-tasks, mental relaxation, nothing more'. 'At least they were milestones on your road,' I protested. 'Droppings by the way,' he amended. 'I can't agree,' was all I could say. 'No one wants you to,' he curtly rejoined. Our conversation became less spasmodic and I listened to him enlarging on world-unification, concerning which he spoke with so much humour and eloquence that I felt I ought to do something about it; but the feeling passed off.

Bernard Shaw called Wells a spoilt child because everything had been made too easy for him and success had come too quickly. But if there was something of the spoilt child about him, he was not a spoilt man, for he never became pompous or self-important or conceited. The only sign in him of early indulgence was that he had no control of his temper. The slightest rebuff or criticism or disapproval would banish his sense of humour and goad him to exhibitions of baffled fury that resembled those of a pampered child when denied some gratification. Yet the people he insulted while in this condition did not take offence because there was no malice in his wrath. 'No one could be angry with Wells for long,' Shaw told me. 'He frankly admits that his temper is hysterical. I remember meeting him the day after the appearance of an outrageous article which he had written on me. Really I'd have been entitled to punch his head. But he was looking small and uneasy, and I just shook hands with him. Another time, when he was very angry with me, he wrote to me that everyone believed me to be homosexual and that he, Wells, had always denied it, but in future he wouldn't.' Shaw and Wells were about as unlike each other as were Chesterton and Belloc, but they were the chief thought-influences of their age. Wells was a lesser Dickens, small and tubby and easily offended; Shaw was a greater Voltaire, tall and lean and impervious to insult.

Considering how much criticism he was forced to undergo, Wells remained curiously sensitive. In some article I referred to his squeaky voice. He wrote me a long letter of complaint, the gist of which was that if ever his voice had been squeaky it was so no longer, that he had trained himself as a platform speaker and broadcaster, and that his voice might now almost be called a baritone. In any case, he concluded, why fuss about the quality of a voice? Had the voice anything to *say*? That was what mattered. I could tell from the querulous tone of the letter that the writer still had a squeaky voice.

I ought to have known that he would throw no light on Shaw, but with the unquenchable optimism of the biographer I called for a talk with him at No. 13 Hanover Terrace, Regents Park, in August 1939, and my diary records: 'Apart from his remark that he did not believe Shaw had ever slept with his wife 'in the fullest sense of the word', I received nothing of interest from him. Mrs Shaw, he said, had had an unfortunate love-affair in early life which had put her against sex, and they made no secret of the fact that they had always occupied separate bedrooms.' One of Wells's sons was there, and over tea H.G. and I had a brief spar on the question of biography. It began with his saying that people thought they were thoroughly educated because they had been to a public school or university. 'D'you think *you* can teach us anything?' was their attitude to him, said H.G. From the bootblack to the Master of the College, he continued, they were just as annoyed when accused of being under-educated as the poor were annoyed when accused of being dirty, gross or inefficient. 'Yet what on earth is the use of an Oxford or Cambridge education?' he asked. I replied that it helped one to take an interest in the Varsity boat-race. This left him unsatisfied, so I thought of something else.

'It produces our bishops,' I said.

'Is that a justification?'

'Well, they hand us at least one good laugh a day.'

'Is that their object in life?'

'I can't think of any other.'

At this point Well's son chipped in, telling us that the Bishop of London had once declared that he would like to make a bonfire of all the contraceptives in the world and dance round it. 'Do you still question the value of a Varsity education?' I asked Wells. He did not seem much amused, but smiled wearily. I then manifested a biographical interest in some of the people who had lived in Hanover Terrace, such as Dickens and Wilkie Collins, and he irritably exclaimed: 'Why do people live in the past?'

'Because the past, which we know, is more interesting than the future, which we don't know,' I replied.

'Isn't the present good enough for you?'

'Yes, quite; but one of its principal charms is that it enshrines the past.'

'What's the use of biography, anyway?'

'What's the use of history, come to that?'

'History is a record of mistakes; it teaches people what to avoid.'

'Biography is a record of life; it shows people how to live.'

'I give it up,' said Wells with a tired laugh.

'I should,' said I, rather pleased with an easy victory.

Following the above spar we calmed ourselves over a cup of tea, and he asked me what my next subject was to be. When I told him that I hoped to write on Shakespeare, he said that the works of Shakespeare had been produced by about a dozen people. In the argument that followed each of us was able to prove to his own satisfaction that the other was wrong. I closed the debate by saying that, whatever might be urged against Frank Harris's book on Shakespeare, he had at least made it clear that the creator of Falstaff and Cleopatra was a man, not a committee. 'Harris', said Wells, 'was a blackguard, a blackmailer, a liar and a bore, who would have murdered his grandmother for sixpence if he had had the courage to do it.' Allowing for the fact that he was still a little heated, I thought this concise summary a somewhat partial view of Harris. Though possibly true, it was not the whole truth, and I begged Wells to supply the proofs of the blackmailing and blackguardism. He did not hesitate.

The story he told me was that shortly after the commencement of the 1914 war Harris's doings in France had compelled him to quit Paris at short notice and take refuge in a country house lent him by the Countess of Warwick in Essex. Wells was then living near by and resumed friendly relations with Harris, who wanted to leave for America. Lady Warwick found Harris sympathetic and allowed him to look through a number of carelessly written and extremely confidential letters which she had received from the Prince of Wales, who afterwards became Edward VII. Harris said that he would advise her what should be done with them, since they were documents of considerable historical interest. But after he had left for America she discovered that he had taken them with him, and when requested to return them he intimated that they had been placed at his disposal with a view to publication. 'It was perfectly clear', said Wells, 'that he intended to serialize them in a magazine he had got hold of, so we brought pressure to bear against his design through diplomatic channels, and a fairly substantial sum was paid to Harris before all the letters were placed in safe custody. So you see Lady Warwick's generous hospitality was rewarded with robbery and blackmail. Not a nice story, but Harris was not a nice man. Do you agree?' I candidly admitted that the word 'nice' had never occurred to me in connection with Frank Harris. On the other hand his blackmailing proclivities had their cheerful side, and I told Wells of an incident Harris had once described to me:

'I was driving past Horatio Bottomley's office when who should emerge from it but the chairman of a company which Bottomley had been exposing in his paper. The man looked crestfallen, and I guessed the cause. Stopping my cab, I walked straight into Bottomley's sanctum. I hadn't been announced, and his surprise at my appearance turned to amazement when I said: 'I want £500 of the sum your recent visitor has just paid you.' He knew me and knew that I knew him. Without a word he opened his safe, took out a bundle of bank-notes, and handed me £500. "How did you know about it?" he asked as I pocketed the notes. "I didn't", I replied, and left him to think that one out.'

Wells was amused, and on this friendly note I left him, sat down on a chair in Regents Park, and wrote an account of my interview.

My wife did most of the research work necessary for my biography of Shaw, and I took about a year to write it. For peace and quiet Colin asked us to stay in his country place, Tenements Farm, near Chipperfield, where most of the book was written in an orchard summer-house; though we passed the month of October 1939 on the Teme at Ludlow in a cottage owned by a charming couple named Thompson, and here I worked in the mornings but spent the afternoons walking all over that lovely district, the absence of motor cars from the roads giving us so much pleasure that for the first time we perceived a virtue in war.

I finished the book by the end of the year and wrote to ask whether Shaw wished to see it before it went to the printer. His reply convinced me that it could not go to the printer until he had seen it. I took it down to his flat and asked how long he would take over it. That depended on how much there was to correct, he said, adding that it might take him five years. I suggested that he meant five weeks. 'Good heavens, no!' he exclaimed. 'It takes me more than that to write a play. Shall we say six months?' I groaned. 'Now go away and start your next book at once,' he continued. 'Nothing is more amateurish than to be unable to do this. I don't know how long I shall be.' In a few weeks I rang up to ask how he was getting on. He did not like this pressure, and said he hoped to finish 'before Easter 2040'. Then I tried Blanche Patch, who told me that he carried the typescript with him from London to Ayot and from Ayot to London, that in the midst of his other work he was constantly taking it out, reading it, labouring painfully at it, making notes with great difficulty, and that she came across chapters strewn all over the house.

He returned it to me by instalments in no chapter-sequence. His early corrections and interpolations were made in pencil, so that I could rub them out, he said, and rewrite them in my own words. But gradually he warmed to the work and made his contributions in ink, using red ink for unpublishable comments. In this way he provided me with much of the material for his socialistic activities, which was my chief need. 'Here is the Fabian chapter,' he said, handing it back to me with countless erasures and additions. 'Your attempt at it was heroic, but nobody who had not been personally through it could possibly have done it. What a job!'

Whenever I tried to rush him, the burden of his song became, 'You've no idea how long this takes'. He spent as much time correcting and amplifying the book as I had spent in writing it, and with the last instalment he assured me that he could have written three plays in the hours he had devoted to arguing with me and emending the statements of my so-called authorities. I replied that posterity would be grateful to me. His comment on that lacked restraint.

The finished work was so long that many excisions had to be made, and even then it ran to some 210,000 words, which drew this from Shaw: 'I should advise you for the sake of your own reputation for readability to cut down ruthlessly.' The publisher having asked me to reduce the length of the book by 35,000 words, I had a session with Shaw which lasted for three hours. Our excisions chiefly consisted of quotations from his letters and dramatic criticisms, but he also blue-pencilled reports of our talks. For the publication of the complete work I have inserted all the best things that were then removed owing to the paper-shortage or to his belief that they were not important enough.

From the many hints that he dropped during the writing and revising of the biography, I came to the conclusion that the one event in his personal life that had brought him regret almost amounting to sorrow was his estrangement from Granville Barker. In addition to their affectionate relationship and mutual admiration, they had been closely associated in Shaw's heyday when he was conquering London at the Court Theatre. These were on the whole his happiest years, and Barker was an inseparable part of them. Later, Shaw generously responded to an urgent appeal by Barker and helped him in every possible way during the proceedings leading up to his divorce; but as everything had not gone according to plan, Barker and his

second wife never forgave Shaw for having done his
level best to give satisfaction to all parties. Thereafter
the new Mrs. Barker hated Shaw and all he stood
for, and Barker weakly surrendered to her will, cutting adrift from his one-time god and all-time bene-
factor.

Shaw gave me a rather sad account of what I believe
was their last meeting in 1932. Barker's first wife, Lillah
McCarthy, who had played Shaw's leading female
creations at the Court Theatre, married again, becoming Lady Keeble, and when she wrote her memoirs she
asked Shaw to provide a preface. 'Naturally,' Shaw told
me, 'I had to send the preface to her ex-husband
Barker, who suddenly blew into my house at Ayot one
day as if he had only been away a few hours instead of
ten years. The Sidney Webbs were with us and Barker
looked rather uncomfortable. He asked if he could speak
to me for a few minutes in private. "I never thought I
would come here again," he said when we were alone,
and he went on to assure me that if Lillah's book were
published he would take proceedings. I replied that he
couldn't, as there was not a detrimental word about
him in it; I warned him that any action on his part
would result in a lot of mud-stirring; and I absolutely
declined to advise the withdrawal of the book. At last
I got a smile out of him; he saw that he hadn't a leg
to stand on, and left me with some approach to friendliness. About twenty minutes later (he must have gone
some distance in his car) he returned to take an effusive
farewell of my wife. As a result of his attitude, all the
references to him were taken out of Lillah's book, much
to the annoyance of both the Barkers when they read it.'

Shaw's loyalty to his old friend remained unshaken,
and when I wrote something about Barker which
implied that his life had been too sheltered and easily
successful for him to understand the distress, bitterness

and tragedy of Shakespeare's life, Shaw took exception to my remarks. 'Shakespeare's lot in life was much the same as yours and mine and Barker's,' he said. 'His father was a prosperous alderman who got into difficulties later in life, so that Shakespeare had to go up to London to earn a living, and got it from the actors whom his father had entertained when they were on the road. There were plenty of books in the house. Shakespeare's mother had social pretensions as "an Arden" and the family demanded a coat of arms and finally got it—*non sans droict*. There is no evidence that Shakespeare was ever hungry or ill-clad. I was worse off, as my father never was successful in business. Barker's father was an achitect turned building speculator. Barker had to leave home and go on the stage at fourteen, Shakespeare not until he was twenty. As to unrequited love, Barker was always falling in love and getting engaged. His infatuation with his second wife and his utter subjection to her for the rest of his life was a tragedy that never befell Shakespeare, who didn't have to fight his way but rose soon by sheer gravitation and never looked back, any more than Wells and Kipling and Dickens. Think of *my* nine years of utter failure!'

Shaw was wrong about my own social background and he had paid little attention to Shakespeare's, failing to relate the suffering of Lear and the rage of Timon to the life and personality of their author. But he was simply defending Barker, for whom he always kept a soft place in his heart; and for that, among many other things, I liked him.

Although I believe this break in their friendship was his most keenly felt loss until the death of his wife, he would not let me refer to it in the biography because both the Barkers were then alive. But it was the only important matter about which he asked me to be reticent. Indeed so outspoken was he in other respects that just before the book was sent to the printer I had what I thought was a brain-wave, and when he referred to the 'unique private history' which he had contributed to my pages I made the suggestion that everything he had written should be shown in the text between square brackets or by indentation. His reply was vigorous and decisive:

'Not on your life, Hesketh! What I have written I have written in your character, not in my own. As an autobiographer I should have written quite differently. There are things that you may quite properly say which would come less gracefully from me. I have carefully avoided altering your opinions except where you had not known the facts. For the rest I have either retained or paraphrased, leaving you to reparaphrase if I had misinterpreted. You can of course in a foreword say that as you know me personally your authority for much hitherto unpublished information is G.B.S. himself at first hand, and that you have consulted me on doubtful points sufficiently to feel confident that your readers will not be misled in matters of fact. A good deal that could not have been made public before has been released by the parties passing from life into history. But if a word is said to connect me with the authorship of the book or its first proposal or its commercial profits, I shall be driven to the most desperate steps to disclaim it. It must appear as Frank Harris's book did, to which I contributed a good deal to save his widow from destitution. If you are not prepared to father my stuff, you can rewrite it; but you must not publish it as mine. You have more than enough ipse dixits in inverted commas to carry you through without that outrage. Besides, what you propose would concentrate all the reviewing and all the credit with publishers on me, and shove you into the background.'

I wrote my note of Acknowledgements on the lines

he suggested, showed it to him, and said that I would tone down some of his more Shavian phrases. Handing me a few final emendations, he said: 'Let nothing tempt you to tone any of this down. Tone it up as much as you like. Don't run away with the notion that your readers—least of all the critics—will spot any difference between your stuff and mine. They won't. In the Harris book they didn't. If the story carries them along they won't start detective work; and, anyhow, my style won't disgrace you. Since you must consider the copyright question as between your executors and mine, I strongly advise you to do what I did in the Harris case. When the book is safely in print, take the copy and burn every scrap of it. It will then be for ever impossible for either of us to lay a finger on any page or passage and say "This is Pearson's copyright and this is Shaw's". It will be all yours without any possible question; and let nothing tempt you to part with it. I have no duplicates. Your prefatory note is all right. If you are unbearably ashamed of some of my sallies you can add "In reporting what he has told me I have endeavoured when possible to use what I can remember of his own vivid phrases." There! Will that satisfy you?'

The book came out at the end of October 1942, and was very generously received by the critics, the doyen of whom, Desmond MacCarthy, devoted two articles to it in *The Sunday Times*. Altogether he criticized seven of my works, and the opening of his first notice of my Shaw biography explains why:

> I have always found it a pleasure to review Mr Hesketh Pearson's biographies. As a biographer he has been attracted to the wits: he takes a great delight in wit and witty men. His *Gilbert and Sullivan*, his *Labby*, his *Smith of Smiths*, were excellent. So was his Life of Tom Paine. That book showed another vein in Mr Hesketh Pearson, strong sympathy with the reformer type, the rebel, the man in

whom religious instincts are fused with political passion, and faith in the Divine with confidence in the betterment of man. Mr Hesketh Pearson was well qualified for writing the life of Bernard Shaw. Whatever else may be thought of this celebrated dramatist, critic, pamphleteer, orator, and enemy of tradition, he is surely the most prolifically witty writer since Voltaire. I don't think myself he is as sensible, but he is far more original. . . .

My biography sold about 30,000 copies in the original English edition, 100,000 copies in a cheap reprint, and a few more thousands in a later edition. It did almost as well in America. At the age of fifty-six, after a longish struggle, I knew success, and would have been on velvet if my earnings had not coincided with heavy war-taxation on both sides of the Atlantic.

Shaw was delighted, telling me that 'the book has created a sort of Shavian furore, and brought me a heap of letters from old people whom it has reminded of old contacts with me.' Also that 'the success of your book has driven the whole trade mad. They all want a book about me, a film about me, anything about me.' As a consequence of this, he changed his tune. Having cautioned me before publication that if a word were said to connect him with the authorship of the book he would take the most desperate steps to disclaim it, he now spoke openly of the help he had given me; and on seeing my copy of it during a visit, he opened it to write on the flyleaf underneath my signature: 'Also his humble collaborator—G. Bernard Shaw.'

13

⊱⊰

Rustication

While Shaw had been tinkering with my book, I had been writing another. In March 1938 we left the house we had shared with the Dennys in Abbey Road and took the ground-floor flat of No. 144 Goldhurst Terrace, N.W.6. But we did not spend more than half of our three-year tenancy there. At that time, owing to the political situation, the noise of the wireless was loud in the land, and we sought peace in Colin's country house for the spring and summer of 1939 while I wrestled with Shaw. Having brought the contest to a close, we returned early in 1940 to London, where Hughie and I did our best to interest publishers in a successor to *Skye High*. At the beginning of 1939, to recuperate from a recent emotional stress, I had taken him for a short holiday to the Cotswolds, during which we thought of writing a second talk-and-travel book dealing primarily with Shakespeare; but the publishers who now considered our suggestion evidently felt that something more exciting than Shakespeare was needed to distract the public mind from Hitler, with whom we were technically at war, and we temporarily shelved our plan. Hughie took a job as master at Marlborough College and moved his family away from Hastings, that part of the coast being declared a Danger Zone. But I could not rid my mind of Shakespeare, all of whose works I read again, and just as he had helped me through my service in the 1914-18 war I felt the need to express my indebtedness to him in the present war, and possibly help others to endure its strain. The blare of neighbouring wireless sets drove us to the peace of Sussex, and at the end of April 1940 we joined our friends Walter and Lydia Havers, who had already spent a month at 'Highfield', Barnetts Farm, Rock, near Washington, where we had pleasant rooms in an isolated house standing on high ground with a view of Chanctonbury Ring.

One must work to live, but one need not overwork to underlive, and the weather was so beautiful that I only wrote the first chapter of my *Life of Shakespeare* while were were at Rock for the months of May and June, spending most of the time walking through the weald and over the downs in country I already knew well, as far west as Duncton, as far east as the Devil's Dyke behind Brighton. Gladys was a good walker, and we averaged from fifteen to twenty miles on a fine day. We lunched on bread and cheese in country pubs, revisiting Arundel, Amberley, Burpham, the Stokes, Pulborough, Midhurst, Thakeham, Steyning, Poynings, Fulking, Beeding, and a dozen other places. We had very little rain, though I find this in my diary:

> 6 May. Another instalment from Shaw arrived. We walked all along the top of the downs from Washington to Houghton. On the way we met two shepherds at intervals. In answer to our query as to whether there would be rain, the first said no, as the sheep ' 'ollered ' on the approach of rain and they were not ' 'ollering ', while the second said there would be no rain in his opinion, which he did not back with that of his sheep. Within ten minutes of the latter's prophecy there was a brisk shower which thoroughly wetted us.

Once the clouds looked threatening, and as a flock of sheep were ' 'ollering ' we descended the downs, entering the Half Moon Inn at Storrington, where we drank good beer and talked with an old labourer, who complained that England had become 'too much of a playground', a sage observation. He said that he and his class had been rooted out of the soil, which had run to seed while wealthy urbanites used the countryside for golf, tennis, motoring, week-ending and cocktail parties. Incidentally, despite the vocal sheep, it did not rain, and we were forced to conclude either that they prophesy dirty weather for a different locality, ' 'ollering ' in Sussex when it is about to rain in the Hebrides, or that they raise their voices because they are thirsty and want rain.

My diary tells me that I started my Shakespeare book on 17 May, the sky being cloudy for the first time since our arrival, but whenever the sun shone work was forgotten:

20 May. Another instalment from Shaw, but the weather was too fine to look at it, and Gladys and I bused to Petworth, where we trotted about, visited a pub, and then took another bus to Duncton. We walked eastwards along the road under the downs, passing through Sutton, where we stopped for a drink, Bignor (my favourite spot in Sussex), Westburton and Bury. From Bury we walked along the banks of the Arun to Houghton, where we had tea on the bank of the river, and then climbed the downs and went along the top to Washington. Another drink and then back to 'Highfield' at about 9.10 p.m. Sixteen miles or so in glorious sunshine, with a strong north-east breeze, the whole countryside sweet-scented and sugared with may blossom.

This passage is typical of most and shows the unexciting nature of my themes. But Hitler's hordes were beginning to submerge France just then, and one of my entries is at least peculiar, though I do not see why I should have been granted a private revelation:

23 May. When I drew back the curtains after putting out the light last night I saw a most extraordinary picture. The

whole of the down on the edge of which Chanctonbury Ring is planted was bathed in a kind of misty glow. The moon, almost full, was on the wane; it was a perfectly cloudless night; yet the entire universe apart from Chanctonbury Down was by contrast dark, and a tree in the foreground seemed quite black. Along the top edge of the Down ran a strip of golden light and from behind the hill a silvery vapour was rising. I have never seen anything quite like it. I might have been peeping from and through the netherworld into paradise. Perhaps it carried a promise. I hope so.

Nothing could have been less promising than what followed. As a last resort the country obeyed their King and attended church on 26 May to pray. We heard from an ex-bank manager in the Frankland Arms, Washington, that the churches had been thronged with people 'most of whom did not know their way about the prayer-book', but that the following Sunday the churches were half-empty again. Some days later we dropped into the Washington pub and met the aforesaid bank manager with a friend. The news had come through that the Germans were in Paris, and for a few minutes we discussed this. But suddenly they began to talk of golf, and for as long as we remained with them the Germans, Paris, the fate of Great Britain and civilization were forgotten while these two argued about links, clubs, shots, and what had happened when a special club was taken for a particular shot and what might have happened if a different club had been used. It appears from my diary that, whatever I may have thought of Winston Churchill as a leader, I did not think highly of him as an orator: 'Heard Churchill broadcast at 9. Very amateurish. He speaks like a gangster clergyman who has gone on the stage, raising and lowering his voice and intoning away like a tyro at the job.'

Monday, 17 June, was a fatal day, and part of what I entered in my diary must be quoted, if only to show that the spirit of Shakespeare still animates his countrymen at moments of crisis:

> The Archbishop of Canterbury called the nation to pray yesterday for the French people. The prayer was answered at midnight when the French army laid down its arms; yet I doubt if the Primate was pleased.

> We heard the news over the wireless at 1 p.m. today in the Half Moon pub, Storrington. We had been there some minutes, discussing the game of cribbage with a son of toil and joking with the landlord about guest-houses, a snob name nowadays used by boarding-houses. I said that I would stay in a guest-house and leave without paying, claiming guesthood. After which, if they summonsed me, I'd make a test case of it. We consulted two dictionaries he had and found that another meaning of 'guest' was one who pays; but I said that the guest-houses had had that put into the later dictionaries, the publishers of which got a rake-off. Just before 1 o'clock several labourers came in with their bread and cheese, ordered beer and sat munching their lunch. There were eight of us in the bar, all told, and we were all dumbfounded, sandbagged, stunned by the news. One or two whistled and then began speaking in monosyllables. But we were just stupefied. At last one fellow, very like my pal Allan Jeayes in appearance, got up and said: 'Oh, well—Come the three corners of the world in arms!' 'But shall we shock them?' I asked. He shrugged his shoulders and went out. He belongs to a type fast disappearing; I should say an old-time radical acquainted with literature, the salt of the earth. We tumbled out shortly after and made for the downs, more or less speechless.

I ought perhaps to add that I am impervious to the herd-instinct, what Kipling calls the law of the pack or the jungle, in wartime or any other time, and think it absurd to work up mass emotion at the expense of the enemy. However wars are caused, whether by the imbecility or poltroonery of politicians, the power-lust of maniacs or the danger of revolution, they could not be fought unless the majority of people were frustrated and unhappy, due to what Falstaff calls 'the cankers of a calm world'. It is therefore a waste of time to talk about the causes, the immediate contrivers and the moral issues of war. Once the thing has started it becomes simply a struggle for survival. Two years before the 1939 war broke out I knew that we would soon have to fight for everything we valued, for our very existence, and was quite unmoved throughout the conflict by all the claptrap which the Press and politicians thought necessary to maintain the fighting spirit of the nation. To call the Hitler gang 'wicked men' and all the rest of it was to me mere childishness. St Paul's remark, 'For all have sinned and come short of the glory of God', is the essential truth.

My practical attitude to war was defined in simple terms at the Black Rabbit pub near Arundel on the last day of our holiday, 24 June. In the course of a long walk, Gladys and I lunched there on bread and cheese and beer. We got into conversation with two or three countrymen about the future of the French navy now that the Germans had reached the south coast of France. More people dropped in, one of whom asked me what I would do if I were in command of the British fleet in the Mediterranean. The answer, said I, was easy. I would advise the commander of the French fleet to tell his government to go to hell and desert to us. If that did not appeal to him, I would suggest that he hand his fleet over to us and take his men on shore, we obliging him, should he desire it, with a display of force to be followed by his surrender. If he objected to that, I would promptly sink his fleet, saving as many of his sailors as possible. The company at the Black Rabbit unanimously voted that I should take command of the British fleet in the Mediterranean. I embraced the honour and stood drinks all round. So much my diary reports. I forget whether my policy was pursued by the British admiral on the spot.

The next day we returned to London; and finding that the windows of all the neighbouring houses in Goldhurst Terrace were kept open so that everyone could benefit from the wireless news from early morning till late night, we accepted an invitation from Colin to occupy a cottage contiguous to his house near Chipperfield, where I could write my book on Shakespeare in relative tranquillity.

Late that summer London was severely bombed and people woke up to the fact that the war was serious. We were lucky to be twenty miles away from the racket, and I felt no urge to go nearer. The nightly explosions in our neighbourhood were enough to keep me up many nights writing till three or four in the morning, as the cottage shook from floor to roof whenever an enemy plane jettisoned bombs meant for London within a few miles of us. But Shakespeare helped to preserve my sanity in a mad world, as he had done in the previous war, and while absorbed in my work I was able to forget the conflict. Gladys and I tramped the countryside pretty well every afternoon and enjoyed many a session with acquaintances at the Two Brewers on Chipperfield Common. Colin was in London during the week, but on Saturdays and Sundays he often drove his wife Madge, his daughter Anthea, and ourselves, to a little pub at Sarratt or Chorley Wood or some other village, where we heard all the local gossip. Hugh Kingsmill and Basil Cameron came to spend several week-ends, and when we lent our London flat to Hughie during his summer holidays I spent one or two weekends with him.

Having finished my book on Shakespeare by Christmas 1940, I settled down to a description of the difficulties I had encountered while writing my Life of Shaw and an exposure of the myths, printed and oral, that had grown up around his personality. This was ultimately published as a prologue to my account of the last decade of Shaw's life, which appeared as *G.B.S.: A Postscript* in 1951.

Early in 1941 we heard from Malcolm Muggeridge that a pleasant house near his own at Whatlington, Battle, Sussex, had been abandoned by its owner and could be had for a nominal rent. I had known Malcolm since 1935, when Hughie introduced him to me at the Horseshoe in Tottenham Court Road, and had stayed with him and his wife Kitty several times. He was a stimulating talker, a robust walker, a hearty laugher and a goodly quaffer. Though his main interest was in politics, he could discuss life and literature with rare appreciation and witty depreciation, and when not in a mood of profound melancholy his company was always invigorating and entertaining. We saw a lot of him in the early war years and found his pessimism more diverting than other people's optimism.

Battle was in the Danger Zone, since the authorities believed that the German invasion would start thereabouts, and many of the inhabitants had been evacuated from the district between Eastbourne and Dover and some fifteen miles inland. This suited us admirably, because we felt that complete repose could only be obtained in a Danger Zone; and Malcolm, being in the Intelligence Corps, was able to sign a 'pass' for our residence there.

We gave up our London flat after an incendiary bomb had damaged it and arrived at Woods Place, Battle, in April 1941, remaining there, with occasional visits to London, until the middle of 1945, when the owners wished to return. It was a delightful spot, a mile from the nearest hamlet, Whatlington, and we were very happy there. The house, partly Tudor, partly Victorian, stands on what the eighteenth-century writers called 'a gentle eminence', looking over fields and woods, with one small trout stream at the foot of the hill to the north, another to the south, and the London-Hastings railway line running between embankments just beyond the orchard and kitchen-garden on the east. We occupied the more spacious Victorian section at the front, leaving our visitors to bash their heads in the Elizabethan section at the back. My study, with a delightful view southwards, was exactly over the front porch. The diary records that on our first morning, Sunday, 20 April, we 'woke to a sound of running water. A pipe had burst, through neglect during the frosts in the winter months, and the place was deluged.' We experienced trouble with our water system all the time we were there, the well-pump constantly refusing to function; and even when we managed to get the mechanism mended the water was of such a colour that having a bath was equivalent to tanning our skins. For drinking water I had to take two buckets to the bottom of a very rough lane, about a third of a mile long, fill them at a spring, and carry them back up the hill. This I did every day for the last three years of our residence, the farmer who had provided us with a churnful at intervals having left after the first year.

I became a manual labourer while at Woods Place, and thoroughly enjoyed the relaxation from mental labour. We had a large kitchen-garden which I dug up twice a year, discovering that four hours of strenuous digging was child's play compared with four hours of concentrated writing; the first exhilarated, the second exhausted. I had already converted part of a meadow into a vegetable garden for someone at Chipperfield; but now I settled down to my herculean labours with the pleasure of knowing that I would benefit from the produce of my hands; and when someone said to me 'Are you digging for victory?' I replied, 'No, for gluttony'. My other toil included the picking of apples and pears, the filling-up of pot-holes in the lane, the dragging of logs up the hill from a wood and the sawing thereof, the sickling of thick undergrowth and brambles in the orchard and elsewhere, the putting up of barricades to prevent a flock of sheep from defiling our porch and front garden, and, when Gladys's sister Bee was not with us, the daily cleansing of the hen-house and feeding of its inhabitants. I enjoyed every minute of it, but I am so constituted that I enjoy everything except illness and boring company. The food problem was constant in wartime and apart from the vegetables, I contributed with the help of my gun. There were about 150 acres of land attached to Woods Place, and although the breeding of game had stopped during the war I occasionally got a pheasant or a partridge, a rabbit or a pigeon, a mallard or a widgeon. I disliked shooting at rabbits because I felt a sort of kinship with them and dreaded wounding them; but the call of the pot was sometimes irresistible.

In the summer of 1941 Hughie came to stay with us for a few weeks. He and I had at last arranged to write another of our strange books. Alan White of Methuen's had promised to publish it, and to give it a wider appeal we had decided to make England, not Shakespeare, its main theme, calling it *This Blessed Plot*. All the same we started off with our trip to the Cotswolds in January 1939 and our talk about Shakespeare as we covered the miles between Fairford and Cirencester. Among other things we exchanged our memories of Stratford-on-Avon, one of mine being censored by Gladys when she read it in type, her reason being that the people concerned might still be alive; but if they are not dead by

this time they have reached an age when the subject
will revive their youth and they may be grateful for
the reminiscence. The incident, which I described to
Hughie, was embarrassing enough to uproot a family
and shatter a love affair:

'It was at a party at Canon Arbuthnot's, then vicar
of Stratford. I was about 13, and most of the others
were a bit older. We were playing games of skill, and
a very pretty girl of 18 had to pick a pin with her teeth
from the leg of the chair on which she was sitting. She
bent right round in a contorted position. There was a
tense silence among the spectators, who included her
parents, the Canon and her fiancé, and her teeth were
about to close on the pin when there was a sharp report.
The girl jumped up and rushed crimson from the room.
The Master of Ceremonies, a youth of 19, did nothing,
for which one can't blame him as the older people
present plunged nervously into irrelevant conversation,
while the rest of us stood about looking sheepish.
Unbelievably fantastic though it sounds, the father and
mother left the next day with their children, and were
never seen in Stratford again. They had lived for some
years in one of the largest houses in the neighbourhood.
The girl's fiancé married someone else.'

Having taken a deep breath, Hughie said: 'And the
Victorians were astounded at the taboos of Central
African savages! I have always found all I wanted in
the way of anthropology among the Victorians them-
selves.' We walked on in silence, presently broken by
Hughie:

'I mustn't pretend to be immune from the particular
imbecilities of the age into which I was born. An
incident comes back to me which would doubtless have
meant nothing to a Latin, but which still causes me
disquietude when I remember it. It was in the spring
of 1920, and I was in France on business, having been

evacuated from the northern branch of the family firm. One night at the chief hotel in St Malo I went along in pyjamas, with a book and a pipe, and a scarf round my neck, to a lavatory which I imagined, as the hotel was a large one, to be one of a number. Like many men I regard a lavatory as a place of study and meditation, a hermit's cell unvexed by the clash of conflicting egotisms; and a distant sound of music coming up from the ground floor deepened my sense of privacy and repose. I had been there a minute or two when someone tried the handle. Presuming that the person would go elsewhere, I went on with my book. Some fifteen minutes later, my pipe finished, I adjusted my scarf and emerged. A pair of eyes was glaring at me from a pretty face. Along the passage was ranged a double row of girls, perhaps thirty in all, and every one of them glaring at me. It flashed across me that this must be the dance interval, and that it must be nearly over. With bowed head I walked between them, pipe in one hand, book in the other."

When *This Blessed Plot* was published the following year, minus the above episodes, the *Manchester Guardian* critic declared that we had 'invented the conversation travel-book as a new art form', a verdict we found no reason to challenge.

Over the years Gladys and I saw much of Malcolm whenever he was on leave and exchanged innumerable visits with Kitty, who lived at the end of the lane leading up to our place and at whose house our parcels, rations and what-not were left, since no driver who valued the springs of his car showed willingness to negotiate our shattering track. A few friends risked the primitive isolation in which we lived and stayed with us at intervals. Joan and Jim Thornton braved the conditions twice; Frank Allen came several times and incidentally made valuable contributions to our larder with my gun; my nephew Teddy (brother Jack's boy) did not mind roughing it and visited us on three or four occasions, though his wife Molly, having emerged from our bath resembling a West African, preferred the bombs of civilization to the waters of Woods Place. Walter and Lydia Havers, Douglas and Nora Jefferies, Ethel and Maud Denny, all sampled the barbarism of the Danger Zone; while my sisters had one look at it and afterwards expressed a wish that we should visit them when they were on holiday at Tunbridge Wells. Both of them were working hard at canteen jobs in and about Bedford. Evelyne's husband, Dane, had been imprisoned by the Japanese at Singapore, and she was living with Elsie, whose husband, Deak, was commanding the Home Guard. They were also looking after father, and told me a characteristic story of him. A landmine exploded in Bedford, a mile from his house, which rocked like a ship in a ground-swell. He was just being helped into bed and demanded of his nurse, 'What's that?' White and trembling she answered, 'A bomb, I think.' 'I disapprove of this gallivanting about in the air,' said he, getting into bed and composing himself to sleep.

In 1941 his mind showed signs of weakening, and sometimes he failed to distinguish between his two daughters. He would be talking quite rationally and then suddenly say, 'When am I going to see my dear wife again?' or 'When are you going to take me home again?' In answer to some question Elsie tried to explain that his first wife was buried at Abberley, his second, our mother, at Bedford. 'And where are my third and fourth wives buried?' he asked. Once he complained that he had not seen Elsie for a year, and almost in the same breath accused her of taking nine pounds from him the day before. Occasionally he spoke lucidly of his Worcestershire days and of his friends there as if he had only just parted from them, but this would be followed by a string of meaningless words. Early the following year he was scarcely capable of utterance; his mind had practically gone; but Elsie wrote to me that 'sometimes he gets quite violent and hits out at anybody or anything.' Near the very end he stretched his arm upwards and spoke his last words: 'I can't reach you, Connie.' He died on Easter Sunday, 5 April 1942, at the age of eighty-eight, and four days later I wrote in my diary: 'Oh, how I hate these services, which always make me cry. Strange and sad to think of the old man, so much in command of his circumstances through life, left up there on the top of the windswept hill, willy-nilly.'

Had he lived to see it, father would scarcely have glanced at my next book, *A Life of Shakespeare*, which appeared on St William's Day, or, as most people prefer to call it, St George's Day, 23 April 1942. He would have picked it up and quickly put it down with a dismissive 'Posh on his hobby!' Having been refused by several publishers, it was at last accepted by Penguin Books, which delighted me because I knew its low price would give it a wide circulation among men serving in the forces. For the first and only time in my life a work of mine brought countless letters, mostly from fellows training in Great Britain or serving abroad in the army and navy, and this warmed my heart, for not only had my hobby made them forget 'the present horror' but it had encouraged them to read or re-read Shakespeare. Although written after my Shaw biography, it was published six months before, and I was pleased when G.B.S. wrote to say that it was the best Life of the poet he had read. I also find this in my diary: '25 April. James Agate in this morning's *Daily Express*, having been asked to name, not the book of the week, but a book for every week, names my *Life of*

Shakespeare. Good for James!' At a later date Agate asked Hamish Hamilton to arrange a lunchtime meeting with me. But I have always made a point of avoiding critics, for a reason I afterwards gave Agate when forcibly introduced to him at our club: 'I don't like critics to have anything against me except my books.' I need scarcely say that the professorial gang became articulate on the subject of my Shakespeare, but their method, as Desmond MacCarthy once wrote, is first to crab an author and then to crib him.

It grieves me to add that this book was the occasion of my only quarrel with Hughie, who had recently been appointed literary editor of *Punch*. As our interest in Shakespeare had been a major bond between us, and I had written a criticism of his work on the theme, I was annoyed when he did not deal with it himself but gave it to another reviewer. I should have remembered Johnson's remark in his essay on Sir Thomas Browne: 'The reciprocal civility of authors is one of the most risible scenes in the farce of life.' An unpleasant exchange of letters took place between us, which I have since destroyed. His excuse was that as the book had been dedicated to him, whatever he said in praise of it would be discounted; to which I replied that the vast majority of readers did not notice either dedications or the names of critics. However I soon realized that such a friendship as ours was far too valuable to be jeopardized by a childish complaint,and proffered the olive branch, which he at once accepted, and our future friendship was untroubled by a memory of my petulance.

Meanwhile I had been writing a biography of Conan Doyle, hardly a subject of great moment, nor particularly interesting in himself, but having expressed myself on two heroes of my manhood, Shakespeare and Shaw, I felt like doing the same for a hero of my youth. In the course of my researches I spent a pleasant day with A. E. W. Mason, who had taken a house near Petworth, and about five pages of my diary are filled with an account of my visit. Bits of what he told me appear in my book on Doyle, but as I had to omit an incident that amused me vastly at the time it can find a place here. Mason having talked for some time, all his reminiscences showing Doyle in an unfavourable light, he suddenly pulled himself together and said: 'Now that I've told you nothing but nice things about Doyle, I'll tell you something nasty', which he did.

The firm of Collins, which had issued my Nicholson and Shaw books, did not care for my one on Doyle, which was accepted by Alan White for Methuen's and published in 1943. I gather that its frankness did not make all the members of the Doyle family skip for joy, but no honest biographer can hope to please everyone, and it happened that I received a wraithlike commendation of the work. As a rule I dream of my characters while writing about them and occasionally remember scraps of conversation with them after waking up. But I dreamt of Doyle some months after two editions of the biography had sold out. He seemed pleased that I had done him justice, telling me to take no notice of hostile criticism; and as I always act in accordance with dreams when they echo my own feelings, I have followed his advice.

Doyle, by the way, had been very fond of Sussex, and at a later meeting Mason and I discussed the various merits of the county at some length. He preferred the western part; and though I consider the downland between Steyning and Cocking the most attractive part of England, which for me means the world, I came to the conclusion while living near Battle that the hinterland of east Sussex was lovelier than that of west Sussex. The wooded hills and dells, the high roads from which one sees the fields unfolding to the horizon, the fascinating little towns, give a sense of opulence and comfort I have not felt elsewhere. But I was in love again—no, not 'again', for as Oscar Wilde says, 'Each time one loves is the only time one has ever loved'—and that emotion transfigures scenery and glorifies the universe. I knew a man who mistook Wigan, the home of his beloved, for the Garden of Eden. Not to be in love is not to be alive, and I for one am unable to unlove those I have once loved, never ceasing to be grateful for what they have given me until the spring of life runs dry.

Although we had delightful woods and meadows to wander through within a mile of our house, very often followed by our cats, Gladys and I frequently went further afield and explored the surrounding villages. The walk along a stream to Sedlescombe was one of our favourites; and we were constantly in Battle, where we soon got to know many of its residents and where we constantly lunched at the George, then run by a charming fellow named Marsh, who was helped by his wife and daughters. I used to think the number of babies we were called upon to admire in the main street rather excessive; but we assumed the peculiarly imbecile expression always to be seen on people's faces when they look at babies or small children, and passed on. I have invariably been good-natured enough to let women do everything for my comfort, and the least I can do in return is to lie like a trooper about the beauty of a baby, which usually reminds me of an underdone beefsteak.

But it appears, from an incident of those days, that the expression on my face does not always carry conviction. One day Freddie Andrews motored over from Middleton for a day's pub-crawl, and we drew up for a drink at a country club, which was refused us as non-members. We argued with the proprietress, and her

scruples were gradually vanishing when she fell back
on her last line of defence. 'How do I know that you
are not a magistrate?' she asked me. 'Do I *look* like a
magistrate?' I scornfully protested. 'Yes, you do!' she
loudly proclaimed. Our roar of laughter settled the
issue, and we remained drinking for some time.

I paid a number of visits to London in connection
with my work, staying either at the Savage Club or
with our friends Eleanor O'Connell and John Wardrop,
who lived at No. 10 Park Village West. I remember
returning there late one night and standing at the foot
of Primrose Hill while the guns at the top were blazing
away at raiders, the ground beneath me shaking with
the detonations. It was very impressive, and I might
have remained there longer if a large piece of metal
had not hit the road within a few feet of me, which
caused me to jump and take a less detached interest
in the proceedings.

Another episode during a week in London is worth
recounting. One evening I walked into the Club and
found the bar empty except for Max Beerbohm, who
was enjoying a glass of wine at a table. I made myself
known to him and he spoke in high terms of my Life of
Shaw. I asked him if his opinion of Shaw's plays had
altered since he wrote about them in the *Saturday
Review*. 'Not a lot,' he replied. 'But I think his greatest
work was his dramatic criticism, most of which I know
by heart. No one has come near him at that job. The
rest of us are pigmies in comparison.' Then we switched
on to other themes, and I told him a war-story of my
own, which I will give here at greater length:

One May evening I was taking my usual walk
between tea and supper through the woods, full of
anemones, in the immediate neighbourhood of Woods
Place. There was a spot some few hundred yards north
of our house where the railway divided a biggish wood,

in the midst of which an old disused brick bridge crossed the line, all marks of a road or track leading up to it on either side being obliterated. I was leaning on the parapet and smoking a pipe when suddenly an army officer emerged from the wood and seemed rather taken aback at finding me there. I knew there were troops billeted near by but I had seen none of them at close quarters except in the local pub. We good-eveninged one another and then he said: 'It appears that I have lost myself. Will you please tell me how to find Mountfield Halt?' I replied that the quickest and easiest way was to walk along the line, as it was only a mile away. He thanked me, and I watched him idly until he disappeared round the railway bend.

That evening there was a special meeting of air-raid wardens at the Royal Oak Inn to hear the latest instructions from headquarters. These were confined to a warning that an invasion was expected, probably by parachutists, and we were again told what to do in that event. Having absorbed the details with our beer, the wardens on duty remained at their post and the rest of us went home. It was a beautiful still moonlit night and I decided to return across the fields instead of by road and lane. One sentence in the warning we had received recurred to me: it stressed the fact that the invaders would probably be in British uniforms, and somehow it made me think of the officer I had met in the woods only a few hours before. Surely, I thought, there had been something not quite English about him. Was it the face? No. The walk? No. The voice, the accent? No. Then I remembered the slightly odd phraseology—'It appears that I have lost myself'. A typical Briton would have said 'Where the hell am I?' And 'Will you please tell me how to find Mountfield Halt?' would have been rendered in the vernacular 'Where's Mountfield station?' I now began to feel alarmed. This chap may have been finding likely spots for flashlighting to airplanes. I must ring up headquarters the moment I got home and report the incident. They would want to know why I had not done so before, and I could reply that the suspicion had only entered my head after thinking over the official message at the meeting that night. On the other hand they might laugh at my assumption that all English officers speak concisely. What ought I to do?

At that instant of my uncertainty I left the sloping wheatfield down which I had been walking and plunged into Tigwood, only known to myself by that name because it reminded me of the gloomy wood where Montague Tigg in *Martin Chuzzlewit* was murdered. Wild garlic grew in this dense spot, which was so dark that even the sunlight failed to penetrate it, except here and there by a few unirradiating bars. With my natural claustrophobia, and a certain timidity in the dark dating from childhood. I had forced myself to go through Tigwood again and again in an attempt to overcome my weaknesses. Woods make curious noises in the silence of the night, and Tigwood specialized in ominous sounds. In spite of a full moon the place was more sinister than ever on this occasion, and as I felt my way slowly along the rough path which bordered a small trout stream the stillness and obscurity were so portentous that the snap of a twig under my foot sounded like a rifle shot. By the time I stepped on to the rickety plank bridge I felt my heart thumping, and the clatter of a loose board brought it into my mouth.

I half-ran up the hill leading to our house, and when I got there I had to stop under the porch to steady my shaken nerves. On reflection I decided not to frighten my wife with my own apprehensions, and not to report my meeting with the officer for fear of ridicule. It was eleven o'clock when I reached home and after a short chat my wife went to bed. During April and May we usually heard the Battle siren wailing an 'alert' somewhere about ten at night, and an 'all clear' between twelve and one. Though the first had not yet been sounded, I decided to sit up as usual until one o'clock. Lighting my pipe, I was soon absorbed in *David Copperfield*, which I was reading for about the sixth time.

At midnight came the 'alert', which struck me as queer, but that was because I felt a bit jumpy. The siren filled the air with its din, and when it ceased the silence was deathly. For half an hour I sat with my eyes on the book, my mind elsewhere, and all I heard was the bark of a fox some three fields off. Usually I enjoyed the peace of our isolation, but tonight it made me feel uncomfortable. The windows, though blacked out with shutters, were open, and towards one o'clock I became vaguely conscious of unfamiliar sounds outside. Blaming my imagination, I drank a stiff whisky. But the sounds were now clearer, and straining my ears I felt convinced that they came from the stealthy tread of feet upon grass. Slipping off my shoes, I went into the hall and listened. The sounds were more definite on the other side of the house, where the grass was longer and rougher. I crept down to the kitchen, and distinctly heard a noise like the tip-toeing of men across the gravel yard.

Clearly it was my urgent duty to report what I could no longer doubt: that the expected parachute invasion had started. Our telephone was in the hall. I lifted it from the table, carried it as far away from the front door as the flex would allow, got in touch with district headquarters, and spoke as softly as possible. I was ordered to stay indoors and ring again if anything else happened.

The suspense of the next fifteen minutes was

indescribable. I waited in the hall nearly suffocating myself in an attempt to catch every movement outside. First I heard the sound of heavy breathing just beyond the door. Next the handle rattled ever so slightly. And then came a bump. I wondered if they were going to set fire to the house, and ignite several such places to assist their landing.

At last a sudden shout gave me the signal of relief. I seized my only firearm, a double-barrelled gun, un-locked the door, flung it open, and beheld several British soldiers convulsed with laughter, while a flock of sheep were scampering away from the house and across the lawn. I sensed the humour of the situation, but could not laugh as heartily as they.

Having given him a brief version of this story, Max and I got back to literature, and while we were chatting the evening was made hideous by the dismal wailings of an air-raid warning. ' 'Tis the voice of the siren; I heard her complain,' misquoted Max as he got up, and with a word of farewell he disappeared. In the war years his broadcasts made him popular, and towards the end of his life he was canonized by the critics, a distinction he had won by writing very little and grow-ing very old.

Gladys and I were in London together when the news that British and American troops had landed in France was broken to us on Tuesday morning, 6 June 1944, as we entered the large empty reading-room of the British Museum. The dome room was not in use during the war, and we worked in a smaller library just off it. We asked whether the landing had been successful. The janitor did not know, but added, 'No news is good news'; to which I replied, 'No news is simply no news.' He called me a pessimist. I admitted to being a mediumist, and left him to ponder on the word.

Up to that time we had only been inconvenienced

by occasional bombs in the Battle area, though I remember an evening when a bunch of incendiary bombs fell on Whatlington, illuminating the country-side, and while I dashed up to the warden's post I heard nightingales singing in the burning wood along the road. But shortly after our return from London, in June 1944 the Danger Zone became dangerous, the first hint of which was recorded in my diary:

15 June. An 'alert' just before midnight and I went out to see what was happening. I fancy it must have been the first appearance of these radio-controlled planes, or tor-pedoes, or whatever they are called, over this country. I saw three of them, and the firing of our red tracer stuff was very poor, well behind them all the way. If it is as I fancy, our scientists will have to think till their heads ache. 16 June. Yes, I was right. Two more of the brutes, or rather robots, woke me up in the early hours. . . . We will of course deal with them in time. The Huns are greatly jubilant.

Then started a period of persistent 'alerts' and 'all clears' for about three months. Air-raid wardens were supposed to be at their posts during these alarms, but as most of them, including myself, lived some distance away, it was decided to keep in touch by telephone, especially as, during the robot spell, we would other-wise have been travelling to and fro all day and all night. We got very little sleep, as we had to be ready at a moment's notice to rush to the scene of some casualty. Very often I did not trouble to take off my coat and trousers, but lay on a downstairs sofa snatch-ing an hour here, an hour there. One of the things dropped near the railway line some two hundred yards from our house, caused a clearing in the wood, drove tree-trunks across the rails, blew our windows in, made the old part of the house change shape, and killed four rabbits. Another fell just down the lane; our ceilings fell with it, and I had to wade through glass from room to room of a near-by cottage. And so it went on. A few diary entries will tell all that is necessary:

> 22 June. I tried to work this morning, after a restless night, but the banging and crashing and thumping and whirring prevented me from concentrating; so I went down to fetch water and paper. The men came to patch up our house.
> 29 June. Lots of robots down. Worked this evening between crashes.
> 30 June. Our Spitfires shot quite a lot of robots from the sky this evening and the neighbourhood shook with their explosions.
> 1 July: Another robot day: what was once thrilling is now boring.
> 5 July. Robots all day.
> 12 July. Today I resumed work on Oscar, though there was more noise than usual.
> 17 July. Read P. G. Wodehouse's *Summer Moonshine*: uproarious stuff. He's a public benefactor; while all the rulers and politicians are public pests.
> 18 July. I dug up potatoes.
> 26 July. The usual robots. These are of daily and nightly occurrence, and our house shakes with each explosion. Worked again.
> 5 Sept. During the robot phase we have been sleeping downstairs, as I had to be ready to dash out on duty at a moment's notice; but in view of the war news I took mattresses and what-not upstairs this evening and we'll sleep tonight for the first time for over two months in beds and undressed.

Between four and five hundred of these flying bombs were brought down in the Rye and Battle area, and we were kept pretty lively. Two of my fellow-wardens, Fred Hunt and Wally Deeprose, became my friends, and we still meet at intervals. Fred now runs the inn at John's Cross, and Wally manages a farm. The Royal Oak Inn was our headquarters, and sometimes it became a Royal Soak Inn. Seeing the wardens leaving the premises one evening to pursue their duties elsewhere, Malcolm said that we were already stretcher cases (*'quis custodiet ipsos custodes?'*) and that the morale of the whole outfit had sunk since my appearance on the scene.

As my book on Shaw was doing well, it occurred to me that I might have a little money to leave if I were blown up by a bomb; so I made my first will and called on my friend Fred Sheppard, who as chief solicitor and coroner of the district could deal with the matter in both capacities. Having read the rough draft, he remarked:

'There's nothing here about cremation. Do you wish to be cremated?'

'Not a bad idea,' I said. 'But as I am making a will just now because I might at any moment be exploded by a flying bomb, perhaps a cremation clause is unnecessary.'

'Certainly not. You may wish to have the bits assembled and then incinerated.'

'I hadn't thought of that.'

'Then shall we say to be cremated if collected?'

This interchange was conducted by him in a courteous bedside manner.

I had been compelled to break off my work for days at a stretch during those months, but while sitting up at night I usually managed to add a few paragraphs, and Chapters 5, 6 and 7 of my *Life of Oscar Wilde* were composed during the height of the robot season.

Quiet had been restored by the end of October, when Gladys and I spent eight days at the Charing Cross Hotel, during which we paid a visit to Shaw at Ayot St Lawrence, did some research work in the British Museum, and heard the gigantic explosions of the rocket bombs.

My book on Wilde was finished in March 1945, published the following year by Methuen's in England, Harper's in America, and was as prosperous in both countries as the Shaw biography. I felt proud of being the means whereby Wilde's reputation as a notable character had at length been widely acknowledged and firmly established. Apart from the fact that he was responsible for my mental weaning, I had long regarded him as one of the three most delightful personalities in literary history, and I had already done my best for the other two; Sydney Smith and Bernard Shaw.

We left Woods Place on 17 July 1945, I with much reluctance, Gladys looking forward to the renewal of her afternoon bridge-parties, which had been suspended during the war.

14

I⚡🌀⚡I

An End

On leaving the country I suffered a spasm of self-pity.
It was not an emotion I had indulged since my nonage
because, like Shakespeare's Richard III, I 'find in myself
no pity to myself'. One could create an effective stage
figure who pities himself because he has no grounds for
self-pity. He would not be liked, since the effect would
be satirical, and the most popular figure in dramatic
literature is Hamlet, who, being drenched with self-
pity, voices that commonest of emotions. I fancy this
momentary deviation from my normal self was due to
a feeling that like my forebears I should have been
born a country squire, the air and life of a city being
alien to my nature. However the sentiment died soon
after my love of London was reborn, and I pampered
my affection for the country by visiting Battle several
times in the next few years with James Mitchell, who
quickly made friends with some of my friends and
enjoyed strolling the distance between the George Hotel
and the church, though he drew the line at more bucolic
pedestrianism.

After spending a fortnight with Eleanor O'Connell
and John Wardrop, my friendship with James enabled
us to set up a new home. His sister Peggy and her
husband, Harrington Evans, lived at No. 14 Priory
Road, N.W.6., within a few minutes of our two previous
residences, and as the lower part of their house had just

been vacated we were able to occupy it. A year or so later they retired to the country and we took a lease of the place, which has since been renewed.

The last entry in my diary is under 6 August (Bank Holiday) 1945: 'I have determined now to stop these daily jottings. They are trivial and stupid, and one day telleth another.' Henceforth I shall have to rely for mere facts on my pocket-books of 1946-60.

One is easily led along the path one wishes to take, and the first thing I did on arrival in London was to start a new book with Hughie, which like the other two could not possibly sell more than a few hundred copies but would give us much pleasure in the writing. This time Douglas Jerrold gambled against a cert, accepted a work that was supposed to be about London for Eyre and Spottiswoode, and *Talking of Dick Whittington* came out in 1947.

Unless I have written in vain, the reader will know by now that I live happily in my own world and am but partly conscious of the world-shaking events taking place around me. We had no wireless set at Woods Place, and on the rare occasions when we wished to hear anything we went down the lane to Kitty's house. Consequently I was wholly unaware of the class of entertainment provided for the masses throughout the war years, and when Reggie Pound introduced a couple of fellows to me at the club one day I did not know their names: Tommy Handley and Ted Cavanagh. In reply to my whispered request for information, Reggie incredulously said: 'Itma, of course!' But I knew nothing about Itma and begged for enlightenment. He gave a sceptical laugh, and the conversation became general. Few of my friends were convinced of my utter ignorance of a show that had apparently made the nation hold its sides in a period of calamity; and not even Colin could quite believe his ears when I related another circumstance. Having received a telephone call from an unknown fellow asking me to lunch at Claridge's with his mother, who had a most important matter to discuss, I accepted the invitation and was duly ushered into a private suite, where over cocktails a most attractive woman begged me to write the Life of her husband. 'Who is your husband?' 'Sam Goldwyn.' 'Who is Sam Goldwyn?' Her eyes started from their spheres: 'D'you mean to say you've never heard of Sam Goldwyn?' 'I am sorry, but such is the case.' Over lunch she gave me many particulars and said she had hoped I would accompany her back by plane. Having confessed that I was then deep in a biography and could consider nothing until it was finished, I asked why she had picked on me to write her husband's Life, her reply being picturesque enough to remain in my memory: 'We took your wonderful biography of Oscar Wilde with us to Florida and read it on the beach, and by the time we had finished it you couldn't tell that book from seaweed.' I did not write on Sam Goldwyn, but his wife probably got a more fitting person for the task, at least someone who knew his name.

My fantastic unawareness of famous folk is matched by my lack of interest in practical matters, and in the autumn of 1947 I nearly had to sustain an amputation on this account. Something happened to cause an abrasion on the top of my right foot, probably a too tightly laced shoe. This set up an itching which made me scratch the place. I had a vague idea, picked up on service in 1917, that iodine healed raw flesh, so I poured a lot of the stuff on my foot, the smart making me dance. A day or two later the swelling seemed to be subsiding, and as the colour of the iodine on my foot offended my aesthetic sense I decided to cleanse it. I had another vague idea that some stuff called Vim removed stains, so I asked Gladys if this were the case. Without conceiving the purpose for which it was intended, she replied in the affirmative. I then scrubbed the top of my foot with Vim, but soon discovered that, if admirable for pots and pans, it was not designed for sores, and this singularly harsh application laid me up, supine on a couch, for a glorious fortnight of Indian Summer in early October. I received little sympathy from my doctor, who said that I should have sent for a mental specialist instead of an ordinary physician.

However I put my incapacity to use by re-reading, some of them for the fourth or fifth time, the novels of Dickens, upon whose Life I was then engaged. For many years he had been a subject for my meditation, and the two things that delayed my writing on him were the sentimentality in which he submerged some of his characters and the idiocy of his attitude to what were known as 'fallen' women. But as time went on I discovered that, just as there is one step from the sublime to the ridiculous, so there is one step from sentimentality to cynicism; and when it was revealed that in later life he had helped a woman to 'fall', and had treated the mother of his large family with censorious callousness, I perceived the interesting connection between the extremes of his writing on one hand, of his nature on the other. This determined me to explain his odd character, especially as I had always been captivated by his sense of comedy. If remarkable people were not radically dissimilar, their biographies would not be worth writing, and I soon discovered that Dickens was unique. Possessing the qualities common to all men, he exhibited each in an extreme degree, the combination resulting in a personality like that of no one else on record. I did not altogether like him, but he fascinated me.

Having recovered from the Vim-iodine treatment and read all Dickens's novels and published letters,

Gladys and I spent ten days in the Dickens country, basing ourselves at the Rochester inn of Pickwick fame. Money troubles having receded owing to the success of two previous biographies, I find on reference to my pocket-books that quite a few holidays intermitted my labours on Dickens. With Joe Maiden and his wife Joko we spent three weeks at Paris and Blois in May 1947, weeks of so much laughter that the sedate citizens of France must have been confirmed in their opinion that the English were mad. A fortnight's holiday with James Mitchell at Falmouth was only marred by a drive we took with Hitler. We assumed he was the authentic Adolf disguised as a chauffeur not only because he resembled him physically but on account of his spiritual affinity, for he managed to run over or miss by a hair's breadth several dogs on his way round the Cornish peninsula, making us so nervous that we started to shout whenever a dog appeared in the distance. Another holiday at Falmouth with Colin included a visit to Land's End and brought forth a poem which he wrote in a Newquay hotel on our way back:

This is land's end. Here in enduring struggle
   granite meets water.
There is no hope in that horizon, for beyond it
   now lies the known;
Not a new world : only a sea stage
   between old things.
Turn back, turn back then, for in the heart of England,
   in your own heart
Is what you seek. The battle or the peace is there
   and there alone.

This poem made a special appeal to me because I have never searched for peace outside myself and have seldom known disquietude in solitude. It has not been my wish to take an active part in the social life around

me. I am usually at my happiest when wandering
through London either in a dream or observing the
architecture of the streets and the human oddities on
the pavements. But mostly in a dream, from which I
am occasionally aroused by the necessity of extricating
myself from a traffic jam or by someone who wishes to
know the way to somewhere. As I am almost invariably
in another world when so accosted, I return to the present
with an effort and then give precise and detailed information, which on reflection some minutes later I usually
discover to be inaccurate. In my contacts with reality I
am liable to misfortune. Once, in Regents Park, I was
brought to earth by a small boy who stood directly in
front of me with a toy gun pointed at my breast. With
a sudden memory of my own youth, and knowing that
nothing would have pleased me so much at the age of
six or seven, I halted until he pulled the trigger, on
which I did a realistic stage-fall backwards and lay flat
on the grass. The little idiot promptly shrieked himself
into a fit of hysterics, and I received a severe dressing-
down from his nurse who said that I was old enough
to know better. As my age was well past sixty at the
time I could not claim to be the child's contemporary,
and my explanation that the action was purely
altruistic, since I had risked hurting myself in the fall,
seemed to increase her vexation. Since then I have not
attempted to amuse small children.

In the early summer of 1948 I continued my Dickens
book at Folkestone, where Gladys and I spent a month
at the Esplanade Hotel, among our visitors being
Hughie, Colin, Joe and his wife Joko. Donald Gordon,
whom we had known from boyhood, was acting in the
Repertory Theatre there, and we quickly made friends
with its two directors, Arthur (always known as Peter)
Brough and his wife Bess. Thereafter several holidays
were enjoyed at Folkestone, which I came to like almost

as much as Brighton, an annual dose of which was imperative. My brother Jack, who had lived in the Argentine since the early 'twenties and married his second wife Dina there, came to England in the middle of 1948, and much merriment ensued. His wit and humour were unquenchable, and laughter accompanied him wherever he went. Early in October I arranged a family gathering at the Star Hotel, Worcester, so that we could visit all the places we had known in childhood. Elsie, Evelyne and I took Stratford in on the way to see Godfrey Tearle's Othello; Harry travelled from his home in Wales; and the lot of us turned up at Worcester on 2 October, staying till the 4th. It was an extremely high-spirited party, with Jack as master of the mirth, and a great calm must have descended upon the city when we left.

A week of October 1948 was passed at Steyning, where Gladys and I saw something of Hughie and his wife Dorothy, who then lived at Partridge Green nearby. Hughie had been very ill but seemed to be much better that autumn, so I was shocked to hear the following April that he had re-entered a Brighton hospital. His essays, *The Progress of a Biographer*, had just been published. To my mind they contain the most perceptive criticism in the language, and I was able to tell him this at our last meeting. Early in May James and I were staying at Battle, and on the 4th I drove over to see Hughie. He appeared hopeful of an early recovery, but for me it was a tearful occasion. He died on 15 May 1949 and a very large part of myself died with him. Soon afterwards Malcolm wrote me a letter about him, to which I replied, and these exchanges continued until there were enough for a book *About Kingsmill* (1951).

Hughie was not at all keen on my next biographical subject and did his best to influence me in another direction. Both of us regarded politicians as the least attractive units in the human comedy, but something about Benjamin Disraeli had always interested me. The mere fact that a Jew should become the chosen leader of a landed aristocracy in a period of snobbish exclusiveness was evocative enough, but added to that his wit delighted me and his mysterious aloofness intrigued me. He was one of the very few people whose name in the index of a book always made me turn to the page on which he was mentioned or quoted, the only others to have that effect being Wilde, Sydney Smith, Shaw, Dr Johnson, Sheridan, Voltaire and the Duke of Wellington. I had enjoyed the book on Dizzy by André Maurois, but on reconsideration felt that the French picture was too romantic and sentimental. After much preparatory work, my own was begun in June 1949 and finished in December 1950. In January of the latter year I was prostrated by the bursting of an internal blood vessel, and during a fortnight of enforced recumbence I re-read all Dizzy's novels. They threw much light on his curious nature. Publication of my biography took place in the autumn of 1951. It sold well in England and better in America.

One effect of its reception here amused me. Quite a few Conservative organizations, including the central one in London, asked me to address them, clearly on the assumption that, as I had written the Life of a famous tory, I favoured their political cause. In the same way many radicals thought I was one of themselves after reading *Labby*, and a number of Socialists identified me with their theories when I wrote on Shaw. None of them could grasp the simple fact that the instinctive biographer is concerned with individuals, not communities or creeds. I have never belonged to a party or a faith, being well aware that the seeds of corruption are sown in the foundation of every institution. I have voted at elections perhaps three or four times, but only because the people who have gained my vote seemed a little less dishonest than their opponents, my recognition of this being based on the personal observation that the deeper conviction with which a man speaks the less is he likely to believe what he says, since he is trying to convince himself. I am inclined to think that anyone who is capable of believing every article of authoritarian doctrine must be either a knave or a fool. We are all knaves and fools more or less, but my particular form of knavery does not take the form of pretending to do good to others, and my particular form of foolery does not include the desire to make others share my opinions, which are the outcome of my peculiar constitution. I think Dizzy an amazing character, the brainiest statesman in English history, and a frustrated poet; intensely interesting on all counts; but his brand of political partisanship is the least interesting thing about him.

I was criticized in the papers for not paying enough attention to the politics of the period, but when Gladys read the typescript her sole objection was that politics occupied too much of the book. As a rule she helped me with my researches into the lives and characters of my subjects, but she had ceased to be active enough for work on Dizzy. By degrees she lost the use of her legs. She spent periods for treatment in two hospitals and a nursing-home, but the specialists and doctors could do nothing for her, and at last she was confined to one room, being lifted from bed to chair every morning and back again every night. I engaged an admirable nurse for her, Miss Lavinia Davis, whose company was as pleasant as her ministrations were efficient, and invaluable help was given by two sisters, Joyce and Jean Ryder, who occupied the garden floor of our house. Joyce was a cashier at our bank, and she tells me that the first time I asked her to cash a cheque she enquired whether I was related to the author of Shaw's biography and that I replied 'with quiet dignity "I am he".' On the two occasions I had to leave home during the last few months of Gladys's life, a male nurse was brought in to lift her. During the whole of her illness she never uttered a word of complaint, and the only thing that worried her was the inconvenience which she believed her enfeeblement caused me. She loved reading and talking to her friends, and she never seemed in the least depressed. When she thought she was dying she told me that I had been a good husband and that she had been happy with me. But she spoke from the goodness of her own heart, which made me weep. Aware that I had not been a good husband, I could believe that she had been happy, for we had had grand times together, never ceasing to love one another. She died quite suddenly on 8 March 1951, and forty years of a deeply affectionate relationship closed with her last breath.

Both she and I had become devoted to Joyce in the last year or two, and when I asked Joyce to marry me it filled me with delight to hear that Gladys had expressed a hope that we should do so. My very considerable seniority weighed upon me, but Joyce assured me that, though I believed myself to be over sixty, my real age was under six. Anyhow, we were married in 1951 and though it is eight years ago it might have been yesterday. My father once said to me that he had been greatly blessed in his two wives, and there was a hint of complacency in the admission. I, too, have been greatly blessed, but my feeling is mainly of wonder.

Joyce and I took a holiday in Ireland soon after our marriage, a fortnight at Killarney, a few days in Dublin, followed by a week at Stratford-on-Avon. While at Killarney we made two journeys round the Kerry Ring in a hired car, and we enjoyed everything about our holiday except a slight misunderstanding which caused us some discomfort towards the end. One day the hall-porter addressed me 'Good-morning, doctor.' I put this down to a mistake on his part or a mishearing on mine, but when he repeated it next morning we referred to the registration book and found that I had clearly written 'Mr'. It was rather pleasant to be called 'Doctor', and as he appeared to find it pleasant too I did not bother to correct him. But at last several other members of the staff used the term, and only laziness prevented me from explaining their error. This went on until our driver, a very nice fellow, asked whether we minded if he visited his brother in hospital while we stopped for a meal at Tralee. Afterwards he told us that his brother had double-rupture, adding 'You will know all about that, Doctor.' Joyce gasped, but I held myself in check and said nothing until he pressed for my opinion on the subject, whereat I told him firmly that his brother must take his own doctor's advice. My fame as a physician having spread beyond the confines of the hotel, we welcomed the morning of our departure, Joyce wondering what I would do if called up in the middle of the night to attend a woman in labour and help the delivery of a baby.

Fortunately for me Joyce enjoyed research work, as Gladys had done, and as I am liable to become impatient with it my biographies owe more to them than I am able to acknowledge. The first to be written on groundwork prepared by Joyce was *The Man Whistler* (1952), an odd choice in view of the fact that painting makes less appeal to me than any other art except perhaps sculpture. But I wished to understand the seemingly irreconcilable qualities of the poet who could paint the tender portrait of Carlyle or the lovely dream-picture of Cremorne Lights and the man whose bitter tongue suggested hate as his primary emotion.

Moreover he was a wit, though a cruel one, and I felt sure that he would amuse me. He did.

Early in 1952 Joyce learnt to drive a motor-car, passed her test, and with a hired car we spent three weeks of May in Folkestone, thoroughly exploring the neighbouring country and seeing a lot of Bess and Peter Brough. Driving had always bored me and I have a tendency to fall asleep at the wheel, so for everyone's sake I became a passenger whenever we took a motoring holiday. In June that year we went on a trip up the Norwegian fjords, during which we made friends with two charming fellow-passengers on the boat, Nellie and John Davis, whom we have since seen on our journeys to Scotland, as they live at Barbon in Westmorland. According to my pocket-book we had 'a rough crossing' back to Grimsby on the night of Saturday, 12 July, but my awareness of it cannot have been keen because I sat up drinking with the boat's captain and on reaching our cabin at about three in the morning I assured Joyce that the captain had six eyes, a physical peculiarity that could not be doubted since I had counted them carefully, not only from right to left but from left to right. One is supposed to 'see double' in a certain condition, but I had gone one better and seen treble.

As an antidote to Whistler, I decided to write on the noblest man of letters in history; and in September 1952 we drove north, staying with my old army friend Dick Hammond on the way and visiting the cathedrals of Ely, Norwich, Peterborough, Lincoln, York and Durham. We spent a week at Kelso, seeing all the places associated with Sir Walter Scott, and then went on to Edinburgh, where in the company of Percy Stevenson we met several Scott enthusiasts and saw all the places connected with him. We stayed at Loch Achray Hotel in the Trossachs, visited Ayr, Dumfries and the *Redgauntlet* country, and finished our tour at Peniarth

Uchaf, my brother Harry's house in the Dysynni valley behind Towyn, Merionethshire. I had spent many happy Christmas holidays there with Gladys and Henry in the late 'twenties and early 'thirties, shooting in the daytime and playing bridge with Harry, Pearl and Dora in the evenings, games which were accompanied by much laughter and considerable disputation. At the end of October we joined my two sisters at Stratford-on-Avon, now a regular autumnal engagement, just as a week at the Royal Crescent Hotel in Brighton had become a permanent spring fixture.

Incidentally Brighton restored me to health in March 1953. Another blood vessel had erupted internally at the end of November 1952, making me so weak that I was moved to hospital. Again I made use of my disability, reading Scott's letters in bed and during convalescence. I was X-rayed, but there were no signs of an ulcer, and the cause of my illness was a mystery until my doctor, Hugh Wetherbee, gave a rational explanation, which made me more cautious in my feeding and drinking habits. I remained feeble until a week at Brighton put me properly on my feet.

Scott occupied us throughout 1953, one chapter of the book being written at The Elms, Abberley, now a hotel, the old building once owned by my family having been burnt down in the 'twenties. We were in Scotland again during May 1954, arranging for illustrations. In the previous months I had read all the Waverley novels aloud to Joyce. Most of them were familiar to me, but she had only read two or three. It was a testing experience and I anticipated protests, but she enjoyed all of them except *The Monastery* and *The Betrothed*, which we agreed were penitential. My *Walter Scott* came out in November 1954. I felt in advance that the subject would not be popular, and my feeling was justified, but Scott was the only person within my knowledge

whose greatness as a writer was matched by his goodness as a man, and I could not resist the impulse to pay
him the homage of an honest biography. One of the
joys of writing for one's own pleasure is to find that it
gives pleasure to other people, and I was delighted when
Orville Prescott, the leading critic of *The New York
Times*, recognized not only what I had tried to do for
Scott but also my idiosyncrasies as a biographer:

> One of the most admired biographies in all English
> literature, and one of the least read, is John Gibson Lock-
> hart's 'Memoirs of the Life of Sir Walter Scott, Bart.' Five
> years ago at a jumble sale conducted by my children's
> school I bought all nine volumes of this formidable master-
> piece. At one dollar for the set I could not resist the
> bargain. Ever since I have repented my impetuous folly.
> The sole benefit I derived from my purchase was a lesson
> in humility. I never quite finished Volume I. I could not
> look at the remaining eight volumes without cringing and
> feeling pangs of guilt. But from now on I am not going
> to let Lockhart bully me any more. I have read Hesketh
> Pearson's 'Sir Walter Scott: His Life and Personality,' and
> I have learned all anyone needs to know about Scott and I
> have had a delightfully good time learning it.
>
> This is an admirable biography—as anyone would expect
> it to be who has read Mr Pearson's other admirable
> biographies of Whistler, Disraeli, Wilde and Shaw. A con-
> scientious scholar and a writer of skill and charm, Hesketh
> Pearson's approach to the art of biography is peculiarly
> his own. His relish in human personality, in the special
> ideas, habits, characteristics and eccentricities which express
> the essence of individuality, is contagious. His worldly
> philosophy and his urbane wit season his pages with the
> flavour of his own tart personality. And his ultra conserva-
> tive, ultra skeptical views on politics and history provide
> numerous opportunities for taking thought.

Another tribute came from a surprising quarter. Max
Beerbohm had already praised some of my earlier books,

such as those on Shaw, Wilde, Whistler and Labouchere, speaking of them to his great-nephew Denys Parsons as 'keenly penetrating work and immensely entertaining' and telling me how much he admired what he called my 'shining skill in narration'. But both period and people were familiar to him and temperamentally akin in wit, and it never occurred to me that he might appreciate a totally different sort of atmosphere and personality. However he closed a letter on another subject with the words: 'Please let me offer you profound congratulations on your Life of Sir Walter. It is a book grandly worthy of its great and lovable theme.'

While still engaged on Scott I was asked by Denys and David Tree Parsons to write the Life of their grandfather, Beerbohm Tree. At first I refused because of my absorption in Scott, but they resumed the subject later and I agreed, for Tree had been the hero of my nonage and his personality included the four qualities that inspire my admiration and affection; good nature, good humour, good sense and good nonsense, the qualities that delight me in Scott, Sydney Smith, Oscar Wilde and Bernard Shaw. Aware that the reading public are not interested in the Lives of past actors, and that the sale of the book would not cover its production expenses, I stuck to my principle of writing only what I wished to write, turned down a lucrative offer to describe the career of a famous industrialist, and started on Tree, whose daughter Felicity (Lady Cory-Wright) kindly placed at my disposal all her mother's letters. These we found packed higgledy-piggledly in twenty-four trunks of various sizes, and we spent a month motoring to and from Knebworth every day in order to pick out what might be of biographical interest from a mass of junk. Sometimes I could not face it and went for a walk through the park or a drink in the pub, leaving Joyce to toil through letters, bills, leases, orders to view houses, programmes, Press notices, photographs, and heaven-knows-what. Hidden in this conglomeration of impedimenta were a few priceless things for our purpose, but Joyce had to work hard to find them.

Max Beerbohm answered whatever questions I sent him, though of course I was already familiar with the personality of my subject and the story of his rise to fame. My one regret was that he had never tackled King Lear, not that he could have rendered the bursts of rhetoric but he had the intelligence to see that Lear starts as sanely mad and ends as madly sane. This is where other actors go wrong, thinking that because Lear becomes technically insane he must be acted as a madman. Yet it is clear that he only comes into touch with reality when he is supposed to have lost his wits. The one actor of today who has the skill to convey this is Michael Hordern, whose Macbeth was the best I have ever seen.

When my book on Tree was finished, trouble started with solicitors owing to the fact that he had not been a monogamist. But after 'great argument about it and about' it was found that I had been reasonably discreet and no alterations were enforced. But this delayed publication, which took place on 1 November 1956, an unpropitious moment, everyone's interest being centred on the landing of a British force to protect the Suez Canal.

While in the last stages of the book my friends Joan and Jim Thornton told me that owing to the death of W. S. Gilbert's adopted daughter, Nancy McIntosh, her executor Mr F. B. Cockburn wondered whether I would care to glance through the Gilbert papers with the object of writing some sort of period history. The idea appealed to me, and Mr Cockburn kindly provided a room in his house where we could inspect the librettist's letters and documents. I was much interested to come across copies of his letters to Sullivan which threw a fresh light on their quarrel, and decided that they justified a full Life of Gilbert. Facsimiles of his early letters were in tissue-paper volumes, having been taken with a copying-press, and one of these volumes appearing to be unused I tossed it to one side with the remark 'nothing there!' But Joyce did not rely on my patience, took it up, and discovered hidden between a number of empty pages copies of Gilbert's strange letters to his mother. They explained much of his nature and not a little of his work, and were our chief 'find', justice compelling me to add that, had it rested with me, what was found would have been lost, the discovery undiscovered.

Having polished off *Gilbert*, we paid our usual visit to Brighton in March 1956, and in May that year we stayed a fortnight with our friends Norman and Germaine Hunter, near Machynlleth, motoring all over Wales during our visit. In June we flew to Iceland, as we were invited to visit the capital, where I would address the University and give another speech elsewhere. The result was a wholly delightful week at Reykjavik, several trips to notable sights in the hinterland, and a hospitality as friendly as it was generous. I do not care for public speaking, but on these occasions I felt less nervous than usual on account of the cordial atmosphere generated by our hosts.

Jack was in England again that summer and came down to Battle with his son Roy, as we were staying for three weeks in the house of Malcolm and Kitty near Robertsbridge. We wished to see the old haunts at Brighton together, so Joyce drove us over and we revived our memories with the help of alcohol. Jack left England just before the death of our half-brother Harry on 20 September, a blow I felt more than I should have thought possible.

Early the following year I made several appearances

on T.V. with the Brains Trust, though I had warned the producer that my own condition could more aptly be described as Brains Rust. Throughout the 'fifties I also did a fair amount of sound broadcasting, in particular a series called *The Last Actor-Managers*, which with additions appeared in an illustrated volume.

I took life fairly easily in 1957, re-reading books on Johnson and Boswell, as well as all their works, for I had decided to write a duo-biography. A lifelong interest had vastly increased my knowledge of the two; and though I knew it would be a difficult enterprise, all the facts were at my finger-ends. We flew to Geneva at the end of May for a sojourn of three weeks in Switzerland. Unfortunately I was not very well during our visit, and for some days after our arrival at Beatenberg I was down with a fever. Joyce nursed me, and when strong enough I read Boswell's *Johnson*, occasionally glancing through our bedroom window at the lovely view of Lake Thun. I remained ill at intervals after our return and for a while my face resembled one of those hideous masks which children delight to wear, all the features bulging. We sometimes spent week-ends at Rushlake Green with our friends Elsa and Alan Thomas, during one of which in August I felt my normal strength return and quite equal to delivering an address 'About Biography' at the Cheltenham Festival in September.

My next subject was my boyhood's hero Charles II, the only monarch in history whose company I would have enjoyed, and with the exception of his grandfather, Henry IV of France, the most civilized human being who ever sat on a throne. For some years I had wanted to paint his portrait in prose, and I now decided to do so. I re-read all the diaries and memoirs of the period, and traced the steps he had taken as a fugitive. During one of our visits to Joe and Joko Maiden in Hampshire, when we always made a point of visiting Salisbury together, we drove over to Heale House on the Plain, where Charles lay hidden for some days before escaping to the Continent, and then went on to Winchester, where Joe showed us the site of the palace which was being built for Charles at the time of his death.

While still in the throes of re-creating Charles II, I was asked by the Edinburgh Sir Walter Scott Club to be its President for 1959-1960. It was a much-prized honour, and I am glad that my portrait of a Scottish King hangs in a gallery which includes the king of Scotland's literature. My work on Charles happened to be issued in the year 1960, when the three-hundredth anniversary of the Restoration was being celebrated, and it amused me when one or two critics assumed that I had written the book for that occasion. But I did not become aware of the coincidence until passing the proofs, and in any case publication should have taken place in 1959, but was delayed owing to a strike of printers.

I am often asked which of my works I regard as my best. No author is the proper judge of his writings, and all that he can honestly say is that he knows which are his favourites. Obviously mine deal with the subjects who contain the four qualities that appeal to me more than any others, and my favourite characters have been imaginative wits and humourists who united wisdom, toleration and kindliness with high spirits, levity and nonsense: Sydney Smith, Bernard Shaw, Oscar Wilde, Walter Scott, Beerbohm Tree. I think that my main characteristic as a biographer is that I possess a not inconsiderable portion of the actor's temperament, and this has enabled me, by sinking my own personality, to understand my characters, to get into their skins and bring them to life, making the reader feel that he has known them personally; so I have often been told. This can only be done by interest and sympathy, and I have therefore been compelled to write on people whose characters attract me, trusting to luck that they will attract others as well.

Up to the publication of *Charles II* I had never written simply to make money, except in the ill-starred case of *The Whispering Gallery*. But in 1959 I accepted a commission for the first time in my life on a subject chosen by someone else, and the book I wrote, *The Pilgrim Daughters*, would not have been undertaken except on a financial basis. I became quite interested in the theme, the title of which sprang out of a conversation with my wife. Before this I had dealt with all the characters in history who had profoundly interested me, except Beethoven, Voltaire and the Duke of Wellington. Ignorance of the German language and a superficial knowledge of the French disqualified me from writing on the first two, while I could not face the voluminous military histories necessary for the third. But there were still a few personalities who had aroused my interest in one way or another, if not enough to make me tackle full-scale biographies of them. Two of these, Rudyard Kipling and Granville Barker, I had managed to bring into *The Pilgrim Daughters*, and there were several others I wished to deal with at about the same length, especially Sheridan and G. K. Chesterton. So I decided to put them into a final volume together with brief biographies of the wits whose Lives I had already written. Whether I shall retain the vitality to complete this[1] is doubtful, like everything else in life, but I console myself with the words of Falstaff:

'Let time shape, and there an end.'

[1] Hesketh Pearson not only completed *The Lives of The Wits* (published by Heinemann in 1962) but also wrote *Henry of Navarre* (published 1963) and, finally, *Extraordinary People* (published 1965).

Index

327